MINNEAPOLIS

"Minneapolis' Enterprises"
by Dick Schaaf

Produced in cooperation with the
Greater Minneapolis Chamber of Commerce

Windsor Publications, Inc.
Chatsworth, California

MINNEAPOLIS
City of Enterprise, Center of Excellence

A Contemporary Portrait By
WILLIAM SWANSON

Windsor Publications, Inc.—Book Division
Managing Editor: Karen Story
Design Director: Alexander E. D'Anca

Staff for *Minneapolis: City of Enterprise, Center of Excellence*
Manuscript Editor: Doreen Nakakihara
Photo Editor: William A. Matthews
Senior Editor, Corporate Profiles: Judith L. Hunter
Production Editor, Corporate Profiles: Albert Polito
Customer Service Manager: Phyllis Feldman-Schroeder
Editorial Assistants: Kim Kievman, Michael Nugwynne,
  Kathy B. Peyser, Theresa J. Solis
Publisher's Representatives, Corporate Profiles: Jan Belshan,
  Tim Burke, Merl Gratton, Henry Hintermeister
Layout Artist, Editorial: Michael Burg
Layout Artist, Corporate Profiles:
  Mari Catherine Preimesberger-Powell
Designer: Ellen Ifrah

Library of Congress Cataloging-in-Publication Data
Swanson, William, 1945-
    Minneapolis : city of enterprise, center of excellence : a
contemporary portrait / by William Swanson. — 1st ed.
    p. 240 cm. 23 x 31
  Bibliography: p. 237
  Includes index.
  ISBN 0-89781-292-1
  1. Minneapolis (Minn.)—Economic conditions. 2. Minneapo-
lis (Minn.)—Economic conditions—Pictorial works.
  I. Greater Minneapolis Chamber of Commerce. II. Title.
  HC108.M7S89 1989
330.9776'579053—dc19   89-5605
                                                    CIP

Windsor Publications, Inc.
Elliot Martin, Chairman of the Board
James L. Fish III, Chief Operating Officer
Michele Sylvestro, Vice President/Sales-Marketing

Contents

Part 2
MINNEAPOLIS' ENTERPRISES

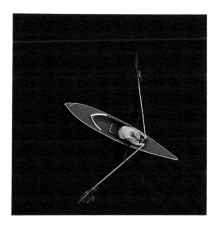

Preface

Viewed from other parts of the country, Minneapolis has until fairly recently, I believe, presented a simple, straightforward, and altogether misleading public image.

At a wedding reception in Boston nearly 20 years ago, I was amused to find myself accorded a certain curiosity, if not heroic status, for having journeyed "so far" for the ceremony. In terms of miles, I might have come from the distant reaches of the solar system. Though the month was September these Bostonians seemed convinced, moreover, that I'd had to dig myself out of 10 feet of snow in order to make my way to the airport; some, indeed, may have assumed I'd traveled at least part of the way (as far as, say, Michigan) by dogsled. Our snow and cold were presumed to be extreme and year-round. I happen to be of Scandinavian descent, and so, they assumed, were all of my fellow Minneapolitans. All of us were believed, for that matter, to be farmers—or whatever people were who lived and worked in a town set smack-dab in the middle of a wheat field. And, finally, though my Boston hosts were apparently too proper to mention it, I'm convinced that they felt that cultural life back in my hometown began and ended with two guys in flannel shirts, bib overalls, and galoshes playing the "Beer Barrel Polka" on a fiddle and accordion.

Thankfully, our image has undergone some considerable improvement during the past several years. Such random phenomena as "The Mary Tyler Moore Show," the emergence of the disparate likes of Garrison Keillor and Prince, the World Series championship of the Minnesota Twins, and several effusive newspaper, magazine, and television stories about "the good life" in Minneapolis (and St. Paul) have combined to suggest to the rest of the world that there is more to our community than can be conveyed by January temperature readings on "Good Morning America."

I suspect that many of us native Minneapolitans were surprised, ironically, to find out just how good we have it. Growing up and living in a community so richly blessed with lakes and parks, outstanding neighborhoods, first-rate schools, and world-class cultural offerings, we may have overlooked the obvious: that Minneapolis is in truth a great city—and, indeed, has been for a long time. Longer, certainly, than the fact has been widely recognized.

We tend, in any case, to be self-effacing people, even when aware

Perceived by some to be a desolate and frozen city, Minneapolis is, in reality, a city of modern office towers and cosmopolitan ideals. Photo by Greg Ryan/Sally Beyer

8

of our civic blessings pleased to let others bring those blessings up in conversation or on the glossy pages of a national magazine. When visitors or new arrivals remark on our verdant parkways and handsome neighborhoods, we are impressed (and perhaps somewhat surprised) by both their enthusiasm and sincerity. Yet when out-of-town writers and commentators rave about our artists, politicians, or baseball fans, we tend, I think, to take these comments not just as compliments, but as verification of something we've known, or felt somewhere deep in our native bones, all the while.

Coming when it does, then, this book is not needed to rescue the city from an ice-encrusted oblivion or misperception. If it helps citizens in distant parts of the country to form a more detailed picture of the city, fine. If it informs newcomers (or prospective newcomers) of the city's history, economy, and amenities, well and good. If it serves former Minneapolitans as a fancy scrapbook, stimulating fond memories of their birthplace or erstwhile hometown, wonderful. As far as I'm concerned, however, the primary mission of this book is to celebrate in word and picture what we have here in these parts, and to remind us that our celebrity, if relatively newfound, is by no means based on strictly latter-day phenomena.

In short, the book's message is this: that from its municipal beginnings to the present day, Minneapolis has been and continues to be both a city of enterprise and a center of excellence.

Photo by Robert Friedman

As told in this volume, the story begins at the Falls of St. Anthony, on the upper Mississippi River. In the late seventeenth century, when the Belgian-born priest Louis Hennepin first laid eyes on the site, the cataract was yet another wonder in a fearfully wondrous wilderness. A century-and-a-half later, it was an attraction for frontier tourists journeying up the Mississippi aboard steamboats. At the midpoint of the nineteenth century, it became both the rationale for the siting of another new community and that new community's original life force.

But St. Anthony Falls is only the beginning. The Minneapolis story is the tale of a steadily developing urban experience. It encompasses the lumber- and flour-milling industries that provided the city with its initial economic foundation and gave birth to such contemporary hometown giants as Cargill and General Mills. It includes mighty institutions like the University of Minnesota, which has played as vital a community role as any such institution in the country; the Metropolitan Council, whose innovative structure and mission have made it the model for numerous imitators around the country; and the Minnesota (née Minneapolis Symphony) Orchestra, one of the premier musical ensembles in the world.

Most importantly, the Minneapolis story, from Father Hennepin's "discovery" of the falls on forward into close proximity to the twenty-first century, belongs to a rich assemblage of men and women. These include the likes of John Stevens, Franklin Steele, and Charles Hoag, among the city's "founding fathers"; John S. Pillsbury, Cadwallader Washburn, Thomas B. Walker, and Elizabeth Quinlan, a few of its early movers and shakers; important creative forces like William MacPhail and Emil Oberhoffer; and more recent keepers of the civic faith like Hubert Humphrey, Curtis Carlson, William Norris, and the family Dayton. These, of course, are only the city's marquee players. The complete cast comprises several generations of homesteaders, entrepreneurs, artists, and working men and women from elsewhere around the United States and dozens of foreign countries. Among the early driving forces were enough transplanted New Englanders to populate half of nineteenth-century Boston!

The narrative of the book moves chronologically from the establishment of the villages of St. Anthony and Minneapolis, to the coming of the waves of immigrants shortly after the Civil War, to the community's turn-of-the-century maturation as a milling, manufacturing, transportation, wholesale, retail, financial, and cultural center, to its mid-twentieth-century renaissance as a regional trade and service hub, to its modern-day status as a technology-driven metropolis of commerce and industry, the arts and the sciences.

En route, according to this story, the community builds strength through economic, cultural, and demographic diversity. It becomes a "city that works" thanks in large part to a remarkable cooperation between public and private sectors and to the pragmatic application of innovative means of getting things done. Its citizens find comfort and good living among its many lakes and parks, in its handsome downtown and various neighborhood communities, as well as in its fast-growing collection of bustling suburbs; they find pleasure and renewal in its culture, civic celebrations, and vast array of entertainments.

There are several outstanding books covering, in considerably more detail than allowed by the scope of this book, the history, development, and various specific components of Minneapolis and the entire Twin Cities metropolitan area. Among those I have enjoyed and found particularly useful are Theodore C. Blegen's *Minnesota: A History of the State*, which provides the essential context for the development of the city as well as many of the key developments and developers; Lucile M. Kane's *The Waterfall that Built a City: The Falls of St. Anthony in Minneapolis*, a fascinating study of the central role played by St. Anthony Falls and its industries over the past century-and-a-half; Joseph Stipanovich's *City of Lakes: An Illustrated History of Minneapolis*, a recent (1982), extensive, and insightful retrospective on many aspects of city life, past and present; a slight but invaluable volume entitled *The Twin Cities of St. Paul and Minneapolis* by geographers Ronald Abler, John S. Adams, and John R. Borchert; and the ever valuable and entertaining *Guide to the Architecture of Minnesota* by David Gebhard and Tom Martinson.

Each in its way both illuminates and gives us good reason to look back and around, to explore and examine, and to be proud of our community, not only for what it is, but for what it has been—and what, with our continued application of energy and innovation, it is yet likely to become.

Photo by Greg Ryan/Sally Beyer

Part 1

Yesterday and Today

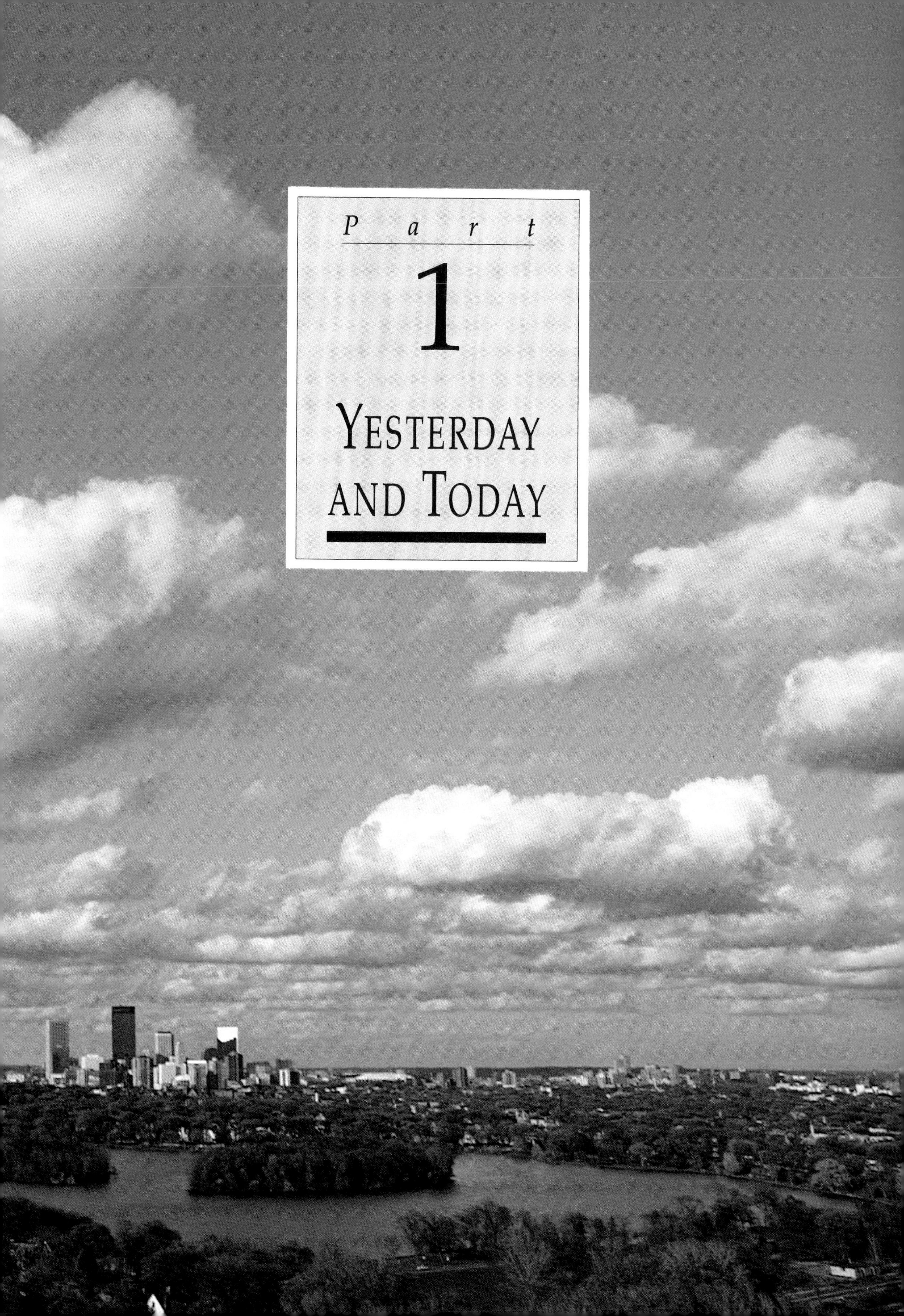

1

The City by the Falls

It was, according to the earliest reports, a beautiful, even breathtaking, sight.

Long before white entrepreneurs began converting its might into milling power, the roaring falls on the upper Mississippi River had a primitive force that drew the awe of the indigenous Sioux and Chippewa and inspired their legends. The Indians called the cataract "the severed rock," after the broken limestone masses of which it was formed, and "the curling" or "falling water." In 1778 a Connecticut Yankee, Jonathan Carver, called it an "astonishing work of nature" —250 yards across and 30 feet from lip to cauldron—whose rushing racket could be heard as far as 15 miles away. Describing the falls and the cluster of small islands just below it, Carver wrote, "[A] more pleasing and picturesque view cannot . . . be found throughout the universe."

The first white man to see the falls was Father Louis Hennepin, a Belgian-born Franciscan priest, in the late 1600s. Hennepin had been exploring the frontier north and west of the Illinois River when he and his companions were captured by Sioux warriors and transported to the shores of Lake Mille Lacs in what is now north-central Minnesota. Some months later Hennepin's captors allowed him to follow the headwaters of the Mississippi southward from Mille Lacs, and in the summer of 1680 he came upon the majestic falls.

On an earlier North American expedition Hennepin had seen Niagara Falls far to the east, and, by comparison, the falls he was looking upon in Minnesota was rather small. Still, he was moved by the spectacle in front of him, which he later described as "terrible" and "astonishing," and named the wondrous "discovery" after his patron saint, Anthony of Padua.

Portions of the upper Mississippi region had been penetrated

The 10th Avenue bridge, foreground, underwent repairs in the early 1900s. The bridge, originally built in 1874, is located next to the larger and more recently built 35 West bridge. Courtesy, Minnesota Historical Society

Father Louis Hennepin was accompanied by Sioux Indians when he first visited one of their sacred places, the mighty waterfall on the Mississippi River; Hennepin later named the falls for his patron saint, Anthony of Padua. Courtesy, Minnesota Historical Society

by French explorers, missionaries, and fur traders since the mid-1600s. Following Hennepin's historic visit near the end of that century, the territory was part of a succession of New World holdings—the property, at one time or another, of the French, Spanish, English, and, finally, the U.S. governments. It was part of Thomas Jefferson's Louisiana Purchase in the first decade of the nineteenth century, shortly thereafter explored by Lewis and Clark and Zebulon Pike, and eventually, in the early 1820s, the site of a permanent white settlement in the sturdy form of Fort Snelling, originally and appropriately known as Fort St. Anthony.

From the fort, situated on a bluff at the confluence of the Mississippi and Minnesota rivers, the falls at St. Anthony lay seven miles upstream. Interestingly enough, the falls' first major "industry" was tourism. Because of its proximity to the fort, which extended the protection of the federal government into the northern reaches of the Midwestern frontier, the falls became, according to historian Lucile M. Kane, "a prime objective of hundreds of artists, writers, politicians, and curious tourists who ascended the Mississippi to see for themselves the cataract Hennepin and Carver had made famous in their books."

The falls may not quite have matched the breathless descriptions rendered by its earliest observers. At 16 feet, the drop of the river at the site was only about half as long as the 30 feet reported by Carver. Nonetheless, it was the most precipitous drop on the entire 2,200-mile course of the Mississippi River and, by all accounts, it was a beautiful thing to behold. In any case, it was a novel and fashionable draw in the newly opened region. Indeed, by 1835, some local boosters were suggesting that St. Anthony Falls would soon be as popular a scenic attraction as Niagara itself.

Despite the visual appeal of the falls, its industrial possibilities were not overlooked by early fort-based settlers who were eager to develop the sprawling military reservation. The falling water could be transformed by mills into power to grind wheat and cut lumber. Thus in the early 1820s, at the direction of the fort's commandant (and eventual namesake), Colonel Josiah Snelling, the first rudimentary mills were constructed at St. Anthony.

The products of those original mills, it should be noted, were solely for local consumption: lumber for construction in and about the fort and flour for the bread of the fort's dependents. But, in Kane's words, "Snelling's mills were . . . prophetic of the future." The vast stands of pine to the north of the falls and the wheat being planted as grist for its mills would soon provide the impetus for the growth of a great city.

Officially speaking, civilian settlement in what would eventually become Minneapolis was prohibited until the early 1850s, when treaties with the local Indians were finally ratified. In reality, however, small groups of settlers, mostly from New England and the more eastern and southern reaches of the Midwest, had begun to hunker down on sites near Fort Snelling and on both east and west sides of St. Anthony's falls.

At about the same time, speculators and squatters, also without the official blessing of federal authorities, began a tiny settlement called Pig's Eye a few miles south and east of the fort.

This is Fort Snelling as it appeared around 1860. The fort was situated on a bluff at the confluence of the Mississippi and Minnesota rivers. Courtesy, Hennepin County Historical Society

Later—and mercifully—the town was renamed St. Paul. Some 10 miles below the falls, St. Paul provided a natural and logical terminus for upper Mississippi navigation. This gave the village a head start in what would prove to be a long and occasionally acrimonious rivalry with St. Anthony—today part of Minneapolis. An early commercial center in the region, St. Paul became the territorial capital in 1849.

Most of the early settlers near the fort were merchants, tradesmen, whiskey-sellers, and entrepreneurs who did business—legally or otherwise—with Colonel Snelling's bustling garrison. There was also a small handful of persons interested in serving the more spiritual and intellectual needs of the virgin territory. Historians say the first white civilian dwelling on what is now Minneapolis soil was the handiwork of Gideon and Samuel Pond.

The Pond brothers, formerly of Connecticut, were missionaries to the Indians. With the military's permission, the Ponds constructed a humble log mission on the east side of Lake Calhoun in 1834. They were soon joined by the Reverend Jedediah Stevens and his wife, transplanted New Yorkers, who set up a mission school on the west shore of Lake Harriet, not far from the Ponds. It is believed that the Stevenses' daughter, born shortly after their arrival, was the area's first white child delivered beyond the walls of the fort.

Meanwhile, on the east side of the falls, the village of St.

This Sioux Indian camp, photographed in 1875, was home to the first settlers of the Minneapolis area. Courtesy, Minnesota Historical Society

Anthony began to take hold despite official prohibitions against civilian settlement. In the late 1830s another New Englander, an entrepreneur named Franklin Steele, finagled a claim on some land adjacent to the falls. There, a few years later, Ard Godfrey (a colleague of Steele's) built the area's first civilian sawmill. A short time after that, using lumber from Godfrey's mill, a man named Roswell Russell built the site's first frame house, where he opened St. Anthony's first legitimate store. Thus, little by little, commercial activity increased beside the falls. By 1850 St. Anthony, with a population of about 300, was an incorporated community in its own right.

In the winter of 1849-50, an erstwhile military man from Vermont named John H. Stevens secured the right to build a home on the west side of the river, just above the falls. Stevens was a protégé of the opportunistic Franklin Steele, who was clearly keen on the commercial possibilities of the entire area. (As part of Steele's arrangement with the military, he agreed to establish the site's first ferry service between east and west banks.) Stevens' story-and-a-half frame house—quite substantial for its day—became the first permanent home in Minneapolis.

As a matter of fact, Minneapolis is said to have become "Minneapolis" at the sturdy Stevens home, which served as a hub of early west-bank activity. There, in 1852, a former Philadelphian named Charles Hoag suggested that the new community, sepa-

While the Sioux Indians had been residents of the Minneapolis area for quite some time before the first white settlers arrived, they were not always accorded the privileges of their tenure. These captured Sioux were held at Fort Snelling. Courtesy, Minnesota Historical Society

What was possibly the first real estate company in the city of Minneapolis was founded by Simon Snyder and William McFarlane. The demand for housing and commercial property soon brought many other competitors into the market. Courtesy, Minnesota Historical Society

rate from the village of St. Anthony on the opposite side of the river, should be called "Minnehapolis." The erudite and inventive Hoag had combined the local Indian word for water—*Minne*—with the Greek term for city—*polis*—then added the "h," presumably to aid in pronunciation. Other denizens of the new community suggested such names as "Lowell," "Albion," "All Saints," and, imaginatively enough, "West St. Anthony." But, after a couple of years of argument, Hoag's more creative designation (minus the "h") carried the day.

The metropolis, later and less formally known as "the Mill City" and "the City of Lakes," was officially christened Minneapolis.

Water, in the rushing form of the upper Mississippi River, was the force that powered the development of both St. Anthony and Minneapolis in those early years. While St. Paul, 10 miles downriver, became the major disembarkation point for traffic from the south and east, St. Anthony, with upstart Minneapolis on its flank, was growing into a crucial commercial milling site for the enormous flow of fresh-cut timber from the north. Soon enough, with the opening and planting of the vast agricultural lands to the west, mills at the falls were busy grinding wheat into flour. Soon, too, that lumber and flour were destined for external consumption.

The possibilities of the great natural site at first outstripped the realities imposed by delayed treaties, military preoccupations, and various financial and political shenanigans—not to mention limitations on the influx of investment capital. There were logistical problems as well. St. Anthony and Minneapolis were not connected by a permanent bridge until 1855, when the redoubtable Franklin Steele and his partners established that first critical connection. It was not, for that matter, until 1855 that Congress finally honored the occupancy rights of the settlers—officially, until then, known as "squatters" —in Minneapolis.

Once officially opened for civilian settlement, the areas on both sides of the river grew with startling swiftness. Minnesota historian Theodore C. Blegen has pointed out that within three months of Congress' action in 1855, some 20,000 local acres were entered for title. Almost as quickly, says Blegen, "[s]treets, buildings, stores, and community activities took form and shape." The financial panic of 1857 stunted the area's growth—but only temporarily. The village was fast becoming a city, with a population of more than 10,000 by 1860.

While the earliest settlers in Minneapolis consisted mostly of transplanted Yankees and Midwesterners, successive waves contained increasing numbers of immigrants seeking a better life in America. Most of the newcomers who arrived in Minneapolis during the 1850s, 1860s, and 1870s came from Scandinavia, Germany, and the United Kingdom. Many were farmers eager to till the fertile territory west of the Mississippi. But many others were drawn by the opportunities offered by the new communities themselves—jobs and, perhaps, great fortunes.

The jobs, if not necessarily the great fortunes, were available in an increasing number of industries. Once the communities were established, a network of separate yet highly interdependent businesses began to take root and grow. Clustered around the mills were the mill-related manufacturers—coopers, for example, whose barrels were essential to the shipping of flour, and furniture-makers, whose products were fashioned from the freshly milled lumber. Spreading out from the riverfront mills and factories were the food markets, dry-goods stores, banks, doctors' offices, and funeral parlors—all the varied components of a viable commercial community. In 1855, reflecting a growing demand for both commercial property and housing, Simon Snyder and William McFarlane established what is believed to have been the city's first real estate company. A number of other real estate agencies (often coupled with loan offices) quickly followed.

Geographers Ronald Abler, John Adams, and John Borchert, in their study of the region's growth, have summed up the dynamics of the time this way:

Sawmills, flour mills, banking, railroads, settlement, immigration, agricultural production, and the development of the Twin Cities are so closely intertwined that it is impossible to say which caused which. Growth or change in any one had immediate repercussions for the others. The repercussions in turn fed more change.

The extension of the railroads onto the Northern Plains was extending the reach of North American civilization overland, beyond the areas served—and, up until now, restricted—by the nation's great rivers. With the railroads came not only homesteaders from Europe and the East Coast but entrepreneurs, workers, new businesses, and much-needed development money from Eastern investors. The railroads also began carrying agricultural

The arrival of the railroad in the Minneapolis area brought an increase in homesteaders and localized transportation. Courtesy, Minnesota Historical Society

production from the Dakotas and western Minnesota to the mills and storage depots of the Twin Cities, where that production was processed and shipped to markets farther south and east.

Only a few decades earlier, the Falls of St. Anthony had been an exotic spectacle, nearby Fort Snelling had been a distant outpost, and both had been on the outermost reaches of American civilization. Suddenly, less than a half-century later, the communities that had sprung up around the two remote landmarks were becoming essential connecting points on the nation's westward spread across the continent.

For the first few years of its existence, Minneapolis played the tail to St. Anthony's dog. St. Anthony and Minneapolis had, in turn, been the scrappy little siblings of the slightly older, somewhat more sophisticated "metropolis" of St. Paul. In Theodore Blegen's words the latter, for its part, had "many early advantages in the race for urban supremacy, such as priority in time, the steamboat trade, the territory's pioneer commerce, the earliest banking, and the political capital."

But in the boom times that followed the Civil War, the tail began wagging the dog. Once the west bank of the river had been opened to homesteading and commerce, Minneapolis grew quickly and eventually surpassed St. Anthony in both population and business activity. Despite the tensions between west and east banks, sober minds on both sides prevailed, and in 1872 the two communities merged into one—Minneapolis. By the 1880s the newly enlarged Minneapolis was poised to overtake its elder, more worldly sibling downriver. Much to St. Paul's chagrin, according to the 1880 census Minneapolis boasted the greater population, with 46,000 residents compared to St. Paul's 42,000. As the gateway to the growing Northwest, Minneapolis was becoming the dominant city in the area.

For all its growth, however, the city's heart throughout the latter half of the nineteenth century remained the Falls of St. Anthony. Historians report that by the end of the Civil War there were at least a dozen sawmills powered by the water, and those sawmills were responsible for 100 million board feet of lumber a year. Flour milling surpassed lumber milling in total production in the 1870s though the latter continued to grow until the turn of the century, when the once apparently limitless "pineries" of north-central Minnesota and western Wisconsin began to thin out and disappear.

Local flour milling had grown fast on the heels of its lumbering counterpart. The city's dozen-odd flour mills were producing more than 250,000 barrels of flour a day by 1870. The mills were also spawning a large number of food- and feed-processing, machinery-manufacturing, and flour-packaging enterprises, which collectively were soon providing more employment than the

Railroads allowed the grain industry to be less dependent on the Mississippi River for transportation, and grain elevators were soon built many miles from the river. Courtesy, Hennepin County Historical Society

flour mills themselves. With the development and proliferation of the railroads, the city's industry was spreading out away from the original Mississippi-side sites. Massive grain elevators, for example, rose along the railroad tracks, often miles from the river's historic banks.

All the while, the mills and their attendant industries were producing more than just the obvious products. They were creating, in addition to flour and lumber, many of the city's great and abiding fortunes, corporations, civic leaders, and private benefactors.

John Sargent Pillsbury was a New England-born retailer who invested in his nephew Charles' flour-milling business in the 1850s. The C.A. Pillsbury Company became one of the world's great food companies (now known simply as The Pillsbury Company), and successive generations of Pillsburys have served as community and cultural leaders. John S. Pillsbury himself was a major contributor to, among other things, the fledgling University of

Minnesota. Besides serving as a longtime regent of the university, Pillsbury was thrice elected governor of Minnesota—the first of several Pillsburys to hold public office through the years.

Cadwallader C. Washburn and John Crosby were partners in the Washburn Crosby Company, founded by Washburn in 1866. The company is known today as General Mills, Inc., another multinational food-processing giant, and successive generations of both early partners have played significant roles in the city's development. Cadwallader Washburn was a native of Maine who served as governor of Wisconsin. As a mover and shaker in the Minneapolis milling industry, Washburn was a tireless innovator and promoter who, during the 1880s, helped transform the city into the nation's foremost grain-milling complex.

Thomas B. Walker was one of the community's early lumber-milling magnates. Yet another transplanted Yankee, Walker turned a large portion of his milling fortune into civic and cultural improvements for his adopted community. Although his money went toward such diverse causes as the Minneapolis public library and park systems and the local symphony orchestra, he is best known today for his namesake, the city's world-famous Walker Art Center, which has its origins in the extensive private collection Walker began in the 1870s. Walker's heirs, moreover, donated land adjacent to the center for the renowned Guthrie Theater, built in the mid-1960s.

Such citizens—and there have been many—clearly contributed a great deal to the city by the falls. Their foresight, willingness to take risks, and community-spirited generosity helped make Minneapolis a great metropolis. Their examples—not to mention, in many cases, the work of their like-minded descendants—

Thomas B. Walker, one of the first lumber-milling magnates in the Minneapolis area, donated much of his fortune for civic and cultural improvements. Courtesy, Hennepin County Historical Society

have done much to perpetuate the city's greatness into the late twentieth century.

Additionally, the lives of these pioneers suggest that Minneapolis enjoyed a cultural advantage from the very beginning: a mature, well-educated, and socially responsible vanguard, raised not on the raw frontier but in the great civic traditions of New England. Not all of these men and women were wealthy when they arrived from the East, but they were persons of vision and ambition. Many had been taught in the fine old schools of the East, then steeped in the law and lore of established business practice. They understood the importance of effective city government and of cooperation between private and public sectors. Equally important, they appreciated the fact that a business is, in the long run, only as sound as the community in which it operates. By and large, they made it a point to tend to both.

Between 1880 and 1890, Minneapolis' population increased by more than 250 percent and reached 165,000. By the turn of the century, the population had topped 200,000. The Civil War and the nationwide financial panics of 1873 and 1893 had taken their toll on Minneapolitans and Minneapolis interests, but the city's headlong rush into the twentieth century continued unabated.

The "Yankee connection" had leveled off, but immigration—primarily from northern Europe and the British Isles—continued at a rapid pace in the new century. So, too, did the arrival of Americans from other parts of the country, especially from the Middle West. There was also a more or less steady influx of rural folk seeking to make a better life for themselves and their families in the city. Despite the diversity of these groups, a remarkable dedica-

This 1876 view of Minneapolis from the Winslow House shows a portion of Nicollet Island in the Mississippi River and, more importantly, the earliest phase of Minneapolis' transformation from a primarily agricultural area into a mixed industrial and agricultural center. Courtesy, Hennepin County Historical Society

tion to hard work and honest labor arose in Minneapolis that remains a hallmark of the local work force to the present day.

The migration from farm to city was by no means unique to this part of the country or, for that matter, to that particular period of history. America had been transforming itself from a predominantly agrarian to a predominantly urban nation since its earliest days. Locally, as elsewhere, the shift from farm to factory (or office or other urban workplace) shortly after the turn of the century was symbolic of the continuing shift from a primarily agriculture-based economy to one with more varied, city-oriented underpinnings. This shift accelerated between the World Wars and took its contemporary form during the second half of the century, but its manifestations were highly visible in Minneapolis by 1900.

Lumber milling had reached its peak during the 1890s. By the end of the First World War it would be all but nonexistent in Minneapolis. Flour milling was on a steady rise until World War I, at which point a number of factors, including the opening of the Panama Canal and greater diversity in domestic agricultural production, began to curtail its local growth.

As milling production flattened out and began to decline, other hometown industries—many of them nearly as well-established if not quite as dominant—became more and more important. Locally owned banks and savings and loan associations became increasingly significant as the amount of local wealth and home ownership increased. Manufacturing burgeoned and took diverse new forms, independent of the mills. Transportation activity heightened dramatically, owing to the city's location as the jumping-off point to the Northwest and Canada. With the astonishing rise of the internal-combustion engine, the city rapidly became a trucking center as well as a hub of rail and river shipping. (Its considerable prominence as a center of commercial aviation did not begin until after the Second World War.)

Minneapolis, at the turn of the century, was already a regional center—drawing people and commerce from the smaller communities and rural areas of the Dakotas, northern Iowa, western Wisconsin, and, of course, outstate Minnesota. Visitors came to the city to do business, to bank, and to shop; increasingly, they also came to be educated, to see medical specialists, or, more happily, to attend plays, operas, concerts, or recitals. Some still came to see the Falls of St. Anthony, though, as a lure for tourists, the cataract by this time possessed considerably less natural appeal than the dramatic Minnehaha Falls in south Minneapolis or the beautiful, many-faceted Lake Minnetonka on the western fringes of town.

For many Upper Midwesterners, far removed from the bright lights and artistic attractions of New York, Chicago, and San Francisco, the Twin Cities of Minneapolis and St. Paul served as a blessed mecca of twentieth-century culture. It was, in addition, a continuing draw for tourists from Eastern centers of civiliza-

tion. Henry David Thoreau paid a visit in the 1860s, reportedly for his health. He is said to have spent some pleasant hours along the then-rustic shores of lakes Calhoun and Harriet. The national Republican party set up a temporary camp here in 1892, when it nominated Benjamin Harrison for president.

The community had featured a fine hotel from nearly its beginning. The Winslow House, which opened in 1857, overlooking the river in St. Anthony, was a deluxe, six-story establishment that was said to be the largest of its kind west of Chicago. After the Winslow House's decline, the grand and glorious West Hotel, on the west bank of the river, was the area's most prestigious hostelry—a home away from home for thousands of visitors over the next 50 years. The original Radisson Hotel, on Sixth Street in downtown Minneapolis, was officially inaugurated by William Howard Taft in 1909.

The Minneapolis Athenaeum opened its doors in 1859, a precursor to the public library; the Minneapolis YMCA started in 1866. Beginning in 1867 the Pence Opera House, billed as the "Playhouse for Pioneers," offered everything from *Our American Cousin* to *Richard III.* The city had a chamber of commerce in 1881, electric lights in 1882, and electric streetcars and its first "skyscraper" in 1889. The city's Grand Opera House was built in 1882; the Minneapolis School of Art opened in 1886. The Minneapolis Symphony Orchestra presented its inaugural concert in 1903.

Trolley transportation enabled cities like Minneapolis to continue to expand business activity long after residential areas filled up. Workers could live on the outskirts of the city and still get to work with ease. Courtesy, Minneapolis Public Library

For those who had come here for good, Minneapolis was becoming something else, too: a solid and secure hometown; a city of clean air, safe streets, and cultural amenities; a community of schools, churches, and tree-lined neighborhoods; and a wholesome place to live, work, worship, and raise a family.

It was also, literally and gloriously, a city of lakes. Many communities could boast richer histories, grander downtowns, milder winters, gaudier nightlife, or greater proximity to the mountains or the sea. Few, however, had so much scenic beauty so close at hand. For thousands of Minneapolitans, the lake was not a half-day's journey away—it was right outside their front door! Most sections of Minneapolis were within walking distance of one lake or another, and the graceful lake names—Harriet, Isles, Nokomis, Powderhorn, Cedar, and so forth—were often used to designate surrounding neighborhoods.

The city's lakes, at least in their original forms, were a gift of nature. Their preservation, development, and maintenance as community treasures, however, required the hand of man. A pair of nature-minded Maine natives—Charles Loring, the city's first commissioner of parks, and Horace Cleveland, a noted landscape architect who had worked in St. Paul—directed the city's purchase of several large parcels of land for use as public parks during the 1880s. Among the extensive acreage thus belonging to the public was the land surrounding Minnehaha Falls near Fort Snelling, the land flanking Minnehaha Creek (which meanders west to east through south Minneapolis), and the land around the five largest lakes inside the city limits. (There are, by official count, a grand total of 15.) In addition, a good-sized tract of swampland southwest of downtown was dredged to become the lovely showcase that is Lake of the Isles.

Both Minneapolis and St. Paul bought the land that ran along the Mississippi River between Fort Snelling and the main Twin Cities campus of the University of Minnesota (near the St. Paul line in southeast Minneapolis) and developed it into verdant parkway. As suburbs extended the metropolitan area outward from the urban core, public concern for water and parkland followed. For instance Hennepin County, which includes the city of Minneapolis and several of its western and southern suburbs, began developing one of the largest county park systems in the nation.

The city's earliest residential neighborhoods were clustered among the mills and other industrial and commercial establishments along both sides of the river. As the industrial and commercial activity increased, so did the need for greater residential space. For the most part, that space developed to the south and west of the original industrial sites. As is the case in most growing cities, the working class congregated in the affordable housing relatively close to their jobs, while the more affluent citizens built their homes somewhat farther from the hurly-burly of the workplace. In the early days of Minneapolis, this often meant that the workers—including the most recent arrivals from overseas—could be found in such teeming confines as Bohemian Flats not far from the mills along the west bank of the river, and their employers along the more gracious expanses of Park Avenue or on genteel Lowry Hill, significantly south and west, respectively.

Over time, the city's neighborhoods expanded to municipal limits beyond Minnehaha Creek to the south and the far side of the string of lakes from Cedar to Harriet on the west. Northern expansion reached beyond Bassett Creek, while to the east it pushed up against the St. Paul line and (south of downtown) the Mississippi River. Inevitably, with the growth of the city's middle class, the lines between poor and rich enclaves blurred. Some areas—such as hilly Kenwood, with its stately houses overlooking Lake of the Isles—were (and still are) more exclusive than others. Yet, by most contemporary measures, twentieth-century Minneapolis boasted a broad range of livable, affordable, and accessible housing, close to both lakes and parks.

Minneapolis grew up with a deep and abiding commitment to education, both public and private. A wide array of churches reflected, over time, less a Yankee influence than the strong spiritual faiths of later arrivals—Scandinavian and German Lutherans; German, Irish, and Polish Catholics; Russian and Polish Jews; and Middle Western Methodists and Baptists. Minneapolis and its environs have never, for that matter, been quite as ethnically homogeneous as outsiders have believed. By the turn of the century, the city's Eastern- and European-born majority was complemented by small but growing numbers of blacks, Asians, and other minorities. In more recent years, Minneapolis has been home to one of the nation's largest urban populations of American Indians—most of the descendants of the area's original Sioux and Ojibway inhabitants.

The city's scenic offerings, cultural diversity, and relative prosperity did not, however, make it immune to the problems of the times. Young Minneapolitans went off to war in 1917 and 1941, and did their best to hold on to their homes and livelihoods during the Great Depression. In the middle 1930s, hundreds of Teamsters and their unionist supporters took to the streets and fought pitched battles with police and employer-organized vigilantes before Governor Floyd B. Olson, who'd grown up on the city's North Side, was compelled to declare martial law. In the mid-1940s an ambitious young South Dakota native, Hubert H. Humphrey, cleaned up a corrupt municipal police department as Minneapolis' reform-minded mayor.

Humphrey, with a group of young colleagues, was also instrumental in the formation of the state's liberal Democratic Farmer

Nicollet Avenue, and much of the rest of Minneapolis, had electric lights in by 1882. Courtesy, Minnesota Historical Society

Labor Party. The DFL became, in short order, the dominant political force in what had once been a Republican stronghold. Humphrey himself, of course, set out on a track that stretched all the way from Minneapolis to the White House. Well, *almost* all the way.

In 1950 the city of Minneapolis stood on the threshold of its first centenary.

Its population had reached an all-time high of more than 500,000, and it was, by all accounts, a vibrant, progressive, livable community. Its downtown skyline was dominated by the 32-story Foshay Tower, which, when dedicated amid enormous fanfare in 1929, was the tallest building west of Chicago. The mills of its founders were no longer thriving, but many of the great companies spawned by those original mills testified to their robust legacy. Pillsbury, General Mills, and Cargill, moreover, had been joined by Honeywell, a manufacturer of thermostats; Dayton's, the area's dominant retailer; and other mainstays of the city's modern economy.

But the city was also poised on the threshold of dramatic change.

On all sides of the Twin Cities new housing developments, businesses, and supporting services were about to spring up, grow, and coalesce into bustling communities—creating what would, within three decades, become a metropolitan area of more than 2 million people. Big-league baseball, football, and hockey would, within less than two decades, join with internationally acclaimed repertory theater and other cultural amenities to give the area a glitter and excitement undreamed of even by its most hyperbolic early promoters. Breakthroughs in medicine and health-care technology at the University of Minnesota and other local medical and scientific centers would, in just a few short years, draw worldwide attention. Innovations in electronics and computer manufacture were already, in 1950, beginning to spark a dynamic new component of the local economy.

Most importantly, as Minneapolis looked ahead to its second century, a new generation of leaders was stepping into position. Some of the names—Pillsbury and Dayton, for instance—were familiar enough, harking back to earlier times. Many others, however, were fresh—names like Cowles, Carlson, Norris, Bakken, and Pohlad.

Some of the new leaders were homegrown. Others, like those pioneering New Englanders, were outsiders. Most, whether old Minneapolis stock or new arrivals, perceived the growth of their individual enterprises and the further development of their community as mutually dependent imperatives.

In that light, looking forward, they all saw an even brighter future for their city by the falls.

Chapter

2

Through Diversity, Strength

The development of Minneapolis as a lumber- and grain-milling center followed a fortuitous logic dictated by geography, natural resources, and human settlement. There was, of course, the waterfall of St. Anthony, providing the essential power for the mills. There were the vast stands of white pine and the oceans of grain to feed the mills. There were the enterprising Eastern businessmen to develop, expand, and improve the mills, and the countless immigrants to help keep the mills turning. It was, in sum, no fluke of history that made the city by the falls one of the world's preeminent producers of flour and milled timber by the end of the nineteenth century.

There is reason to believe, however, that the continuing development of Minneapolis and its "twin" sibling, St. Paul, benefited from other less obvious, more coincidental factors and influences. University of Minnesota geography professor John Borchert has pointed out, for example, that railroad technology during the latter half of the nineteenth century was allowing North American industrial and commercial centers to be located farther apart than ever before. The Twin Cities, says Borchert, grew up on the fringe of contemporary American settlement, where such centers were, quite literally, few and far between.

According to Borchert, the story of the Twin Cities could have worked itself out differently. "Had the region's population and wealth been more dispersed among a larger number of

Minneapolis area residents are modern examples of the diversity and strength that have enabled the city to grow from a milling and lumber town to the present metropolitan center, with more than 360,000 residents living within the city. Photo by Ed Bock

St. Anthony Falls has been a source of power since the days of the first grain mills in Minneapolis. Today, water is harnessed for hydroelectric power plants. Photo by Greg Ryan/Sally Beyer

smaller centers, there would have been a net loss to the [entire] Upper Midwest economy," Borchert explains. As it happened, the whole region profited handsomely from "an extraordinary concentration of . . . resources" in Minneapolis and St. Paul. And the Twin Cities, "in terms of entrepreneurial skill and information, in terms of money and human capital, reached some sort of critical mass by the 1920s."

A good thing that was, too. By the 1920s the city's once mighty lumber-milling industry had all but disappeared, following the demise of the region's pine forests. At the same time flour-milling, the other pillar of the city's pioneer economy, was leveling off as grain growing, processing, and transporting technologies made the likes of Kansas City and Buffalo more competitive milling centers. As historian Joseph Stipanovich has pointed out, it was the city's good fortune that the decline of local flour-milling was not as precipitous as the decline of its lumbering counterpart, because the former generated much more employment and revenue. Still, in a one- or two-industry town, any such decline could have been troublesome.

But the milling industries, by the second decade of the new century, had produced a legacy that would ensure their places in local history. Through a process of merger and concentration, the Twin Cities' millers perpetuated themselves as a handful of large, multinational companies like Washburn Crosby (General Mills), Pillsbury, and Cargill. Through a process of spin-off and synergy, they continue to spark and encourage the diversification of the local economy.

Diversification, in fact, had begun decades earlier, with the establishment of flour-barrel manufacturing and other mill-related industries, as well as with the local advent of shopkeepers, hoteliers, real estate companies, newspapers, and the various components of a growing "small business" community.

Among the city's early developing industries, a logic, again, prevailed. A fast-growing city is likely to have, for instance, a fast-growing construction trade to meet its demand for new mills, elevators, and factories; civic and commercial buildings;

Although the lumber milling industry had declined by the 1920s, flour milling continued to remain strong, a business which proved to be able to provide more employment and greater revenue. Photo by Robert Friedman

communications and transportation facilities; and schools, churches, and homes. Minneapolis in the late 1800s was certainly no exception. Following the same logic was the local development of banks and investment firms to fuel the community's growth, and insurance companies to protect it.

The First National Bank of Minneapolis, now part of the regional giant, First Bank System, was founded as the Bank of Minneapolis in 1857. Northwestern National Bank, precursor of First Bank System's regional rival, the Norwest Corporation, was founded on a $2,000 deposit from milling executive William Hood Dunwoody in 1872. Northwestern National Life Insurance Company, another pioneer, opened its doors in 1885.

The city's late nineteenth- and early twentieth-century development as a regional retail center was especially dramatic in light of the raging competition between the Twin Cities. St. Paul, the older of the "twins" and, since 1858, the state capital, had the early advantage in both wholesale and retail trade. But as Minneapolis' population and regional influence began to eclipse St. Paul's in the 1880s, so did its wholesale and retail muscle. By 1900 Minneapolis' wholesale volume was twice that of St. Paul's, and the Mill City was the retail hub of the Upper Midwest.

Like the milling business, the city's retail trade was driven by a relatively small group of energetic pioneers. They included the energetic Elizabeth Quinlan, an Irish immigrant and erstwhile clerk who, with another clerk, Fred Young, founded the city's first ready-to-wear women's clothing store in 1894. Young-Quinlan was a local institution in its distinctive quarters on Nicollet Avenue for more than 80 years. The pioneers included, too, a Scotsman by

FACING PAGE: Styles of the past blend with those of the new in Minneapolis, as the IDS Tower provides a contrasting backdrop for one of the area's many examples of older architecture. Photo by Ed Bock

BELOW: Construction has traditionally been a busy trade in Minneapolis due to the city's constant growth. Photo by Thomas K. Perry

Pleasure boats make their way through the St. Anthony Lock along the Mississippi River. Photo by Will Goddard

the name of William Donaldson, whose "Glass Block" on Nicollet Avenue was one of the most dazzling emporiums in the region for decades. Donaldsons department stores were mainstays of Minneapolis' home-based retail community until their purchase, in 1988, by Chicago-based Carson Pirie Scott.

Then there was George Draper Dayton, who came to Minneapolis from the western part of the state in the 1880s. Dayton was a banker who had constructed a six-story building on the corner of Seventh and Nicollet around the turn of the century. A short while later, he moved a dry-goods retailer that he had purchased onto the site. In 1903 the store's name was changed from Goodfellow's to Dayton's Daylight Store, and, a short time after that, to the Dayton's Dry Goods Company. Soon, because of the store's commitment to innovative retailing and customer service, the shorter name, "Dayton's," became virtually synonymous with full-service department store shopping throughout the Upper Midwest.

Other industries grew swiftly, too. The Twin Cities had become a railroad center during the second half of the nineteenth century, owing to its mills, its location, and the drive of such leaders as James J. Hill, the fabled "Empire Builder." One of the more interesting rail enterprises, dating back to the 1880s, was the Minneapolis, St. Paul & Sault Ste. Marie, the forerunner of today's Soo Line. While most railroads at the time were land-grant lines, the original Soo was developed by private money, which also paid for its initial right-of-way. The line was the brainchild of such local entrepreneurs as William Washburn (brother of Cadwallader Washburn), who sought the most competitive route by which to ship products back East.

As it diversified, Minneapolis industry reflected both the technological opportunities of the times and the logic imposed by its environment. Moving energetically into the new century, the city's industrial ranks soon included nearly every kind of manufacturer and service industry then operating in rapidly urbanizing America. Perhaps Minneapolis would forever be known as the Mill City, but by the 1920s mills were only a part of the local story. Historian Joseph Stipanovich, citing the federal government's *Census of Manufacturers* in 1929, says:

[W]hile flour and grain-mill products were still the most valuable products in the city's economy, printing and publishing came second. The products

Valspar Paint has been one of the many local companies working to make Minneapolis more attractive. The Valspar building is known for its vivid paint scheme. Photo by Will Goddard

crafted in the city's foundries and machine shops were the third most valuable items produced in the city, while railroad car construction and repair, the assembly of electrical machinery and related apparatus, furniture making, the processing of butter, and preparation of spices and coffee all ranked in the top 10 most valuable activities, measured by the worth of output.

A healthy share of the city's diversification was, in Stipanovich's words, "aided not only by the investments in basic research by various firms tackling particular problems in the market but also by research carried out at the University of Minnesota." Established as a land-grant institution during the 1860s, the U of M was, during its early years, primarily a liberal arts center. But, as Stipanovich points out, by the late nineteenth century the school's Board of Regents "included representatives of the Minneapolis milling interests . . . and their influence was instrumental in the development of applied research . . . [T]he tackling of industrial research problems by the university greatly aided in the development of the economy of the entire state."

Just often enough, however, the diversification of the Mill City operated by its own peculiar imperatives, independent of prevailing logic and institutional assistance. Such was the case of Minneapolis-based Honeywell, one of the modern world's high-technology titans, whose guiding light had his business roots in the decidedly *low*-technology manufacturing of wheelbarrows.

The famous Honeywell thermostat itself was the invention of a Minneapolis man whose business was originally the manufacture of fire extinguishers. In 1883 A.M. Butz came up with the idea for a device that would automatically regulate furnace and boiler temperatures. Butz's idea was brilliant—a marvel of practical know-how—but the fledgling Consolidated Temperature Controlling Company, built around that first thermostat, couldn't make a go of it. Only through the increasingly frequent infusions of cash provided by William Sweatt, a local wheelbarrow-maker, did the company manage to survive. Impressed by the possibilities of the thermostat, Sweatt invested $1,500 in Butz's enterprise in 1891. In a few years—more by default than by design—Sweatt was the company's sole owner.

Despite the company's inauspicious beginnings, the thermostat was, by the first decade of the new century, an idea whose time had clearly come. The hard-working, innovative Sweatt added a clock to the device and marketed the "new" thermostat aggressively, and slowly but surely the company began to prosper. Sweatt's sons, Harold Wilson Sweatt and Charles Baxter Sweatt, joined the firm in 1913 and 1916, respectively, and the firm opened sales offices around the country. In 1927, following a merger with an Ohio-based competitor, the fast-growing, international-minded Minneapolis Heat Regulator Company took a new name: the Honeywell Heating Specialties Company.

The Minneapolis-St. Paul International Airport has passenger service to more than 80 major U.S. cities, as well as direct international flights. Photo by Steve Schneider

Today, a century after its modest inception, Honeywell Inc. is a $7-billion corporation that designs and manufactures computer systems and electronic control equipment with a wide range of applications. The company, with nearly 80,000 employees scattered around the world, is still headquartered in Minneapolis.

On September 15, 1929, a former city planning engineer named A.C. Godward filled a full page of the *Minneapolis Journal* with a vividly detailed—and remarkably foresightful—picture of his hometown in the year 1979. Anticipating the city's growth over the next 50 years, Godward wrote:

We are not limited as to resources or possibilities of expansion. Our expansion is dependent upon whether or not Minneapolis continues to give its entire trade territory a comprehensive service of an acceptable type . . . This district extends over half a million square miles of productive land, and contains one and one-quarter million families, or nearly 7,000,000 people . . .

It is the responsibility of Minneapolis to serve this trade territory in the processing of its raw material, marketing of its goods, manufacturing the necessities for the people in its trade area and the jobbing and wholesaling of supplies needed by its people when such supplies cannot be economically manufactured at home.

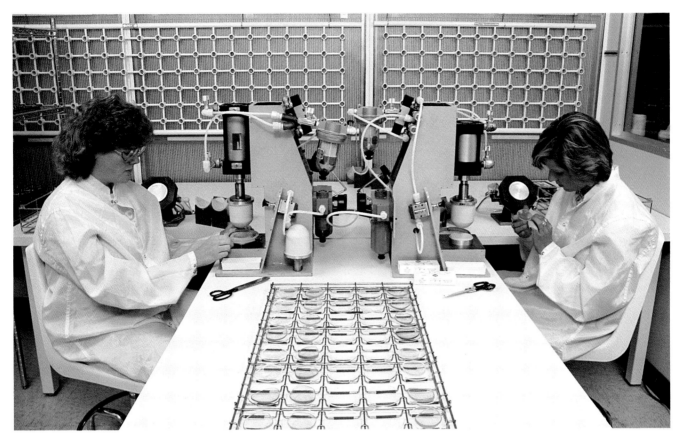

Employees at one of Minneapolis' many and varied high-tech companies, Benson Optical, put the finishing touches on eyeglass lenses. Photo by Ed Bock

If Minneapolis continues to give this service to its trade territory efficiently and economically, it will prosper; if it does not, then the competition of other cities, also strategically located in relation to this trade area, will retard the growth of our city . . .

Godward would no doubt be pleased by what actually existed at the distant end of his 50-year telescope. Minneapolis did, in fact, live up to its "responsibility" to serve its trade area as the planner prescribed, prospering through its diversity. It could be argued that, if anything, Godward was too cautious, having limited his projections to contemporary industries and to a trade area of only 7 million people. He had no way of sensing, of course, a future driven by the microchip; no way, for that matter, of anticipating the possibilities of the "global village."

In the half-century that unfurled after Godward's predictions, Minneapolis became a thoroughly modern city, powered by a multifaceted, technology-driven economy.

The city suffered with the rest of the world through the Great Depression. In Minneapolis, as elsewhere, businesses failed, fortunes vanished, and lives were ruined. Wilbur Foshay, a flamboyant local financier emblematic of the "anything's possible" euphoria of the 1920s, went to prison following a mail-fraud conviction in the early years of the heartbreaking 1930s. A bloody Teamsters strike in 1934 helped change the city from what had once been a rigidly "open-shop" employer's bastion to a more equitable community in which power was shared by business interests and labor unions. World War II, following hard on the heels of the Depression, put the city back to work again and sparked the resurgence of its established economy. But, here as elsewhere, business life would never be quite the same again.

Aviation technology burgeoned in the late 1940s and early 1950s, as locally based Northwest Airways (later Northwest Airlines) and North Central Airlines (since merged with Republic Airlines, now part of Northwest) became prominent national carriers. The old Wold-Chamberlain Field was overhauled, enlarged, and rechristened Minneapolis-St. Paul International Airport, making the Twin Cities a hub of trans-global freight and passenger transportation.

Communications technology blossomed during the same postwar period in the form of expanded regional radio coverage and the revolutionary phenomenon of television. Interestingly, the local development of commercial radio was the handiwork of the Washburn Crosby milling company, which bought a two-year-old station called WLAG in 1924. The company changed the station's call letters to WCCO—for "Washburn Crosby Co." —and was soon transmitting commercial jingles for Wheaties breakfast cereal over the regional airwaves. During the next several decades WCCO, under independent management, became one of America's mightiest stations, beaming its lively signal to distant points across the country. In 1948, under the innovative direction of the Stanley Hubbard broadcasting company, KSTP provided the region's first commercial television service. Within a short time, all three major networks were represented by Twin Cities-based stations.

The local opportunities provided by the postwar technology boom were not limited to either air lanes or airwaves. Six months after the end of World War II, a former navy engineer named William Norris and a small group of engineers and technicians formed a company called Engineering Research Associates (ERA) and set up shop in a former radiator plant in south Minneapolis. The company soon had a contract to develop the first general-purpose computer system for the federal government.

The system, called Atlas, propelled ERA—and its stunned electronics industry competitors—into the modern computer age. ERA, for its

The microchip revolution has helped accelerate the growth of the Minneapolis area, home to computer companies such as Cray Research and Control Data Corporation. This installation is part of the computer network at The Pillsbury Company. Photo by Ed Bock

part, evolved into the Univac Division of the Sperry Rand Corporation, while the farsighted Bill Norris, after guiding Univac, set off on his own. In 1957 Norris formed his own electronics company, called it Control Data Corporation (CDC), and began building what at the time were the world's biggest, fastest computers. Control Data, with headquarters in suburban Bloomington, soon became one of the area's most prominent corporate citizens, employing thousands of local managers and workers and contributing to the development of numerous spin-off ventures.

At about the same time Norris and his partners were developing super-computers on the city's South Side, an enterprising engineer at the north end of town was paving the way for another high-tech breakthrough. Initially working out of a garage owned by his brother-in-law, Earl Bakken developed the world's first wearable, battery-powered cardiac pacemaker. Bakken's company, Medtronic, Inc., eventually became the world's largest manufacturer of implantable pacing devices.

Like Norris' Control Data, Bakken's Medtronic stood an industry on its head with its startling technology. Like CDC, Medtronic became a catalyst in the development of a larger, highly sophisticated, electronics-based complex of industries in the postwar Twin Cities. Since the 1960s Medtronic, spin-offs like locally based Cardiac Pacemakers, Inc., the University of Minnesota Hospital and Clinic, and dozens of other private and public companies and institutions have transformed the Twin Cities into one of the foremost concentrations of medical-industrial resources on earth.

Not only serving A.C. Godward's regional trade area, Medtronic, CDC, and many other local high-tech wonder companies were, suddenly and quite literally, serving the entire world.

The postwar diversification of the Minneapolis economy involved more, however, than such breathtaking, state-of-the-art aviation, communications, and electronics technology. In a few noteworthy cases, it "merely" entailed new applications of existing, rather mundane products and services.

There was nothing either new or particularly exciting about the trading stamp, for example, when a 23-year-old Minneapolis soap salesman named Curtis Carlson happened upon the item in the late 1930s. Trading stamps, he quickly discovered, had been circulating with limited success for some 50 years, primarily via department stores. With each purchase from a participating merchant, the customer was given a number of stamps, which were pasted in a collection book and later redeemed for cash.

It was Carlson's ingenuity that took the lowly trading stamp, applied it to the grocery business, and, through hard work, aggressive marketing, and continuing innovation, revolutionized *both* the stamp and grocery industries. Carlson's reasoning was simple: A bunch of carrots is a bunch of carrots, regardless

PREVIOUS PAGE: Postwar diversification and growth of technically oriented industries has rocketed the economy of Minneapolis skyward. Photo by Robert Friedman

ABOVE AND FACING PAGE: Summer means berry season around Minneapolis, where strawberries and raspberries grow in abundance. Photos by Robert Friedman

of where they are bought. What, then, could be used to distinguish one grocery store from another—short of a costly (and generally self-defeating) price war? Trading stamps, of course! And what, besides a few dollars in cash upon redemption, could make collecting the stamps an irresistible habit among consumers? An eventual reward of high-quality "premium" merchandise, that's what!

After several years of pushing his idea, Carlson made the concept work—first in small, neighborhood grocery stores and gas stations, then in national chains of giant supermarkets. The energetic entrepreneur built one of the nation's largest private companies on the foundation of his Gold Bond Stamps. The multinational, $5-billion-plus Carlson Companies, based in the Minneapolis suburb of Minnetonka, has since expanded to comprise hotels and restaurants, worldwide travel services, a wide array of incentive and promotion firms (including the original Gold Bond Stamps), and extensive real estate developments. But it can all be traced back to that fresh approach to an old idea.

Breakthroughs shattered familiar ways of doing business in a number of other local industries, too—and often with far-reaching effects. In the early 1950s the Twin Cities was fast becoming a far-flung metropolitan area, as young, increasingly affluent families built or bought homes in successive rings of suburban developments. Like most of America's urban centers, Minneapolis faced a serious—indeed, potentially crippling—loss of retail trade downtown, where department stores and hundreds of other merchants had sold their wares since pioneer days. People living (and often, working) in suburban Fridley, Richfield, or Hopkins wanted to shop conveniently and close to home. For many of these new suburbanites, downtown Minneapolis was neither.

The grandsons of pioneer retailer George Draper Dayton pondered the situation. The big Dayton's department store at Seventh and Nicollet had been the centerpiece of downtown retail activity for half a century, but the suburban shift was now challenging its survival. The Dayton brothers' eventual solution was as

simple as it would soon prove to be significant. On 500 acres of cornfields in the southwest suburb of Edina, they would develop a whole new concept in retailing: the nation's first all-enclosed, all-weather shopping mall. That first mall, called Southdale, opened in 1956 with great fanfare and at a not-insignificant cost of $20 million. Dayton's stood at one end while Donaldsons was at the other, thus perpetuating the long-standing rivalry between the two stores. Dozens of smaller, more specialized stores and shops were situated around a huge, handsome atrium between them.

The mall was a spectacular success and several other similar suburban "Dales" followed during the 1960s and 1970s, forever changing the shopping patterns of the Twin Cities and adding to the metro area's overall economic health. That the feared deterioration of the Twin Cities' downtowns never happened to the ex-

Metropolitan expansion suffered as many families moved to the suburbs in the 1950s and following years, taking economic support away from the downtown. In the city's resilient style, Minneapolis nevertheless grew into a strong city. Photo by Greg Ryan/Sally Beyer

tent once predicted is further testimony to the ingenuity of local business leaders.

Innovation throughout the last half-century's diversification also kept Minneapolis in the forefront of the nation's agribusiness activity. The latter-day incarnations of the city's founding companies may not have been doing much actual milling alongside the Falls of St. Anthony in the second half of the twentieth century, but they were doing nearly everything else with grain and its products—and then some.

The story of the modern millers—venerable but significantly updated local companies such as Cargill, Pillsbury, General Mills, International Multifoods, and Peavey—is another tale of problem-solving ingenuity and diversification. Each of these companies, in Joseph Stipanovich's words, "adjusted to the changing market conditions in the United States and around the world and upgraded their products and selling activities to remain competitive." As a result, Stipanovich adds, "Agribusiness continued to be a major

facet of Minneapolis' economic vitality."

How well these companies have managed their growth and diversification since the "good old days" on the banks of the Mississippi can be measured, at least in part, by their sheer modern size. All are billion-dollar companies in the late 1980s.

The modest grain-handling enterprise founded by Will Cargill in 1865, for example, is now one of the largest privately owned companies in the world, with annual sales estimated in the neighborhood of $33 billion. The company, now headquartered in the Minneapolis suburb of Minnetonka and employing more than 50,000 persons around the world, has long since diversified its operations. Its major businesses now include the storage, handling, and processing of a variety of agricultural commodities.

Today's Pillsbury Company is a $6-billion corporation that is now part of the British-based conglomerate, Grand Metropolitan PLC. With more than 100,000 employees and worldwide distribution, the company is still headquartered in Minneapolis. Its contemporary operations comprise consumer products, agri-

While Minneapolis has one of the largest concentrations of high-tech businesses in the nation, milling, machinery, and other industries bring diversification. Photo by Will Goddard

products, and restaurants.

General Mills, Inc.—formed in 1928 by the merger of several regional milling operations, including the old Washburn Crosby Company—boasts annual sales of more than $5 billion and has more than 75,000 employees worldwide. Of the major local millers, General Mills, famous for such twentieth-century staples as Cheerios, Wheaties, and Betty Crocker cake mixes, has gone the farthest afield from its pioneering products. GMI has, over the past few decades, expanded into such widely diverse fields as restaurants, toys and games, and fashion and apparel, although it recently narrowed its focus to consumer goods and restaurants. General Mills' stock is publicly traded on the New York Stock Exchange.

In a recent economic profile of the city, the Greater Minneapolis Chamber of Commerce makes the point that with more than 1,300 "technology-intensive" companies in the area, the Twin Cities has "one of the largest concentrations of high-technology businesses in the nation." At the same time, says the chamber report, "The diversity of local manufacturing operations is evidenced by the presence of electronics, milling, machinery, medical products, food processing, and major graphic art industries."

For additional documentation of the area's modern-day diversification, one need only examine a recent listing of *Fortune* magazine's famous "500." In 1989, Minneapolis and St. Paul were credited with no fewer than 15 *Fortune* 500 industrial companies (based on 1988 sales).

The 15 local industrial companies (accompanied by their national ranking and basic industry) included the following: 3M (34th, diverse manufacturing), Honeywell (60th, electronics), General Mills (76th, food products), Control Data (125th, computers), Land O'Lakes (179th, dairy products), International Multifoods (231st, food products), CENEX (287th, agribusiness), Deluxe Check Printing (296th, printing), Bemis (319th, packaging manufacture), Pentair (370th, electric tools), Cray Research (385th, computers), H.B. Fuller (408th, adhesives), Medtronic (424th, medical products), Toro (438th, lawn equipment), and Jostens (450th, commemorative jewelry, graduation accessories).

Local companies named to the *Fortune* service 500 in 1988 were: Super Valu Stores and Nash-Finch (1st and 36th, respectively, among diversified services companies nationwide); First Bank System and Norwest Corporation (22nd and 31st among commercial banking companies); TCF Banking & Savings (27th among savings institutions); St. Paul Companies (27th among diversified financial companies); IDS, Northwestern National, and Minnesota Mutual (18th, 35th, and 42nd among life insurance companies); Dayton Hudson (9th among retailers); Northwest Airlines and Soo Line (10th and 32nd among transportation companies); and Northern States Power (48th among utilities).

Not reflected in these tallies, yet of crucial importance to both the metropolitan area's economy and its quality of life, are a number of other local "industries."

Innovative and generally superior health-care institutions, for instance, have for many decades drawn Upper Midwesterners to the Twin Cities for diagnosis and treatment. In the 1950s, the astonishing heart-surgery and organ-transplant technology pioneered by the staff of the University of Minnesota Hospital transformed the area into one of the world's leading medical centers. The long and fruitful relationship between U of M scientists and local industry—so important to the development of the state's milling, agriculture, and mining components—was yielding significant results in health-care technology in the postwar boom years. Such diverse companies as Medtronic, 3M, and Control Data, in league with the university and other public and private institutions, were making the Twin Cities nothing less than a "medical Silicon Valley."

During the 1970s, the Twin Cities also became a closely observed "laboratory" of innovative health-care delivery systems. A local physician, Dr. Paul M. Ellwood, Jr., coined the phrase "health maintenance organization" (HMO). Along with a number of colleagues and disciples, Ellwood was soon acknowledged as one of the nation's leading proponents of prepaid health-care plans. HMOs, "preferred provider organizations," and other "alternative" health delivery and payment systems took hold in Minneapolis. Together with the explosion in related technology and a large, existing health-services component, they have helped to make health care one of the largest industries in the state.

Like health care, education has long been a mainstay of the state and local economies. From the beginning, Minneapolis business leaders have recognized the critical importance of a well-trained work force and an enlightened citizenry, as well as the essential contributions of academic research and development. And, from the beginning, the business leaders have supported local education accordingly.

Education, meanwhile, has become a significant component of the local economy itself. The enormous Minneapolis and St. Paul campuses of the University of Minnesota together employ nearly 20,000 persons (not counting students); two dozen other public and private schools, colleges, and universities in the area employ additional thousands. Drawn by the community's progressive approach to its schools, a number of education-related businesses—running the gamut from computer software companies to private research and consulting firms—have, in addition, set up shop in the Twin Cities.

On the lighter side, sports and entertainment have continued to be a potent regional drawing card—and an important part of the community's economic composition. A sparkling array of cultural amenities—including the renowned Minnesota Orchestra, Guthrie Theater, and Walker Art Center—have added immeasurably to the region's much-acclaimed "quality of life." This also provides appealing incentives that local companies can use to recruit and retain well-educated managers and employees.

Professional and amateur sports likewise add glitter to the city's commercial and industrial appeal. The Twin Cities has been an official big league community since the early 1960s when, largely through the efforts of area business executives and institutions, local professional franchises were established in baseball, football, and hockey. In the fall of 1989 the city became home to a new National Basketball Association franchise, the Minnesota Timberwolves, coached by Bill Musselman.

In the late 1970s many of the same executives and institutions (including the *Minneapolis Star Tribune* and other members of the local media) led the drive for the construction of a new, entirely covered, downtown stadium. And since 1982, the Twins, the Vikings, and the University of Minnesota football team have played their home games—come rain, snow, or shine—in the Hubert H. Humphrey Metrodome. In early 1989 the Metrodome was the site of the National Collegiate Athletic Association's Midwest Regional basketball finals, and in 1992 the facility will host the NCAA's "Final Four" basketball tourney.

When the owners of the Minnesota Twins talked of moving the franchise out of state during the early 1980s, local business leaders again displayed their determination to keep their town in the major leagues. Senior Minneapolis banker, entrepreneur, and civic leader Carl Pohlad eventually stepped forward and bought the Twins in 1984, vowing to make the long-dormant club competitive. Three seasons later the Twins defied 150-to-1 odds and won their first World Championship ever. By some estimates, the hoopla surrounding the American League playoffs and World Series games generated upward of $100 million for the local economy.

Minneapolis has always been a community congenial to the birth and nurturing of small businesses. Many small businesses splinter off from huge, high-profile corporations and, over time, become major players in their own right. Since the Second World War, the city has been the scene of a large and very profitable number of spin-offs, particularly in the dynamic high-tech industries. For example Cray Research, a builder of new generations of super-computers, is a spin-off of Control Data, itself a spin-off of the Univac Division of Sperry Rand during the 1950s. The origins of CPT Corporation, a local multimillion-dollar manufacturer of word processing systems, are rooted in Honeywell. Golden Valley Microwave Foods, a world leader in the development of foods for microwave ovens, was launched by a former Pillsbury employee.

The drive for a new, entirely covered, downtown sports stadium was started in the late 1970s by local business leaders, and since 1982 the Twins, Vikings, and the University of Minnesota football team have called the Hubert H. Humphrey Metrodome home field. Photo by Robert Friedman

RIGHT AND BELOW: The home field of the Minnesota Vikings is the Hubert H. Humphrey Metrodome, where sellout crowds, protected from inclement weather, gather to watch professional football. Photo by Steve Schneider

The list could go on, but the message is happily succinct. Minneapolis is, as it has always been, a great place for entrepreneurs.

Minneapolis' economy has never been shockproof. Similar to the experiences of other great American cities, the Mill City has all too frequently felt the pinch of financial panics, crashes, recessions, and depressions. Its close ties to the region's farms and associated agribusinesses have given the community a mostly stable foundation, although when agriculture suffers, many local businesses feel the effects. But by and large, because of the historic diversity of its economy, Minneapolis has been remarkably surefooted on its march through the twentieth century.

"The absence of a major heavy-industry base . . . means the city can make rapid shifts without losing massive capital investment locked into areas that cannot easily be transformed into other types of economic activity," Joseph Stipanovich has argued convincingly. In Stipanovich's words:

Minnesota Twins fans proudly call the Metrodome "Homerdome," as well-hit balls seem to carry farther in the enclosed stadium. Here the Twins host the Oakland Athletics. Photo by Steve Schneider

The small scale of business endeavor in Minneapolis, with thousands of firms producing various goods and services around a nucleus of 200 or so very large firms, and the concentrations in trade, services, and financial activities both suggest that large numbers of entrepreneurs could easily make the transition to the wholly new areas of enterprise that may present themselves as technology continues to revolutionize the world . . .

By the late 1980s the economy of the city and the surrounding metropolitan area had never been more vibrant or diverse. The list of the Twin Cities' 100 largest publicly traded corporations included retailers and wholesalers; food processors and marketers; energy companies and utilities; transportation, finance, insurance, health-care, construction, and communications companies; and manufacturers of everything from super-computers and medical devices to toiletries and toys. The roster of the area's top 100 privately held corporations spanned an equally broad range of industrial and commercial activity.

Within the growing high-technology segment of the local economy, the variety of offerings was amazingly extensive. In the late 1980s Twin Cities-area technology companies were developing, manufacturing, and marketing—among literally thousands of products—large and small computers, computer components and accessories, heart valves and hearing aids, fluid material management systems, wireless security equipment, multi-image printers, electronic scales, and telecommunications systems. Interestingly enough, only six of *Corporate Report Minnesota* magazine's 1988 "High-Tech 100" companies were founded before 1950. More than half of the listed companies had been in business for less than 20 years.

Not documented on such lists were the thousands of mom-and-pop operations—grocers and pharmacists, dry cleaners and photo processors, auto dealers and repair shops, and so on ad infinitum—that have long played essential roles in the diversified local economy and continued to thrive in the eighties. These, in turn, have been complemented in recent years by scores of innovative retailing and service establishments—shops, for instance, specializing in snazzy stockings or undergarments, or products celebrating Minnesota life—that have been inspired and given life by the proliferation of upscale specialty malls throughout the metro area. Less visible have been the growing numbers of entrepreneurs who work out of their homes and garages, producing children's books and women's fashions, board games and computer software.

The story of the Minneapolis economy is, of course, far from over, as the city poises itself for the leap into the twenty-first century. The theme, however, remains reassuringly familiar: Through diversity there is strength.

A Community That Works

Some attribute it to a chilly climate, some to geographic isolation. Others point to the flinty pragmatism and civic-mindedness of Yankee pioneers, still others to the communal instincts and solid work ethic of the area's European-born settlers. The "it" is that much remarked-upon quality of cooperation that has distinguished Minneapolis from so many of its urban counterparts over the past century and continues to make the city work today.

The development of the entire nation has been a testimony to a unique—albeit sometimes uneasy—alliance between public and private institutions, organizations, and individuals. Many historians and observers believe, however, that in the Twin Cities this public-private alliance has been exceptionally fruitful. The various components of this alliance don't always agree with one another, nor are their joint efforts inevitably successful. But in the Twin Cities these components, working together, have built a record of civic achievement over the past 120-odd years that is a model for metropolitan areas most everywhere.

In the community's earliest days, the coming together of the few small elements of pioneer society bore some of the intimacy of a family gathering. John H. Stevens' house on the west bank of St. Anthony Falls (not yet officially "Minneapolis") variously served as a meeting hall, general store, bank, land office, church, theater, and inn. Stevens himself was a military man, civic leader, and entrepreneur; the man, as well as his house, was emblematic of the functional combinations required in those formative times. That the new community's name was eventually coined under Stevens' roof seems, in retrospect, only right and appropriate.

Early Minneapolis was an outpost far removed from the established concentrations of "civilized" society. For the most part, settlers here were forced to make do with what they had on

Minneapolis' philosophical roots go back to the roots of the nation: its early settlers came from New England, bringing with them an ultra-American belief in thrift, education, and free enterprise. Photo by Will Goddard

hand or to make something new from scratch. In either case, by absolute necessity, sharing and cooperation were the operative commandments.

The New England-born entrepreneurs who composed the community's early leadership were nothing if not practical. Many of them were well-educated in the imperatives of both private enterprise and public governance, and understood the need for communal cooperation. Mindful as they were of their own commercial interests, they were also firmly committed to local democratic institutions. For instance, they knew that effective public schools produced enlightened citizens and productive workers, and that both were required for the community's orderly growth. Such growth was, among other things, good for business.

Glancing backward from the perspective of the late twentieth century, one might easily underestimate the formative role of those pioneering Yankees. After all, modern Minneapolis is widely perceived as a homogeneous Scandinavian enclave—which, with its thousands of Johnsons, Petersons, and Nelsons, it is to a significant degree. Yet before the Swedes, Norwegians, and Danes began arriving en masse in the 1870s and 1880s—and for many decades after— Minneapolis might, to all intents and purposes, have been a far-flung, admittedly very rustic extension of, say, Bangor, Maine. The community was on more than one occasion described as the "New England of the West." And Minnesota historian Theodore Blegen has recorded what was apparently a common enough sentiment, conveyed by a toast made at a New England Society of the Northwest meeting in the late 1850s. The toast expressed the hope, writes Blegen, that "New England industry, New England enterprise, and New England thrift shall build here a glorious superstructure of education and Gospel truth."

The lofty moral tone of that toast is instructive. In the sec-

Many observers see in Minneapolis a shining example of cooperation between the private and public sectors for the good of both. Photo by Ed Bock

ond half of the nineteenth century, what was more or less a Puritan ethos informed local work habits, lay behind the high priority given local education, and helped set the bedrock commitment to a new Republican party devoted to robust free enterprise and the abolition of slavery. Surely not all of the community's transplanted New Englanders were moralistic Republicans; not all could, for that matter, boast of a Scripture-based integrity in the conduct of their civic and business affairs. Yet there is little doubt that certain high ideals were honored by those early city fathers, and that those ideals influenced, on a number of fronts, the development of their young community.

In addition to the community's basic industries, the erstwhile New Englanders set up churches, meeting halls, and various selective or voluntary associations like the Masonry, Good Templars, Young

RIGHT: Brushing snow off busy downtown streets is not a comfortable job, but facing the rigors of work and weather is an old Minneapolis tradition. Photo by Greg Ryan/Sally Beyer

Much of Minneapolis was built through cooperation that began in the town meetings, clubs, and associations founded by the city's Yankee leadership. Out of these gatherings grew the park board system, the 1892 Republican National Convention, and the Minneapolis Institute of Arts. Photo by Steve Schneider

Costumed interpreters' helpers peer out of the window of the officers' quarters at historic Fort Snelling. Soldiers from the fort constructed the sawmill and flour mill that were among the embryonic beginnings of Minneapolis. Photo by Greg Ryan/Sally Beyer

Men's (and later, Women's) Christian Association, and prestigous Minneapolis, Minikahda, and Lafayette clubs. Like the churches and meeting halls, writes Joseph Stipanovich, the clubs and associations "served several purposes" :

They provided, of course, a framework for social intercourse among the city's social elite. They also formed a sophisticated information network that provided, through informal means, a backup to the formal channels of business and political interchange. It was through these and associated institutions of the churches and politics that the city leaders established consensus on a variety of social and political issues.

Out of that consensus evolved the city's park board system, various legislative and congressional campaigns, the 1892 Republican National Convention, and the Minneapolis Institute of Arts.

Stipanovich and other historians credit the same Yankee establishment for the creation of the city's earliest social-welfare organizations—most notably, local charities and settlement houses. Many of those charitable institutions bore the familiar old New England names of local industry, like the Washburn Memorial Orphan Asylum (founded in 1886 with funding and land provided by the brothers Cadwallader and William Washburn), for example, and the Pillsbury Settlement House (created before the

turn of the century by Charles and John S. Pillsbury). Other prominent New England-born names attached to those early social-
welfare institutions included Crosby, Heffelfinger, Brackett, and
MacMillan.

The immediate impact and continuing influence of the Minneapolis Yankees was enormous. Stipanovich writes:

*Their influence was out of all proportion to their numbers. At their peak
in 1890 they numbered only 10,000, a small fraction of the city's total population, but their wealth and prestige and deep roots in the American past
combined to maintain their position of civic leadership. As a result they
greatly shaped the evolution of the city . . . Their stamp was left on almost
every major civic institution, either because they created it and controlled it
for decades or because their values served to guide it for countless more.*

Many observers insist that
the early Yankee ethic prevails
here to this day. It helps account, they say, for the ability
to consummate important business agreements on the basis
of the participants' word and
handshake, and for the way in
which considerable amounts
of money can be raised for so
many civic and charitable
causes. It also helps account,
they could add, for the persis-
tent conviction that nearly any
local problem can be resolved
with the liberal application of
ingenuity, hard work, and public and private resources.

*Captain of the Anson Northrup excursion
boat, Tom Owens contemplates the Mississippi
River. Downtown is visible in the background;
its many attractions draw visitors from around
the world and generate business for Owens
and others. Photo by Greg Ryan/Sally Beyer*

The "workability" of Min-
neapolis has, virtually from the city's beginnings, depended on a
sharing of civic responsibility—or, viewed from a slightly different perspective, on the voluntary contributions of several significant community players. Individuals like the brothers John S.
and George A. Pillsbury stand out because of their extraordinary
contributions to local business, politics, culture, and philanthropy
(not to mention the continuing contributions of a number of
their equally generous progeny). So do the institutions that such individuals have helped to create.

Perhaps best known among those institutions is the University of Minnesota, which has made immeasurable contributions
to local education, culture, and industry. Chartered in 1851, the
institution took several years to present itself as a university
worthy of its name. John S. Pillsbury, the flour-milling magnate,

took the lead in the various reorganizations required to open the school's doors as a full-fledged land-grant university in 1869. Blegen describes Pillsbury as "hard-driving and large-minded."

It could be argued that few state universities have played as large a role as the University of Minnesota in the development and continuing health of a major city. While many such schools are situated in smaller communities, away from the hustle and bustle of a metropolis, the U of M has, from its beginnings, been situated close to the Twin Cities' heart. Well-established residential neighborhoods and industrial sectors crowd around the school's huge main campus, the Mississippi River lies at its feet, and downtown Minneapolis is within easy walking distance. The university is—and has long been—an integral part of the Twin Cities.

Besides educating successive generations of citizens over the past century, the university has played an essential role in the growth of Minnesota's agriculture, milling, and mining industries. As one of the world's great research institutions, it has additionally made numerous advances in such fields as medicine, engineering, and computer science, among others. Its Minneapolis campus was for many decades home to the renowned Minnesota Orchestra, and continues to be the site of major art and cultural attractions. Its more than 200 areas of study have produced such

World-renowned for its contributions to scientific research, the University of Minnesota is also a center of creativity and culture. Courtesy, University of Minnesota

The university continues to provide the same world-class training that has produced prominent individuals from athletes to astronauts. Photo by Steve Schneider

prominent individuals as entrepreneurs Curt Carlson and Earl Bakken; political leaders Hubert Humphrey, Walter Mondale, Arvonne Fraser, and Roy Wilkins; medical pioneers Dr. C. Walton Lillehei and Dr. Christiaan Barnard; journalists and writers Eric Severeid, Carl Rowan, and Garrison Keillor; athletes Patty Berg and Dave Winfield; entertainers Henry Fonda and Linda Kelsey; astronaut Donald Slayton; and clergywoman Jeannette Piccard.

The institution's importance to the community—as well as the community's importance to the university—can be measured in part by the fact that in recent years it has ranked high among the nation's public universities in voluntary private support, the lion's share of which has come from local donors. Local business leaders, headed by the indefatigable Curt Carlson (class of '37), recently raised more than $365 million in private money for the institution. Carlson himself wrote his alma mater a check for $25 million.

Such sharing, cooperation, and interdependence involves other local institutions and organizations, too. Many, like inner-city Augsburg College, founded by Scandinavian Lutheran settlers in 1869, hark back to the city's pioneer days. Others, like the Minneapolis Urban Coalition, established by concerned citizens during the racial unrest of the mid-1960s, have shorter histories. Most of them, however, have an urgent sense of civic cooperation and responsibility in common. Nearly all are enthusiastically supported by the communities they effectively serve.

One of the more unusual local organizations is the widely acclaimed Citizens League, a nonpartisan aggregation of business leaders, community activists, and academicians dedicated to studying and proposing solutions to some of the area's knottier problems

The state university grew up right in the thick of the Twin Cities area. Today students can easily walk from the campus to downtown Minneapolis to work, shop, or enjoy the city's galaxy of cultural attractions. Photo by Steve Schneider

of public policy. Since its founding in 1952, the league has provided much-needed and widely respected analyses of such diverse issues as property taxes, public education, and health-care utilization. Funded by the dues of its 3,000 members, donations from local businesses, and a variety of foundation grants, the group, though without any official standing, enjoys the consistent attention of public- and private sector policymakers of nearly all political persuasions.

The organization that has drawn perhaps the greatest amount of outside attention, however, is the Twin Cities' Metropolitan Council, created after considerable discussion (much of it sparked by the Citizens League) by the Minnesota State Legislature in 1967. To some observers, the council is proof positive of the determination of the community's various components and jurisdictions to join forces for the common good. *Fortune* magazine, for instance, wrote:

RIGHT: A light covering of snow in late winter does little to impair university activities. Photo by Greg Ryan/Sally Beyer

What is really impressive about the Twin Cities—and instructive to other cities willing to learn—is that they have buried enough of their enmity to work together. With their suburbs, they have forged a new and so far quite successful strategy for the management of a whole urban region. The centerpiece of this rare achievement is the Metropolitan Council, first of its kind in the U.S.

The Metropolitan Council has not replaced the governing bodies that control the seven counties and literally hundreds of municipalities, townships, and school districts that make up the modern-day Twin Cities metro area. Instead, it devotes its energies to such broad metropolitan issues as highways, mass transit, airports, sewage disposal, and regional planning. The council's emphasis is generally on the big metro picture—and on the future. As Steve Keefe, the council's chairman, told a reporter not long ago, "The Metropolitan Council is the one place . . . where you really do take a long-term look at things. There really are people in this agency every day thinking in sophisticated ways about where we are going to be in 15 years."

Government at all levels of the community is generally oriented to problem-solving and future improvement. It is also, even in some of the most skeptical eyes, remarkably open and clean. The old Yankee ideals notwithstanding, over the course of the city's entire 120-plus-year history, this has not always been true. Around the turn of the century, for instance, Minneapolis' city hall was controlled by a former physician named Albert Alonzo Ames. "Doc" Ames' corrupt administration gained national notoriety when journalist Lincoln Steffens exposed it in his series of muckraking reports, "The Shame of the Cities." Political and police department scandals were not uncommon during the first several decades of the twentieth century, or until an energetic young politician named Hubert Humphrey was elected mayor of Minneapolis in 1945.

Humphrey's administration was not without controversy—his merger of the state's Democratic party with more radical organizations, followed by the purge of the new Democratic Farmer Labor Party's more radical members, resulted in a good deal of factional bitterness. But Humphrey, while going on to the larger arenas of the U.S. Senate and vice presidency, helped establish a long line of bright, progressive, and honest politicians whose direction and influence remain important forces in the local and state governments to this day. These include former state attorney general, U.S. senator, and vice president Walter Mondale; former governor and cabinet member Orville Freeman; former mayor Arthur Naftalin; former congressman and current mayor Donald Fraser; and feminist leader and educator Arvonne Fraser.

An interesting aspect of the city's recent political history is the fact that whether city hall has been in Republican or Democratic hands, the critical alliance between public and private sectors has remained intact and effective. Ideology has rarely gotten in the way of major community problem-solving and improvements. Far more often than not, old-fashioned pragmatism has prevailed over more contemporary partisan concerns.

To live and work in Minneapolis has, for countless numbers of its citizens, meant taking on an energetic part in the larger life of the community. The pragmatic pioneers who shaped the city's personality in the 1800s seemed to draw scant distinction between the private citizen and the public servant. The successive waves of immigrants, with their strong beliefs in hard work and civic re-

The Lake of the Isles and the city's powerful skyline illustrate Minneapolis' broad range of merits—a gracious quality of life in the midst of a vigorous, expanding economy. Photo by Ed Bock

City Hall has long redeemed itself from the scandals of the early part of the century, winning the respect of the populace for exceptionally honorable public service. Photo by Robert Friedman

sponsibility, made cooperation and community service a way of life in their adopted city. Those who could afford it often gave generously of their fortunes. More important, however, were their widespread contributions of time, ideas, and constructive energy.

The city's relative isolation surely contributed to the early "can-do" mentality. Minneapolis' manageable size and the absence of divisive ethnic or political strife have helped make things work efficiently in more recent years. And a diverse and expanding local economy had made all manner of improvements and attractions not only desirable but possible—indeed, almost inevitable—for more than a century.

The people of Minneapolis, however, have been the force that has made Minneapolis a special community from its beginnings. Whatever their diverse motives, interests, and political affiliations, Minneapolitans have usually been able to set aside their differences and work for the betterment of the entire city. The early settlers deemed a strong, growing community essential to the strength and growth of their businesses. Similarly, the various groups of immigrants and native-born men and women who followed them accepted the belief that a vibrant city was synonymous with a better life. The streets of Minneapolis were never paved with gold, but, for countless thousands of its citizens, those city streets provided routes of golden opportunity.

The natures of their specific contributions have differed as dramatically as their individual backgrounds. George A. Pillsbury, for example, did not join his brother John and son Charles in Minneapolis until he was 68 years old. The elder Pillsbury had enjoyed a successful career in New England, but, instead of simply living off the fruits of his labors, he journeyed west and started anew in the burgeoning flour-milling business run by his family on the banks of the Mississippi. Hardly a man to settle anonymously into his new surroundings, George Pillsbury, like his brother John, jumped into local politics. He was elected the city's mayor in 1884. Like his brother, he was also a driving force in the development of the University of Minnesota.

William H. Dunwoody, meanwhile, was a native of Philadelphia who joined the leadership of the Washburn Crosby Company as a young man in the 1870s. Dunwoody established the Minneapolis Millers Association and helped open the European market to the products of Minneapolis mills. Also active in a number of civic and educational improvements, he left, as part of his legacy, the city's highly valued Dunwoody Institute for vocational training.

Charles Loring, originally from Maine, was a prominent local businessman who, during the 1880s, directed his considerable intelligence and energies toward the community's plentiful—but as yet mostly undeveloped—lakes and open spaces. During the course of the next several years, as the city's first park board president, he presided over the extensive development of its lakes and parks. His remarkable achievement of helping to make the Mill City also the "City of Lakes" has been memorialized by one of the community's loveliest spots—downtown's Loring Park.

In more recent years, the civic contributions of New England-born business leaders and benefactors have been complemented and enhanced by those of locally bred citizens. Some of the latter, like Curt Carlson, who once delivered newspapers on the city's South Side, and Earl Bakken, who initially serviced medical equipment at the U of M Hospital, reflect the community's considerable Scandinavian influence. Others, like John S. Pillsbury, Jr., retired chairman of the Minneapolis-based Northwestern National Life Insurance Company and a longtime contributor to both the political and cultural health of the city, have extended the Yankee heritage well into the present. Still others, such as Italian-food entrepreneur Rose Totino, have added greatly to the economic, cultural, and educational vitality of the entire area.

Many of the city's recent leaders began making their presence felt amid the diversification and prosperity that followed the end of the Second World War. Some of those young executives, entrepreneurs, and political activists were newcomers seeking fresh opportunities in the thriving Twin Cities, while others were moving into the historic positions of power and

influence shaped by previous generations of their own families. New arrivals and old names alike, they were soon perpetuating the Minneapolis tradition of working together to get things done.

Like many American cities, Minneapolis was faced with a deteriorating core during the mid-1950s, when young urban families were moving in droves to the burgeoning suburbs. The Dayton department store family, active in downtown Minneapolis affairs since the early 1900s, recognized the massive demographic relocation and established the nation's first all-enclosed shopping mall in suburban Edina in 1956. But characteristically, even while extending their operations beyond the city limits, the Daytons did not abandon the city's heart. Quite the contrary. The Daytons were instrumental in the city's much-acclaimed downtown redevelopment.

Donald Dayton, a grandson of founder George Draper Dayton and, at the time, chief executive of the giant home-grown retailer, helped create the Minneapolis Downtown Council, which became the driving force behind the creation of the Nicollet Mall. With its pedestrian walkway, picturesque trees, kiosks, sculptures, and contemporary shops and restaurants, the mall was a significant factor in the postwar downtown rejuvenation and a model for other urban redevelopment projects all over the nation.

Most observers agree that the key to the development of the Nicollet Mall—and much of the other central-city activity that followed the mall's lead—was what one reporter has called the community's "make-things-happen style." The Daytons, both as an organization and as individual citizens, were the catalysts. Long respected for their energetic, farsighted brand of corporate citizenship, the Daytons had for decades led by example. When they got behind the drive to inject new life into downtown Minneapolis, most of their peers—including most of their competitors—quickly and enthusiastically lent their influence and dollars to the enterprise.

A number of major redevelopment projects in the Twin Cities downtowns during the past three decades have followed a similar pattern. A spark is provided by a respected businessperson, political leader, civic organization, or, more often than not, some ad hoc combination of all of the above. Then, following no small amount of both formal debate and informal discussion, the community's diverse forces close ranks behind the idea.

Describing the process behind the overall redevelopment of the Twin Cities' cores, geographer John Borchert writes tellingly:

City government, large corporations with local control and inner-city headquarters, major hospital and medical centers, and neighborhood resident organizations . . . joined in the effort. Major developers were attracted from other centers of investment capital in the United States and Canada. The city governments and specially created authorities funneled federal subsi-

dies to target areas . . . The cities borrowed heavily to buy land, clear it, prepare it for new development—and to make accompanying public improvements and embellishments. The private organizations, in turn, made heavy commitments to new construction . . .

Never before had the problems of [urban] aging, maintenance, preservation, and replacement been recognized so clearly and attacked with so much coordination and money.

By the late 1980s, many of the leaders of Minneapolis' postwar boom had retired. Their number included several of the Dayton brothers; John Pillsbury; Stephen Keating, former chairman of the modern Honeywell Corporation; William Norris, founder and chairman of Control Data Corporation; and John Cowles, Jr., former publisher of the *Star Tribune* daily newspaper. All, along with dozens of their corporate colleagues, had been instrumental in the redevelopment of the city's commercial and industrial core as well as in the development of some of the city's major cultural amenities and social organizations. To name just a few of their

A businessman became an avid creator of lakeside parks, and the City of Mills became the City of Lakes. The name of Loring Park commemorates the achievements of the city's first park board president, Charles Loring. Photo by Ed Bock

achievements, Minneapolis' internationally acclaimed Orchestra Hall and Guthrie Theater were built and the highly regarded Urban Coalition was formed under their civic stewardship.

Fortunately for the continued well-being of the city, some new—and some not so new—names have been rising in their predecessors' places to meet the community's latter-day challenges.

When the original Griffith-family ownership of the Minnesota Twins began thinking about finding a new hometown for their team during the early 1980s, a local envelope company owner and University of Minnesota booster named Harvey Mackay headed a blue-chip group of business and civic leaders dedicated to keeping the franchise in the Twin Cities. One of the group, banker and entrepreneur Carl Pohlad, eventually stepped forward and bought the club, promising to keep it at home. To the near-hysterical delight of the entire community, not to mention to the great and abiding pleasure of Pohlad himself, the Twins, in their third season under new ownership, shocked the experts and became the 1987 World Champions!

When the 20-year-old Nicollet Mall needed a fresh shot of vitality, Robert Dayton, a great-grandson of George Draper Dayton, spearheaded the development of a dazzling, $75-million specialty retail development on the mall called the Conservatory. Bob Dayton had gone out on his own years earlier and opened one of the city's premier women's fashion shops. Now, in the late 1980s, he was injecting new energy and prestige into the mall pioneered by his father and uncles. The step was both innovative in its design and familiar in its civic impact. Once more a creative Minneapolitan with clout had found a way to merge commercial self-interest with community improvement.

The city's historic institutions have likewise kept pace with the times. On one very old, very informal level, the staid and solid Minneapolis Club, established by the city's Yankee pioneers well before the turn of the century, is still the forum for a sizable amount of the civic "action-planning" that goes on among the community's movers and shakers. The University of Minnesota and the Citizens League—as well as the likes of Dayton Hudson Corporation, Honeywell, and General Mills—are still among the community's primary sources of ideas, leadership, and funding.

Another increasingly important resource is the Twin Cities' large collection of private, corporate, and community foundations. According to one recent estimate, more than two dozen local foundations were contributing more than one million dollars a year to a wide variety of causes. Foundation dollars help fund local colleges and universities, cultural and recreation centers, medical and scientific research, and food and shelter for the poor and homeless, among many other local and regional causes and recipients.

Four decades ago the Dayton family pioneered the notion of

corporations giving 5 percent of their pretax earnings to charity. Nowadays dozens of locally based companies are giving at the 5 percent-plus level, while several dozen other Twin Cities firms make annual contributions of between 2 and 5 percent of their pretax profits.

Today, driven by the growth and diversification following World War II, Minneapolis is a full-fledged corporate headquarters city. In fact, only Stamford, Connecticut, is home to more *Fortune* 500 companies on a per capita basis. A large number of these "hometown" corporations feel a deep sense of "ownership" when dealing with local groups and institutions. Upper-echelon executives moving into town from other locations are quickly made aware of the responsibility that accompanies that ownership. George Pillsbury recently explained the phenomenon to *Town & Country* magazine by saying, "The heirs of the founders have inculcated a tradition of social responsibility to the point where an outsider is told, 'If you or your company want to make it in Minneapolis, you'd better participate.'"

Marilyn Nelson, daughter of Curt Carlson and a tireless civic leader in her own right, said in the same article: "You hear a lot of talk today about 'corporate culture.' Well, we have a *community* culture. It's like joining the crew of a fast-moving scull: you have to grab an oar, and once you get the pace, you belong."

In downtown Minneapolis, evidence of the community's determination to work together to get things done continues to build. An enormous hole that had once been the site of Donaldsons department store and the Northwestern National Bank gaped like the socket of a missing tooth for several years following an enormous fire. After a false start or two, downtown forces marshaled their resources during the late 1980s and began to fill the gap. In

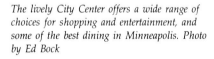

The lively City Center offers a wide range of choices for shopping and entertainment, and some of the best dining in Minneapolis. Photo by Ed Bock

1988 Norwest Corporation opened its handsome 57-story office tower on one part of the site, while a number of upscale retailing operations including Saks Fifth Avenue were making plans to move into sparkling new facilities on the other.

A few blocks to the south, meanwhile, construction began on a new $200-million convention center. (The entire complex is scheduled to open in late 1990.) A few blocks to the west, construction started on a new basketball arena, the home of the Minnesota Timberwolves franchise of the National Basketball Association. Under spirited discussion were ambitious plans for additional retail facilities on the Nicollet Mall and a light-rail mass transit system that would link downtown Minneapolis with several suburban locations, the Twin Cities' international airport, and downtown St. Paul.

All of these projects and more are, to a significant degree, the result of the progressive "can-do" mentality that has impelled and shaped Minneapolis development for more than a century. The sheer size and dazzle of the new construction would no doubt astonish the city's pioneers, but the community spirit and civic cooperation that has given rise to the recent spate of construction would probably not surprise them at all.

Minneapolitans fill the streets for a parade celebrating the surprise victory of the Twins in the 1987 World Series. The triumph was a fitting reward for the diligent efforts made by local leadership to keep the team in the city. Photo by Ed Bock

Competitors in the Summer Aquatennial
Triathlon enter the waters of Lake Nokomis.
Photo by Greg Ryan/Sally Beyer

Chapter 4

A Commitment to Culture

The Twin Cities' renown as one of the nation's leading centers of the arts has been so potent during the latter half of the twentieth century that it is tempting to believe that the community's outstanding cultural amenities sprang fully developed, like the goddess Athena, from the rich Minnesota soil.

In fact, like its industries, its local government structures, and its many other progressive institutions, most of the Twin Cities' contemporary music, theater, dance, and visual arts offerings have grown from humble seeds planted by its nineteenth-century pioneers and nurtured over the succeeding decades by generations of committed citizens.

The impulse to seek the aesthetic beauty and spiritual enrichment offered by the arts was not unique to early Minnesotans and their offspring. But the community's geographic isolation and its Yankee and northern European heritage combined to provide a receptive environment for that impulse. And Minneapolis' varied and vibrant latter-day economy, numerous corporate and private patrons, and the loyal support of its populace have helped ensure a perennial flowering of the local arts.

It is interesting to note that one of the many functions of Colonel John Stevens' house in Minneapolis during the 1850s was that of a theater. One can easily imagine wintry evenings enlivened by lines from *A Midsummer Night's Dream* in the firelit parlor of Stevens' frame home beside the falls. Theaters and music halls were built throughout the Upper Mississippi territory before, during, and after the Civil War, and touring companies traveled the circuit of eager small-town audiences. Minneapolis alone, writes Theodore Blegen, boasted as many as 10 theaters and music halls in the four decades following its incorporation.

The Pence Opera House, which opened in 1867, featured some of the most popular dramatic productions, lectures, and

Claus Oldenburg's distinctive Spoonbridge and Cherry *sculpture is a recent addition to the Minneapolis Sculpture Garden, located near Loring Park in downtown. Photo by Greg Ryan/Sally Beyer*

ABOVE: Many cultural celebrations in Minneapolis reflect various ancestral origins, all of which have heavily influenced many aspects of the area. Photo by Steve Schneider

FACING PAGE: The Minneapolis Symphony Orchestra makes its home in Orchestra Hall, a lavish venue utilizing bold architectural styling to emphasize acoustics. Photo by Steve Schneider

music recitals to be found anywhere during the period, including the plays of Shakespeare and the violin mastery of Ole Bull. The well-developed cultural instincts of the community's Yankee stock resulted in the visits of many prominent Eastern artists and performers, such as the legendary stage stars Edwin Booth and Sarah Bernhardt. At the same time, many of the productions were offered in the languages of the various local immigrant groups. Blegen has pointed out, for instance, that Ibsen's *Ghosts* was first performed in the United States—not in the playwright's native Scandinavia—by a troupe of Norwegian and Danish actors whose historic 1882 tour included Minneapolis. Vaudeville and burlesque were, in their heyday, popular local draws as well, and moving pictures quickly captured the local fancy when they were introduced in the early twentieth century.

Classical music found a permanent and important home in the Twin Cities upon the creation, at the turn of the century, of the Minneapolis Symphony Orchestra. A number of local and traveling musicians had performed before large and appreciative audiences here since the earliest settlement days. Several fine academies of classical music had taken their places in the community during the previous few decades. (One of them, the prestigious MacPhail School of Music begun by the multitalented William MacPhail in 1888, recently celebrated its 100th anniversary!) But it was the formation of the Minneapolis Symphony, during the first few years of the twentieth century, that made the Twin Cities a world capital of great music.

In this instance the driving force was a German immigrant named Emil Oberhoffer. Legend has it that Oberhoffer and his wife found themselves high and dry in the Twin Cities following the failure of the traveling Gilbert and Sullivan company of which they

This Siberian tiger has plenty of domain to survey, thanks to thorough advance planning of the habitats that allow their residents to feel at home. Photo by, Greg Ryan/Sally Beyer

were a part. Trying to make a living in his adopted home, the energetic and versatile musician sang in local restaurants, played the organ and directed the choir in local churches, and gave recitals at St. Paul's Schubert Club (founded in 1882 and already a pillar of the cultural community in the Minnesota capital). In 1896 Oberhoffer became director of Minneapolis' Philharmonic Club, and from the club's podium began to seek the support he needed to make his vivid dream of a hometown symphony orchestra a reality.

Oberhoffer was probably not the first—he was certainly not the last—local impresario to go to the community's movers and shakers for help. The enthusiastic support from the local business and governmental leadership for worthwhile civic projects and institutions has long been a hallmark of life in these parts. Oberhoffer was no Yankee with well-established ties to members of the Minneapolis Club, but the city's Yankee-bred elite circa 1900 were receptive to his impassioned pleas and eventually gave him the financial assistance he sought.

The Minneapolis Symphony Orchestra played its first concert on November 5, 1903, in the city's cavernous Exposition Building (site of the 1892 Republican National Convention). During the next several years, under the baton of maestro Oberhoffer, the orchestra became a local cultural mainstay, performing at the Minneapolis Auditorium, then later at the University of

Minnesota's Northrop Auditorium, and finally in its current home, Orchestra Hall.

The orchestra has long been more than just a local phenomenon. Beginning under Oberhoffer and continuing through his illustrious successors to today's musical director and principal conductor, Edo de Waart, the ensemble, by virtue of its eagerly awaited annual tours, has become a resource of the entire state and a familiar favorite around the world. Its statewide "ownership" was belatedly acknowledged when its name was changed, a half-century after its founding, to the *Minnesota* Orchestra.

The experience of Emil Oberhoffer and his symphony orchestra is instructive in several respects. First and most obviously, of course, it represents the great vision, persistence, and creative vigor that has been responsible for so many of Minneapolis' grand cultural institutions. Second, and nearly as importantly, it displays the crucial—and continuing—encouragement of those institutions at virtually all levels of the local (and often regional) population.

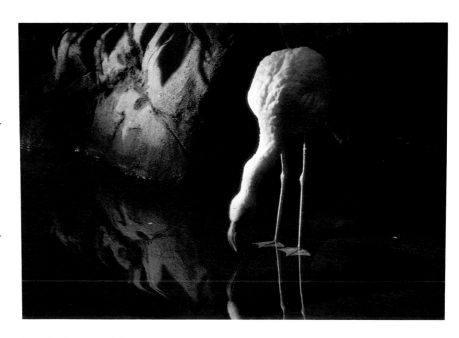

No matter what season of the year, this flamingo and other inhabitants of the Tropics Trail at the Minnesota Zoo enjoy a balmy 70-degree climate. Photo by Thomas K. Perry

In some instances an institution is born with a silver spoon in its mouth—that is, it enjoys the financial backing of a well-heeled founder. A good case in point is the city's internationally acclaimed Walker Art Center. The center is the magnificent extension, nearly a hundred years after its beginning, of local lumber miller and financier Thomas B. Walker's personal collection of fine art. Walker's fortune, coupled with the ongoing generosity of his heirs, has propelled the center into the first rank of the world's contemporary art galleries.

In other cases, an institution is started with the inspiration of its founder and the financial support of wealthier backers. The Minnesota (née Minneapolis Symphony) Orchestra is a prime example. In still others, the founding financial support comes from the public, by way of legislative funding, or from public or private foundation grants. The beautiful Minneapolis Institute of Arts, which grew out of the local Society of Fine Arts, is a beneficiary of both public and private support that provides evidence of the latter.

However they evolve, the community's outstanding cultural institutions have a way of attracting not only the region's continuing support, but of attracting or inspiring new institutions. The presence of the Minnesota Orchestra—and more recently, the Saint Paul Chamber Orchestra, headquartered on the east side of the river since its founding in 1959—has been at least in part responsible for the development of numerous other musical ensembles: large and small, professional and amateur, "downtown" and in the city's neighborhoods and suburbs. The "demand" for great music created by the major orchestras, as well as the part-time availability of many of the orchestra's musicians, has encouraged a plethora of welcome additions to the local music scene.

The community's bountiful theatrical history—in conjunction with its well-rounded cultural base and the enthusiastic financial support from local patrons—resulted in the creation of the world-famous Guthrie Theater in the early 1960s. The great Irish actor and director, Sir Tyrone Guthrie, chose Minneapolis as the site of the new North American repertory theater that would bear his name following a persuasive appeal mounted by a group of Twin Cities civic, industrial, and cultural leaders. The group, which included such familiar local forces as the retailing Dayton brothers and newspaper publisher John Cowles, Jr., pledged to raise $1.5 million for the theater's development, in addition to $400,000 in cash and a parcel of land adjacent to the Walker Art

The Minneapolis Institute of Arts showcases 25,000 years of art from around the globe on its three floors of gallery space. Photo by Steve Schneider

Center donated by the Thomas B. Walker Foundation.

Guthrie was convinced that Minneapolis was the perfect location for his theater. Over the next couple of years, the money was raised; a striking, ultramodern, thrust-stage theater facility was constructed; and the first production—a startlingly contemporary presentation of *Hamlet,* directed by the eminent Tyrone Guthrie himself—was presented to enthusiastic critical and popular reviews in 1963.

In the quarter-century since its opening, the Guthrie Theater, like the Minnesota Orchestra, the Walker Art Center, and the Minneapolis Institute of Arts, has become virtually synonymous with high culture in mid-America. Like its neighbors, in fact, the Guthrie has made an international name for itself, as it has presented a broad array of world-class productions of the works of such diverse authors as Shakespeare, Molière, George Bernard Shaw, Tennessee Williams, Arthur Miller, Bertolt Brecht, and Noel Coward. It has, additionally and true to form, helped perpetuate the reputation of the Twin Cities as a cultural mecca.

When existing arts organizations have needed updates and improvements, the community, likewise true to form, has generally been eager to provide them. In the early 1970s the local business community, led by the Daytons, the Cowles family, Curt Carlson, and dozens of other local patrons, raised some $10 million for the construction of a spectacular downtown concert hall for the Minnesota Orchestra. Strategically located near the south end of the Nicollet Mall, Orchestra Hall, inaugurated in 1974, is now recognized as one of the finest halls on earth. Besides serving as home base for the orchestra, it also functions as the performance site for dozens of other attractions year-round, including the Saint Paul Chamber Orchestra; touring jazz, pop, and blues artists; and a variety of both local and visiting dance ensembles. Despite its name, the building is truly a center for all of the performing arts in the Minneapolis area.

The local arts have also had a highly significant economic impact on the entire metropolitan area. A recent study showed that the various local arts organizations contribute, by conservative estimate, close to $400 million a year to the Twin Cities regional economy.

Today, as the community looks forward to the 1990s, its arts and cultural attractions are as diverse as their varied antecedents. The major orchestras and art museums have played important roles in the local cultural scene for decades. In the years following the Second World War, however, new music and dance organizations, theater companies, museums, and galleries have blossomed and matured on the banks of the upper Mississippi, making the area more culturally diverse than ever.

A sampling, by no means complete, of the contemporary roster of artistic and cultural amenities could include a dizzying array of classical musical groups, such as the Minneapolis Chamber Symphony, which performs at various locations around the Twin Cites; the Plymouth Music Series, performing a variety of mostly classical music year-round from its home base at Minneapolis' Plymouth Congregational Church; the Minnetonka Symphony Orchestra, one of several outstanding, semiprofessional suburban ensembles performing in the area; the Concentus Musicus Renaissance Music Ensembles, performing with period instruments and costumes; and such estimable St. Paul-based organizations as the Minnesota Opera Company, which presents a season of Italian and German masterpieces as well as some lighter and more contemporary works, and the Schubert Club, which serves as host to many great international artists including, in recent years, Vladimir Horowitz and Beverly Sills. Offering a large choice of strictly vocal music are such locally based (but often widely traveled) groups as the Dale Warland Singers, the Bach Society of Minnesota Chorus, the Apollo Club of Minneapolis (approaching its 100th birthday), and the Metropolitan Boys Choir.

Many critics believe that the Twin Cities is blessed with some of the finest dance attractions available anywhere in America. Northrop Auditorium, on the Minneapolis campus of the University of Minnesota, has long been a home away from home for outstanding touring companies like the Joffrey Ballet, the American Ballet Theatre, and the Moiseyev dance troupe as well as for performers such as Mikhail Baryshnikov and Twyla Tharp. (In addition to serving as the permanent home of the Minnesota Orchestra prior to its move to Orchestra Hall, venerable Northrop was, for many years, the site of annual performances by New York's dazzling Metropolitan Opera Company.)

ABOVE: The Ordway Music Theatre hosts lavish productions, like this Minnesota Opera version of The Pearl Fishers. Photo by Greg Ryan/Sally Beyer

RIGHT: The Theater in the Round, located near the University of Minnesota, is a local favorite offering traditional and contemporary drama. Photo by Ed Bock

The Twin Cities has for several years been the home of such nationally acclaimed organizations as the Nancy Hauser Dance Company and School. More recently, such locally based organizations as the New Dance Ensemble, with its emphasis on modern dance, and the Ethnic Dance Theatre, which develops original productions from traditional ethnic dances, have developed widespread reputations and followings.

Well known in drama circles everywhere is the locally based Children's Theatre Company, which operates out of state-of-the-art facilities attached to the Minneapolis Institute of Arts, just south of downtown Minneapolis. Founded as both a drama school and a theater, the CTC has evolved into a source of stunningly inventive drama and comedy for audiences of all ages. Recent offerings have included highly memorable productions of such familiar stories as *Pinocchio* and *Treasure Island,* and original presentations of newer "classics" like Tomie de Paola's *Strega Nona* and Dr. Seuss' *The 500 Hats of Bartholomew Cubbins.*

Other theatrical attractions include the contemporary plays staged by such local groups as the Cricket Theatre, founded more than 20 years ago; the innovative Illusion Theater, headquartered in the handsomely renovated Hennepin Center for the Arts in downtown Minneapolis; the always-surprising Mixed Blood Theater, set in an erstwhile firehouse near the West Bank of the U of M; the Theater in the Round Players, a local

The Minneapolis Sculpture Garden is spread over seven-and-one-half acres and features more than 40 sculptures as well as a glass conservatory. Photo by Ed Bock

favorite producing an eclectic mix of traditional and contemporary drama for more than three decades near the university campus; the Old Log Theater, a perennially popular setting for a variety of mostly lighter musicals and plays, located on the shores of Lake Minnetonka west of the Twin Cities; and the Brave New Workshop, home of the irreverent satirical revues staged for the past 30-odd years by the irrepressible writer and comic Dudley Riggs.

Many of the original plays and revues produced by these and other Twin Cities theater groups have been taken on tour throughout the United States and abroad, often playing to enthusiastic audiences and receiving glowing critical notices.

Fine art, meanwhile, is readily available throughout the metropolitan area. In addition to the stunning galleries of the Walker Art Center and the Minneapolis Institute of Arts, the works of major national and international artists can be found in such varied settings as the Minnesota Museum of Art in downtown St. Paul; the suburban lawns and downtown corridors of General Mills, Inc., and First Bank Corporation; on the campuses of the University of Minnesota, Augsburg and Macalester colleges, and other Twin Cities centers of higher learning; and the grounds of the spectacular new Minneapolis Sculpture Garden across the street from the Walker-Guthrie arts complex.

The rediscovery and renovation of a number of old warehouses and commercial buildings on the northwest edge of downtown Minneapolis during the past 20-plus years has, among other things, created a thriving local "artists' quarter." Set among a string of newly popular cafes and pubs, rehabilitated office space, and fashionable shops are several outstanding storefront galleries that provide an important outlet for artists and artisans from all over the Midwest. To the local buying and collecting public, these galleries offer a wide range of drawings, paintings, photography, prints, sculpture, and other creations, some of it done by well-known names and much of it museum quality.

Citizens with an interest in antiquity, in the physical sciences, in social or natural history, and in many other such phenomena can satisfy their curiosity at still other locations around the Twin Cities.

The Science Museum of Minnesota in downtown St. Paul, for example, offers everything from outstanding dinosaur exhibits to hands-on displays of the latest electronic technology. The museum's new domed Omnitheater surrounds its audience with astonishing cinematic effects, such as detailing an astronaut's journey through space or exploring the depths of the world's seas. The James Ford Bell Museum of Natural History, on the University of Minnesota campus in Minneapolis, offers visitors fascinating dioramas featuring Minnesota flora and fauna in lifelike settings. And the American Swedish Institute, housed in the elaborate, castle-like mansion built by Swedish-American newspaper magnate Swan Turnblad in the early 1900s, offers visitors a glimpse of both the Swedish experience in America and the traditional arts and crafts of Old World Sweden.

The vibrant cultural experience offered by the Twin Cities is by no means confined by brick and mortar, by professional arts, or even by much of a history. The community's wealth of public rituals and civic celebrations is in many ways as rich and varied as its more formal arts structures and institutions.

Appropriately enough for the City of Lakes, its largest and best-known community fete is the Minneapolis Aquatennial, which has been celebrated in, on, and around its abundant fresh water since 1940. The Aquatennial has evolved over the past several decades into a two-week midsummer extravaganza featuring gala Grande Day and Torchlight parades through the city's downtown streets, numerous picnics, ice cream socials, celebrity appearances, arts and crafts fairs, athletic contests, fishing and boating events, a sand-castle sculpture competition, and much more—all capped off by an exciting fireworks display over the heart of the city.

Everybody, regardless of community boundary, attends the Minnesota State Fair, one of the largest state fairs in the nation. That the fairgrounds are situated roughly equidistant from downtown Minneapolis and downtown St. Paul seems of little concern to the more than a million-and-a-half persons who come from all over the state for the late-summer festivities each year.

The state fair is an important annual event, as might be expected in a state with a strong agricultural history. In recent seasons, however, the seemingly numberless events and attractions have included far more than just livestock exhibits and tractor-pulling contests. For instance, the lineup of first-rank celebrity entertainers has the glitter of a Las Vegas or Atlantic City revue, featuring performers like Bob Hope, Willie Nelson, and the Beach Boys. State fair displays are now nearly as likely to boast sophisticated home-built electronic equipment and state-of-the-art farm machinery as blue-ribbon apples and prize-winning dairy cows.

Milk carton boat racing is just one of the events held each year at the Minneapolis Aquatennial, the community's largest fete. Photo by Greg Ryan/Sally Beyer

Many of the community's annual celebrations honor a specific nationality or ethnic heritage. Especially prominent in the Twin Cites are the Norwegian and Swedish festivities that take place in Minneapolis streets and parks every May and June. The local Norwegians call their big day *Syttende Mai*—the 17th of May, commemorating Norway's independence and constitution—and celebrate it with speeches, songs, and dances. *Svenskarnas Dag,* celebrated on a Sunday in late June, is when local Swedes gather for speechifying, singing, and dancing. The celebrations often feature appearances by a notable politician or aspiring office-seeker who does not necessarily bear a Norwegian or Swedish name— testimony, if nothing else, to the continuing Scandinavian influence in local civic affairs.

In June 1988 an ambitious celebration called "Midsummer, a Festival of Music" was inaugurated in the Twin Cities. Billed as "Minnesota's largest-ever music festival," the initial, 1988 edition honored the area's Swedish heritage, coinciding as it did with the nationwide observance of the 350th anniversary of the first Swedish settlement in the United States. The music itself ranged from classical to contemporary, from Swedish traditional to American modern, most of it presented on the idyllic grounds of suburban Bloomington's Hyland Lake Park Reserve.

Meanwhile, Minneapolis' annual Viennese Sommerfest, initiated a decade ago as the summer festival of the Minnesota

Local Norwegians celebrate Syttende Mai *with song and dance. The holiday commemorates Norway's independence. Photo by Kay Shaw*

A portion of the 1,500,000 annual visitors to the Minnesota State Fair make their way through the fairgrounds on a late afternoon. Photo by Steve Schneider

Orchestra, continues to delight large audiences in and around Orchestra Hall. Sommerfest typically features the glorious music of Mozart, Haydn, Brahms, and Johann Strauss, performed by members of the Minnesota Orchestra and various guest artists. The four-week event includes morning "Kaffee Konzerts," special children's programs, early evening "Serenades," and more traditional evening performances, with pre- and post-concert wining and dining in the lovely Peavey Plaza "Marktplatz" adjacent to Orchestra Hall. Like the Aquatennial, Sommerfest, in its relatively short lifetime, has become a summertime "must" in the Twin Cities.

Besides such gala community-wide events, the Twin Cities has become, in the past several years, virtually addicted to any number of smaller, more narrowly focused annual happenings—

Riders disappear in a swirl of color at Valley-fair amusement park in Shakopee, just outside Minneapolis. Photo by Greg Ryan/Sally Beyer

ABOVE: : Minneapolis' standing as a leading center for the arts is a result of many successive generations of residents placing a high priority on cultural amenities. Photo by Ed Bock

FACING PAGE: Intricately detailed architecture in Minneapolis shows the influence of the area's early settlers. Photo by Greg Ryan/ Sally Beyer

neighborhood festivals, art fairs, craft exhibits, antique shows, fund-raising balls, writers' conferences, publishing seminars, guest lectures, and the like—that dot the community calendar from January through December.

Some of these more modest events are not appreciably different from their nineteenth-century counterparts, insofar as they are energetic attempts to enhance and expand the community's aesthetic livelihood. If, as local boosters proclaim, these attempts are a bit *more* successful in Minneapolis than in some other communities, it may be evidence of the region's above-average percentage of high school and college graduates— not to mention the comparative affluence of its well-educated populace—as much as of the influence of its civic-minded pioneers. At any rate, the interest in and support of all kinds of small-scale cultural events is widespread in this community, and seems, happily, to be self-perpetuating. The more events there are, the greater the public's exposure. The greater the public's exposure, the greater the demand for more events. Or such appears to be the case.

Not surprisingly under these circumstances, the community has developed a reputation as a notably hospitable home base for individual artists and craftspersons. Part of the appeal is

undoubtedly the relative quiet and easygoing pace of the community, at least in comparison with such bigger, noisier, and more diverting cultural centers as New York and Los Angeles. The opportunity to air one's mind out while strolling around one of the city's lovely lakes—or to stimulate the creative urge by spending an afternoon with Rembrandt and Cézanne at the Institute of Arts—serves as a considerable attraction to all manner of artistic souls.

There is also the example and encouragement of other artists—which for many younger persons just getting started is all but indispensable. Fledgling novelists, short-story writers, playwrights, and poets of all ages and backgrounds find both at The Loft, a highly respected Minneapolis support and educational group for writers from all over the Upper Midwest. Somewhat less formal examples of support and nurture can be witnessed among the artists' cafes and lofts of the city's downtown warehouse district, where novices and newcomers mingle with their more experienced and successful colleagues.

Minneapolis has its own arts commission, established in 1975, which serves as both an advocate for local artists and arts groups and an advisor to the city's leaders on such issues as the public use of the arts. A gaggle of other, more specialized groups—like the Minneapolis-based Playwrights' Center—offer local artists support and promotion. Funding often flows from both public and private sources, the latter including hometown companies and foundations.

Occasionally there is an artistic force so vital that it creates a new local "industry" —or becomes one in its own right. Such is the case with a Minneapolis-bred musician named Prince Rogers Nelson. Better known around the world as simply Prince, the flamboyant rock star and moviemaker has, over the past few years, been instrumental in the development of his hometown as one of the nation's foremost pop music and film centers. Along with locally based Grammy Award-winning record producers Jimmy "Jam" Harris and Terry Lewis, and several other local pop musicians, Prince has made Minneapolis the rhythm-and-blues equivalent of country music's Nashville. In 1987 Prince opened his own world-class recording and film studio, Paisley Park, in suburban Chanhassen, thus ensuring the area's continued prominence as an important artistic center.

Prince is only one of the most recent of the Twin Cities' creative forces to make it big in the larger arena of international arts and entertainment. In a sense, his artistic line goes back at least as far as Emil Oberhoffer, father of the Minnesota Orchestra. Like Oberhoffer, Prince's success is a tribute to his own imagination, talent, and hard work—yet also to the commitment of the entire community to the care and encouragement of its lively arts and culture.

The Good Life by the Lakes

St. Anthony Falls is all but hidden from public view now, the riverside mills mostly gone or transformed into upscale commercial properties, the pioneer houses of John Stevens and Ard Godfrey only quaint reminders of an earlier, simpler time. Still, one cannot help but wonder about the impressions that a Jonathan Carver, a Cadwallader Washburn, a Stevens, or a Godfrey would have upon experiencing the city of Minneapolis today as it approaches the end of the twentieth century.

At first sight, of course, they would be shocked. The dimensions of the place and the effects of the intervening technology would surely stun those early visitors and settlers. But, given enough time to reflect upon the changes, perhaps they would not be so terribly surprised. Many of the pioneers believed that even in its earliest manifestations, there was the promise of a great city here on the edge of the northern plains. Their belief and their enterprise on the community's behalf combined to form what amounted to a self-fulfilling prophecy.

They would not be surprised to see a thriving downtown, nor to learn that downtown continues to be the heart of the larger community, because downtown, hard by the falls, was the city's physical and spiritual birthplace. In many other large American cities, they would come to understand, downtowns have faded and crumbled and been all but abandoned in favor of industrial and commercial centers in the suburbs. But in Minneapolis, downtown has shaken off the threat of deterioration and blight, added to its opportunities and offerings, and kept itself vibrant. They would probably not be surprised by the development of the city's neighborhoods, because Minneapolis has long offered the promise of a good place to live. They would probably not even be surprised by the burgeoning of multiple

Progress has marched carefully in Minneapolis, leaving plenty of open spaces for rest and refreshment. Loring Park, southwest of downtown, is one beautiful example of the city's commitment to recreation and a fine quality of life. Photo by Ed Bock

Even the newest twentieth-century developments in Minneapolis have their roots in the age-old spirit of enterprise and growth native to this great city. Photo by Ed Bock

rings of suburbs, because the dynamics of the community's progress and growth (if not the dimensions) seem to have been a central assumption of the pioneer mentality.

What they would find today is a modern Twin Cities metropolis of some 2.2 million inhabitants; an amazingly diversified (and thus highly resilient) economy; a vital conglomeration of urban neighborhoods and satellite communities; a showcase of contemporary education, arts, and entertainment; and a quality of life that many latter-day observers believe to be second to none in the entire nation. It would seem an obvious and appropriate presumption to suppose that those pioneers, whatever else they might be thinking as they stepped out of the hypothetical time warp, would be very pleased indeed.

ABOVE RIGHT: Bright lights of the holiday season welcome downtown Christmas shoppers to Nicollet Mall, the major retail corridor of the city. Photo by Greg Ryan/Sally Beyer

An early observer writing in the 1870s described Minneapolis as "wide-awake and flourishing," the "elegance and cost of its private dwellings, its spacious stores . . . its huge factories and thundering machinery" combining to provide ample evidence of "solid prosperity." A similar description would be fitting today, albeit with less emphasis on the "huge factories and thundering machinery," and would nicely apply to the historic downtown heart of the city.

"Wide-awake and flourishing" could, in fact, be the motto of downtown Minneapolis circa 1990. Even longtime residents, approaching the city's center from the neighborhoods or the suburbs, remark on the current growth spurt made strikingly graphic by the ever-changing skyline. When many of those residents were growing up in or around Minneapolis, that downtown skyline was dominated and therefore symbolized by the 447-foot Foshay Tower, completed in 1929. Today they are often hard put to spot the distinctive obelisk (modeled after the Washington Monument), standing as it does literally in the shadows of the massive IDS, Norwest, Pillsbury, and Piper Jaffray towers which seem to reach nearly twice as high into the sunshine.

The evidence of new construction and renovation is visible everywhere downtown, from the historic banks of the Mississippi on the northeast side to the old warehouse district on the northwest to the civic auditorium area on the southwest to the traditional industrial section on the southeast.

Actually, as local architects and authors David Gebhard and Tom Martinson have pointed out, downtown Minneapolis "is the product of three economic booms—in the 1880s, the 1920s, and the period from the late 1950s to the present."

In their fascinating 1977 study, *A Guide to the Architecture of Minnesota,* Gebhard and Martinson explain, "Each of these bursts of activity reflected strong attempts to mold or remold certain aspects of the city into specific urban forms." The first, they say, followed the "speculative logic" and "laissez-faireism of the times," with the streets and buildings generally organized by function (office blocks, retail operations, warehouses, etc.) in what amounted to "an all business, no frills world." In the early 1900s some grander concepts, many of which originated from the Chicago World's Fair City Beautiful

movement, were discussed by city planners, although few ever saw the light of day. By the 1920s, however, the Foshay Tower and a handful of other large buildings were under construction, and the city soon "had (in a minor way) its own skyline of skyscrapers."

The last—and by far the most striking— "edition" of the city's downtown had its origins in the period immediately following World War II, gathered momentum in the late 1950s, and, in Gebhard and Martinson's understated phrasemaking, "is still going on." The redevelopment of the Gateway district on the northeastern edge of downtown effectively replaced the city's most notorious "skid row" with a number of striking buildings, including the Northwestern National Life Insurance headquarters (designed by Minoru Yamasaki), the Federal Reserve Bank Building,

ABOVE: This Paul Granlund sculpture is one of the many attractions for shoppers at Nicollet Mall. Photo by Greg Ryan/Sally Beyer

RIGHT: The Pillsbury office tower (left) is a modern contrast to the city hall building (right) in downtown Minneapolis. Photo by Robert Friedman

LEFT: Both the history-minded and seekers of nightlife have welcomed the rebirth of the riverside mill district as a prime dining and shopping area. Photo by Greg Ryan/Sally Beyer

the Minneapolis Public Library, and The Towers condominiums. The restructuring of downtown's major shopping street into the pedestrian-friendly Nicollet Mall broke new ground in urban renovation—and kept the downtown retailing establishment competitive with the many attractive shopping centers sprouting in the suburbs.

More recent additions to the ongoing boom have included the 51-story IDS Center (with its spectacular Crystal Court shopping, dining, and "commons" area); the massive, modernistic Hennepin County Government Center (across the street and in dramatic architectural contrast to the turn-of-the-century, Romanesque Revival City Hall); the City Center office and shopping complex; the Pillsbury, Piper Jaffray, and Norwest office towers; the Lincoln Centre and International Centre office buildings; the Conservatory shopping and dining complex; the Plaza VII hotel, dining, and shopping center; the Hubert H. Humphrey Metrodome; and the Minnesota Supercomputer Center.

In the postwar metamorphosis of downtown Minneapolis, some treasures have unquestionably been lost. Buildings of a style and opulence no longer possible to duplicate have occasionally been razed to make room for more contemporary, more functional facilities, and the trade-off has not always been aesthetically pleasing. But many of downtown's newer structures— Orchestra Hall and the Plaza VII Building, for example—have happily combined form and function and set a fresh, contemporary style for the city. And the past has not all been lost, as great amounts of private investment capital, public redevelopment monies, and far-reaching entrepreneurial imagination have gone into the rehabilitation of warehouses, mills, and other historic downtown buildings nearly a century old.

During the past decade, to the delight of preservationists and more contemporary-minded citizens alike, increasing developmental attention has been focused on the city's downtown riverfront. After decades of relative neglect, efforts have been made, on both the east and west sides of St. Anthony Falls, to return the river to the city—and vice versa. The deluxe, 100-room Whitney Hotel, for instance, brings elegant hospitality back to the riverbanks that, a century earlier, boasted the legendary Winslow House. St. Anthony Main and Riverplace both offer lively shopping and dining attractions in handsomely restored facilities in the riverside mill district. Planners hope that the old Milwaukee Road Depot will eventually be transformed into a dazzling complex of restaurants, shops, hotels, and residences, overlooking—and thus celebrating—the mighty river.

For many years beginning during the 1960s, visitors from out of town—especially those from more southerly climes—made much of the city's extensive "skyway" system, which links downtown buildings via a series of heated (and air-conditioned) "tunnels" located a story above the sidewalks and streets. The ingenious system allows coatless and hatless shoppers to move from one downtown store to another in climate-controlled comfort, no matter what the "real" weather outside. By the late 1980s, however, the skyways of both Minneapolis and St. Paul have become so familiar—in Minneapolis alone, more than 80 downtown buildings and parking ramps occupying some 35 city blocks are part of the skyway system—that the remarkable conveniences are now virtually taken for granted by all but the most ingenuous visitor.

Indeed, to some observers the skyways are symbolic of the city's modern-day connectedness, linking one contemporary (and often competing) element with another, the old with the new, above the hurly-burly of the busy downtown streets.

Moving out and away from the bustling downtown, one can find oneself in a quiet residential neighborhood, on a noisy playground, or alongside a sparkling lake, with a swiftness of transition that may seem downright magical. Twin Citians have long enjoyed the luxury of moving between work and home or recreation without a long and nerve-wracking commute. In recent decades, suburbanites coming into or going out of the city's center have become accustomed to the longer freeway jaunts generally associated with big cities, but even those trips have not yet ap-

The rich colors of an idyllic residential landscape are only a short trip away from the downtown business area. Photo by Robert Friedman

proached the extremes encountered in New York, Chicago, and Los Angeles.

There has long been an ease of daily living in Minneapolis that belies the popular image of hardworking Yankee and Scandinavian pioneers struggling to stay fed and warm on the unforgiving tundra. Even in the depths of winter, a music-loving resident on the South Side is, quite literally, only minutes from a seat in Orchestra Hall. In the summer, that same resident (or a North Side counterpart) is only minutes from an evening of major league baseball at the Metrodome. Those minutes—say between 15 and 30—include parking and walking time. Extending these hypothetical trips from downtown in any direction to the city limit adds only a few minutes.

Transporting oneself from home to one of the city's lovely parks or beautiful lakes is, generally speaking, even simpler. In many neighborhoods a car isn't even required. A South Side couple, for instance, may live but a half-block from a well-equipped playground popular with their children

This broad and uncrowded stretch of 53rd Street seems never to have heard of blaring horns or snarled traffic. Photo by Steve Schneider

and a mere quarter-mile from Lake Harriet or Lake Calhoun. On a bicycle they may, winding down after work, take an hour's spin around Harriet, Calhoun, Lake of the Isles, and Cedar Lake, one lake leading into the next along the park board's well-maintained bike trails. Or on foot, in jogging shoes, they may follow the south shore of nearby Lake Harriet, then cut west-to-east across the width of the city under the huge, shady trees of Minnehaha Parkway, which follows Minnehaha Creek, which ends at the roaring precipice of Minnehaha Falls just above the river. Or they may follow the creek from Harriet to the falls—or from Harriet *west*ward, all the way to Lake Minnetonka—in a canoe or kayak. They may, for that matter, fish for northern pike on Lake Calhoun.

Not surprisingly, this being the City of Lakes, many of Minneapolis' residential neighborhoods are oriented to local lakes and streams and named accordingly. Calhoun-Isles is a convenient example, comprising Lake Calhoun and Lake of the Isles as well as Cedar Lake (just to the west of Isles) along the western edge of the Minneapolis-St. Louis Park boundary. In addition to the lakes, Calhoun-Isles features some of the city's most desirable residential sections, including prestigious Kenwood with its winding, tree-shaded streets and many gracious Victorian homes. At the north end of Kenwood stands the Walker Art Center-Guthrie Theater complex, overlooking lovely Loring Park and the southwestern fringes of downtown.

South of Calhoun-Isles is the Harriet-West Minnehaha Parkway neighborhood, which centers, of course, on Lake Harriet (with its distinctive band shell, meandering walking paths, popular summertime concerts, and dreamlike sailboat regattas) and the western portion of Minnehaha Creek (with its winding parkway and hiking and biking trails). David Gebhard and Tom Martinson have pointed out that as early as the 1880s, city parkland developers Horace Cleveland and Charles Loring argued that "the acquiring of land and the construction of parks and parkways not only would add to the beauty and livability of the city but would be a sound investment for the city and for private speculators in that adjacent lands would tend to increase in value and would also become desirable places to live." The argument was well-grounded. And the result, in the words of Gebhard and Martinson, was that "[t]he development of south Minneapolis beautifully illustrates how on occasion beauty, money, and public

ABOVE: With lovely homes, fine schools and playgrounds nearby, and easy access to natural recreational areas, Minneapolis' residential neighborhoods are as apt a setting as any for the American Dream. Photo by Steve Schneider

FACING PAGE; This scene by the shore of Lake Calhoun epitomizes the area's high quality of life: fine neighborhoods, lush green parks, and year-round recreation from skating to sailing. Photo by Ed Bock

and private interests can be combined for everyone's benefit." The Harriet-Parkway area—for more than half a century a much-favored residential area—provides proof to this day.

Following Minnehaha Creek due east across south Minneapolis, one eventually reaches the Nokomis neighborhood, where Lake Nokomis and its slightly smaller "twin," Lake Hiawatha (both of them, like Minnehaha Creek and Falls, named after Ojibway characters in Longfellow's enduring "The Song of Hiawatha"), sparkle like blue gems amid abundant parkland greenery and handsome, well-tended, mostly single-family dwellings. A popular public golf course wraps around the south and west shores of Lake Hiawatha, while acres of tree-studded park, picnic, and recreation areas make Lake Nokomis one of the most popular gathering spots in town. Both Nokomis and Hiawatha, like most of the lakes throughout the city, have well-kept public beaches for sunbathing and swimming. (For wintertime fun, many city lakes offer skating rinks with warming houses, plus an extensive network of specially groomed trails for the increasingly popular sport of cross-country skiing.)

Moving northward from the Nokomis area, the West River Parkway provides additional parkland for strolling, biking, picnicking, or simple lazing about along the lovely bluffs of the Mississippi. (The East River Road, on the St. Paul side of the river, is very nearly a mirror image of the West, offering Twin Citians a pleasant afternoon going up one side and then down the other.) Turning westward at the Lake Street Bridge, one soon encounters the Powderhorn neighborhood, with its Powderhorn Lake, its surrounding park, and its mostly blue-collar residential area that ex-

Miles of well-kept trails draw Minneapolitans away from their firesides for the hardier pleasures of cross-country skiing. Photo by Thomas K. Perry

tends to the southern fringes of downtown.

North, northeast, and east of downtown there are fewer lakes, but still plenty of parkland and playgrounds—and additional attractions not found elsewhere in Minneapolis. The Near North and Northeast areas encompass, for example, some of the city's oldest precincts, with a variety of traditionally ethnic neighborhoods and historical points, including the picturesque, multi-styled, nineteenth-century Grain Belt Brewery and the St. Anthony of Padua Church, which dates back to 1861. Also on the Near North Side lies wonderful Theodore Wirth Regional Park, with its pretty lake, challenging public golf course, extensive trails and parkway, and idyllic Eloise Butler Wildflower Garden and Bird Sanctuary.

Due east of downtown, flanking the river as it cuts northwest to southeast through the city's midpoint, is the historic Southeast neighborhood, which comprises the sprawling Minneapolis campus of the University of Minnesota and charming residential enclaves like Prospect Park (long a favorite of U of M faculty and staff). The ever-bustling university area has many unique attractions of its own. These include a variety of year-round artistic and cultural programs, seasonal collegiate sporting events, and a surprising array of unusual shopping, dining, and entertainment opportunities.

The older neighborhoods of north and northeast Minneapolis cherish such historic landmarks as the nineteenth-century Grain Belt Brewery, with its eye-catching mixture of architectural styles. Photo by Greg Ryan/Sally Beyer

ABOVE: Businesspeople add to the clientele of the stylish cafes and shops that cater to students in the university district. Photo by Greg Ryan/Sally Beyer

FACING PAGE: Whether for ice-skating or water-skiing, lakes in the Minneapolis area function as a source of continual recreation. Photo by Steve Schneider

The so-called Seven Corners area, immediately adjacent to the West Bank campus, was once notorious for its "Snoose Boulevard." In its early days a teeming neighborhood of mostly Scandinavian immigrants, Snoose Boulevard, by the 1950s, had become the eastern terminus of the Washington Avenue skid row. In the 1960s, along with the Dinkytown area near the East Bank campus, Seven Corners became a center of coffeehouses and radical student activity—and, as such, a showcase for the likes of a young Bob Dylan. Today Seven Corners is a thriving theater and dining area that is still popular with students—despite its latter-day respectability.

Like most American cities (including its sibling across the river), Minneapolis proper has lost population during the past several decades. In 1950 the city reached its numerical zenith, with a population of more than 520,000. Since then, that number has declined to about 360,000. During the same period, however, the population of the total Twin Cities metropolitan area has jumped to about 2.2 million, which makes it the 16th largest in the country.

It is misleading, though, to think of the community's hundred-odd suburbs and satellites as merely individual, virtually indistinguishable explosions in the postwar baby boom. While many did indeed spring up—seemingly out of nowhere—during the past three decades, and while most have shared an almost supernatural

flowering during this period, many others boast histories nearly as long (and, some would say, certainly as glorious) as those of the central cities themselves. And while some Twin Cities suburbs look pretty much like some others, many more are as distinctive as the urban neighborhoods they surround.

Many, as might again be expected, were settled on or close to a lake, and are identified closely with that lake. West of Minneapolis, for example, are the several distinct communities surrounding Lake Minnetonka—the metro area's largest and probably most heavily used body of water. The huge lake's extensive shoreline turns and twists around numerous bays and peninsulas, creating surprisingly diverse settings for a surprisingly diverse string of small cities, towns, and villages. Many of the lake's communities trace their histories back to the 1800s, when the lake was a fashionable resort site for tourists from all over the nation. A much-used streetcar line linked Minneapolis and the lake, which for the better part of a century featured various attractions including romantic steamboat cruises, a colorful amusement park, and big-time entertainment.

The city of Minnetonka, on the lake's eastern edge, is today one of the Twin Cities' larger suburbs, with a population of about 45,000, a substantial number of growing residential areas, and an increasingly popular array of shopping, dining, and entertainment complexes. Minnetonka is also the home of a significant number of major corporations, including the world's largest privately held company, Cargill, Inc., which began as a pioneer Minneapolis grain-milling operation in the mid-1800s.

Much smaller, but more distinctive, are such other Lake Minnetonka communities as Wayzata, Excelsior, Shorewood, Tonka Bay, Orono, Deephaven, and Minnetrista. Hilly and vaguely eccentric Excelsior, on the lake's southern shore, retains the influence of its nineteenth-century New England settlers and offers its many visitors what has long been the lake's only large-scale shoreline park. Wayzata, on the northeast shore, offers both a popular lakefront business, dining, and entertainment district and a secluded lakeshore sanctuary for many of the fabled names of Minneapolis social and commercial history. Mostly residential Orono and Deephaven, meanwhile, are a mix of old and new, opulent and modest, suburban and semirural neighborhoods.

North and northwest of Minneapolis, the lakes are smaller and less of a regional draw. Nonetheless, owing to their proximity to the city and a growing number of corporate headquarters, northern suburbs such as Brooklyn Park, Brooklyn Center, Anoka, Fridley, Coon Rapids, and Plymouth have been enjoying tremendous growth during the past couple of decades. Some of them—Brooklyn Center, Anoka, and Fridley, for example—are now considered mature communities, each with its own distinct business district, corporate component, and civic histories and celebrations. Others, like

Communities of suburban Minneapolis find their location a relaxing break from the bustle of the city. Photo by Robert Friedman

Coon Rapids and Plymouth, are still very much in their developmental stages, their recent, mostly rural pasts rapidly becoming a memory as new houses, schools, commercial centers, and industries pop up and proliferate from boundary to boundary.

Similar growth is readily apparent to the south and southwest of Minneapolis. Four decades ago Minneapolitans could drive due south out of the city on Portland Avenue, pass through a sparsely populated "bedroom community" called Richfield, and find themselves standing in an open field, recently planted with corn. Here and there in that field were wooden stakes signalling the imminent approach of a housing development and, on Portland Avenue itself, the beginning of a shopping center.

That field was called Bloomington.

Today Bloomington is Minnesota's third-largest city, with a population of about 85,000. Stretched out, east to west, along the busy Interstate-494 "Strip," Bloomington is now home base to several of the metro area's dominant companies, including Control Data, Jostens, and International Dairy Queen, as well as to the Minnesota North Stars hockey team and the Metropolitan Sports Center. (From 1961 until 1982, when the Metrodome opened its doors downtown, Bloomington was also the home of the Twins and the Vikings, who played in the late lamented Metropolitan Stadium, now the construction site of an enormous new retail, entertainment, and office complex.) Its eastern end borders on the Minneapolis-St. Paul International Airport, and this proximity helps make the suburb one of the Twin Cities' major hotel, restaurant, and entertainment areas.

Residentially, Bloomington offers virtually everything from the 30-year-old, single-family pastel ramblers that originally filled the erstwhile cornfields on the suburb's east side, to some of the metro area's largest and most expensive contemporary homes on the hillier, more recently developed west side. Also on the west end of town is the sprawling Hyland Lake Park Reserve, with its beautiful lake, trails, play areas, and skiing facilities.

PREVIOUS PAGE: Not all lakes draw great numbers of people looking for recreation. Those lakes less popular with humans are usually more popular with wildlife. Photo by Robert Friedman

BELOW: Autumn colors provide notice of changing seasons, a vivid reminder of the four very different seasons found in the Minneapolis area. Photo by Robert Friedman

Canterbury Downs racetrack outside of Minneapolis is a popular weekend attraction. Photo by Steve Schneider

As new a major community as Bloomington is, however, it is a virtual old-timer alongside a few of its suburban neighbors. Eden Prairie, Burnsville, Apple Valley, and Eagan are all second- or third-tier Minneapolis suburbs that have exploded—both commercially and residentially—in little more than the past decade. In these locations, too, onetime farmland has given way to massive housing developments, shopping centers, office complexes, and service areas; here, too, the choice of homes and amenities spans a wide range of possibilities, priced from the low end to the high. And here, too, what was once "way out in the country" is now often only a half-hour's drive to the urban core, thanks to the continuing expansion of the metropolitan freeway system begun in earnest during the 1960s. Even such traditionally rural communities as Chanhassen, Chaska, and Prior Lake—too distant to be "suburbs" in the conventional sense—have assumed more "suburban" roles.

Perhaps the best-known Twin Cities suburb, however, is neither the oldest, the largest, nor the most scenically situated. Edina is, in fact, old, having celebrated its centenary in 1988. It is, in addition, comparatively large, with a population of about 48,000. If it does not share Wayzata's lakeside vistas, it does have the considerable advantage of being located on the southwest edge of Minneapolis proper, with easy access to downtown and the city's lakes. And with its own tree-shaded parks, ponds, and streams, it is scenic in its own right.

Edina is home, though, to some of the area's handsomest neighborhoods and grandest residences. It has, moreover, during the postwar boom, become one of the most potent commercial centers in the Twin Cities. It was in Edina that the Dayton brothers located the first all-season shopping mall, Southdale, in the middle 1950s, thereby establishing the community as a fashionable place to shop for everything from haute couture to gourmet foods. And it is in Edina that many large companies have, in the past two decades, established corporate headquarters in gleaming new office towers and complexes.

The extraordinary growth of the suburbs as individual entities since the end of World War II has clearly been the result, here as elsewhere, of vast numbers of young urban families moving to the fresh, often more spacious residential developments sprouting beyond the city limits. As the young families have migrated outward, away from the city's historic center, so have the businesses

that employ their breadwinners, as well as the schools, hospitals, retail establishments, restaurants, and entertainment centers that serve them. It is a process that has become both symbiotic and self-perpetuating.

Sporting events in the Minneapolis area are not limited to professional events, as Little League remains a favorite summer program. Photo by Ed Bock

The linking of these individual entities has in part been the result of the metro area's ever-expanding freeway system and, in part, an extraordinary area-wide sensibility that has manifested itself in, among other things, the Metropolitan Council. Though not always as tangible as the six- and eight-lane strips of concrete freeway that crisscross the Twin Cities, this metropolitan sensibility has been at least as important in bringing the various—and increasingly far-flung—communities together.

It is an interesting phenomenon. Ask a random sample of

Twin Citians where they're from, and they'll likely say, "Minneapolis," "Bloomington," or "White Bear Lake" —a specific hometown or, in some cases, neighborhood. Ask, however, about their weekend plans, and they'll probably reply that they've got tickets for the Twins' game at the Metrodome or for a Sommerfest concert at Orchestra Hall, or perhaps that they're taking the family to the Minnesota Zoo in Apple Valley, the Science Museum in downtown St. Paul, or the Canterbury Downs Thoroughbred racetrack in Shakopee. To be sure, the still-manageable size of the metro area—relative to the likes of Chicago or Los Angeles—facilitates this level of crosstown activity, but there is more to it than that. No matter how loyal they may be to their individual communities or neighborhoods, Twin Citians seem genuinely pleased to belong to the metropolis at large.

The Metrodome is located in downtown Minneapolis, but this has not kept away Twins and Vikings fans from throughout the metro area (or, for that matter, from all around the Upper Midwest). They come to cheer on, of course, the *Minnesota* Twins and the *Minnesota* Vikings, just as classical music enthusiasts applaud the *Minnesota* Orchestra at Orchestra Hall or the Ordway Music Theatre. There is much in this part of the country to distract the sports fan or concert-goer; the ease with which Twin Citians commute between home and the ballpark or concert hall is rivaled by the ease with which they can hitch up their boat and trailer and head for a lakeside cabin "up North." If the quality of the attraction is up to their expectations, they will—they *do*—support it enthusiastically, no matter in which end of town it is playing.

And, indeed, first-rate attractions can be found all over the metropolitan area. The various athletic, cultural, and entertainment opportunities have already been discussed, as have the many civic celebrations and the vast array of shopping complexes that reach the four corners of the Twin Cities' seven contiguous counties. Mention must also be made of the growing variety of outstanding restaurants and bistros that have, in the past several years, added to the area-wide traffic flow.

The restaurants range from longtime favorites like Murray's steakhouse in downtown Minneapolis and perennial award-winners like St. Paul's Blue Horse to newer and enthusiastically welcomed establishments like the D'Amico Cucina cafe in Minneapolis' warehouse district and Sasha's Deli on the pleasant shores of Lake Minnetonka. The arrival, over the past decade, of large groups of Southeast Asian refugees has increased the number and quality of ethnic restaurants (not to mention ethnic gift shops and food markets) throughout the metro area. As a happy result, Twin Citians now find it just as easy to enjoy a delicious Vietnamese dinner as Italian or French cuisine.

The Twin Cities' metropolitan consciousness, however, comprises more than just recreational or leisure-time amenities. When

PREVIOUS PAGE: No matter what season, Minneapolis area landscapes can become dramatic scenery. Photo by Robert Friedman

131

hometowners and visitors alike speak of the area's quality of life, they generally are thinking first about such weighty concerns as education and health care. In both categories, Twin Citians have a good deal to be proud of, from one end of town to the other.

According to a recent economic profile assembled by the Greater Minneapolis Chamber of Commerce, the entire metropolitan area comprises nearly 50 public school districts, offering kindergarten through grade-12 education, and more than 250 private elementary and secondary schools. Four out of five Twin Citians 25 years and older are at least high school graduates, and the state's high school graduation rate is the highest in the entire nation. Moreover, the metro area includes 13 four-year colleges and universities, 6 community colleges, 9 publicly supported technical institutes, and several proprietary schools offering trade and technical training. The postsecondary institutions—including, of course, the local campuses of the University of Minnesota—draw students from all over the region.

The metropolitan library system is recognized as among the finest and most complete in the United States. The area actually includes more than a dozen public systems, with individual branches numbering nearly a hundred. The various systems are linked by the comprehensive Metropolitan Library Service Agency, which allows cost-free borrowing privileges between one system and another. The University of Minnesota and the other local colleges and universities have extensive library and research facilities of their own, many of which are open to the public.

The Twin Cities is famous for its innovative and progressive health-care facilities, which draw patients from not only around the region, but from around the world as well. A recent Metropolitan Council survey counted a total of 32 hospitals and 9 health maintenance organizations operating in the seven-county metro area. Local state-of-the-art health-care facilities include the internationally renowned organ-transplant center at the University of Minnesota and such newer but already high-profile institutions as the Phillips Eye Institute at Minneapolis' Metropolitan-Mount Sinai Medical Center and the International Diabetes Center at the Park Nicollet Medical Center in St. Louis Park. Because the predations of injury and illness recognize no municipal boundaries, the waiting rooms of the Twin Cities' hospitals and clinics—according to their individual treatment specialties—contain patients from all over the metro area.

Finally, it is important to remember that the Twin Cities metropolitan area has a stable and vibrant heart. In the final analysis, the vitality of downtown Minneapolis may well account—as much as the freeways and an overall metropolitan mentality—for the widely acclaimed "livability" of the area as a whole. In Minneapolis, the center is holding, and the good life by the lakes remains a shining reality.

Winter is the time for ice sports on the local lakes. Many offer such niceties as skating rinks with warming houses. Photo by Ed Bock

Afterword

"I have not lived in Minneapolis for forty-five years," wrote Harrison Salisbury, veteran *New York Times* correspondent, distinguished author, and peripatetic world traveler, in 1976, "but I think there has hardly been a day of my life that I did not think of it."

The Minneapolis that Salisbury thought about while living in the several distant and exotic places he has lived has, for the most part, disappeared. The big, imposing Royalston Avenue house in which he grew up just north of downtown was long gone in the middle 1970s, when he returned to reminisce about the old days—as were, indeed, many of his boyhood haunts as he remembered them. Like most long-absent sons and daughters, Salisbury was saddened and even angered, if not entirely surprised, by the changes that had occurred since he had left home.

Change, of course, is the way most living things—including cities—grow, renew, and reinvigorate themselves. The issue, it seems to me, is not so much change per se—change is inevitable— but how change is managed and the nature of its results.

Now approaching the midpoint of its second century, Minneapolis is a city in the process of significant change: reflected in its stunning downtown skyline, in the composition of its new generation of public and private leaders, in the ethnic richness of its population, and in various other local phenomena. Then again, Minneapolis has always been a city that not only accommodates change, but seems to thrive on it. It had evolved, after all, from a frontier milling town into a diversified center of commerce and culture by the end of its first hundred years.

The triumphs of the city's people, collectively and on their own, reflect their willingness and ability to make the most of change. In many cases, they have anticipated economic and social trends, establishing, for instance, a municipal park system that would allow present and future generations to enjoy the exceptional natural beauty of the region, and service and shopping areas on the leading edge of major demographic movements. In other instances, they have reacted to downturns and diminutions of markets and industries by creating fresh enterprise to take the place of the old and to maximize the benefits of incoming technology. It can be reasonably argued that Minneapolis' success has been directly proportional to the willingness and ability of its citizens and institutions to insist that change be translated, sooner or later, into development and improvement.

As the community at large continues to change, it's worth noting that many of the smaller, more personal pleasures remain quite the same. I am speaking now of strolling along the sun-dappled walkways of Lake Harriet on a Sunday afternoon; of ice skating on Lake of the Isles or at Powderhorn Park; of driving beneath the canopy of elms, oaks, and maples along the Minnehaha Parkway on a bright autumn morning; of listening to the transcendent glory of Handel's *Messiah* as performed by the Minnesota Orchestra and chorus at Christmas. These are among the many hometown

A pleasure boat passes beneath the Lake Street bridge, connecting St. Paul and Minneapolis over the Mississippi River. Photo by Greg Ryan and Sally Beyer

pleasures I have recalled when I've lived in other parts of the world, and are what I still consider among the bedrock of my personal Minneapolis experience.

Minneapolis has been called a small town in the process of becoming a big city. If so, it is our continuing challenge to preserve the best of the "small town"—including that variety of sweet, personal pleasures—while developing the best of the "big city." Not every community has been able to handle the transformation. Minneapolis, I believe, is one that can. That *has.* That *is.*

In any case, the Minneapolis story continues without a definitive ending. In relation to most of the great urban centers of the world, Minneapolis is still young, still growing, still developing its special resources and character. We are, all of us, encouraged to participate in that development—and to read on.

Part

2

MINNEAPOLIS' ENTERPRISES

Chapter **6**

Networks

Minneapolis' communication providers keep information circulating within the area.

U S WEST, Inc.,
142

Star Tribune,
146

KMSP-TV,
148

AT&T,
150

Photo by Ed Bock

U S WEST, INC.

Created in 1984 as one of seven regional companies to emerge from the court-ordered breakup of the Bell System, U S WEST is today one of the world's largest and most diversified telecommunications companies. The traditional 14-state region it serves extends from Minnesota to the Southwest and the Pacific Northwest. The traditional service mission it handles includes the familiar telephone operations of Northwestern Bell, Mountain Bell, and Pacific Northwest Bell—now merged and reorganized by customer-focused markets rather than geographic territories and operating under the name of U S WEST Communications. In addition, various subsidiary units and new business ventures have made U S WEST a truly international technology leader.

Through expansion and diversification, U S WEST has used its strong base and century-long heritage of customer service to grow into new communications areas, typically as an outgrowth of its traditional communications businesses. Beyond conventional telephone service, U S WEST is ac-

tive in directory publishing, cellular mobile communications, business communications, software, commercial real estate, and financial services. In all, U S WEST employs nearly 70,000 men and women—more than 7,500 of them in Minnesota, some 70 percent of those in the Twin Cities. It responds to the needs of some 9 million customers with a full spectrum of telecommunications services.

Though headquartered in Colorado, U S WEST is one of Minneapolis' largest employers and has made the city a key operating center for a number of its subsidiary companies. The largest among them is U S WEST Communications Group, the holding company that coordinates the former activities of Northwestern Bell, Mountain Bell, and Pacific Northwest Bell. Together, the market unit companies of U S WEST Communica-

From left: Tom Madison, president, Information Markets Group; Eric Selberg, vice-president and chief executive officer of Minnesota operations; and Ron James, vice-president, Large Business Service Unit.

tions Group account for more than 90 percent of the parent company's annual revenues. They are charged with providing high-quality local telephone service as well as in-state long-distance service within specified calling areas and local connect service to interstate long-distance companies.

The reorganization of its three regional phone companies into U S WEST Communications was the result of a great deal of research and planning. Through internal examination a new strategy was developed to give customers what they want, where they want it, and packaged in the way they desire. It is part of a company-wide transformation from a product lines orientation to a communication solution approach.

The reorganization of services by customers rather than geography allows U S WEST Communications to serve customers under three broad market headings: the Consumer Division, the Business Division, and the Carrier and Information Provider Division. Each division is active in the Twin Cities, and (in addition to the group's

headquarters) several major business units make their corporate homes in Minneapolis:

—One of the largest and most active is the Large Business Services market unit. Its charter is to provide services to organizations with 100 or more employees. Its mission is to help its customers move and manage information and, by doing so efficiently and cost effectively, create a competitive advantage for their firms.

—Two organizations within the U S WEST Communications Carrier and Information Provider Division also call Minneapolis home. One is the Exchange Carrier market unit. It serves the needs of independent local-exchange companies in U S WEST's 14-state business region by providing network, connections, and value-added services to help them run their businesses.

Also based in Minneapolis is the Technical Operations service unit, a support organization that packages and assembles switching, transmission, transport, and customer premises equipment elements for the group's market units.

A major reason behind the decision to locate the headquarters of U S WEST Communications and its Large Business Services market unit in Minneapolis is the concentration of large, *Fortune* 500-scale businesses there as well as the diversity of the area's business and technology sector. The greater Minneapolis area is home to more major corporations than any other city in U S WEST's 14-state operating region. In addition, Thomas Madison, president of the group, was formerly president of Northwestern Bell.

"As we formulated U S WEST Communications," Madison recalls, "our strategy was to focus our efforts to better understand customer needs and then satisfy them. Our goal is to be the preeminent supplier in terms of the qual-

Judi Scott, director of sales for U S WEST Direct in Minnesota, helps a customer with his directory advertising needs.

ity of the products and services we provide in the markets in which we compete. We want to be more responsive to our customers. We want to be more flexible in the ways we serve our customers. And we plan to compete by finding ways to say 'yes' to our customers, by giving them what they want when and how they want it."

The Large Business Services unit consolidates formerly separate, business-oriented functions from Northwestern Bell, Mountain Bell, and Pacific Northwest Bell. Its primary attention is given to meeting the "information-intensive needs" of some 12,000 large corporate customers throughout U S WEST's 14-state region, a process that includes not only basic products and services but also support activities such as maintenance and research into new types of service

and technology.

One of the most promising new technologies being introduced within U S WEST is ISDN: the Integrated Services Digital Network. As its evolution continues, ISDN will provide the realization of a high-tech dream—the integration of voice, data, image, and facsimile transmissions, either separately or simultaneously, over conventional copper wire and optical fibers in the nation's existing telecommunications network.

In recent years Minneapolis has been the site of one of ISDN's first major operating tests. With further development, the lessons learned there can be applied in business today and may soon offer greater capabilities to the

143

Ron Sanders, region general manager of U S WEST Cellular, uses his cellular phone day or night.

home.

In addition to the Large Business Services unit, the Business Division of the U S WEST Communications Group also includes market units that concentrate on serving the needs of small businesses (fewer than 100 employees), government and educational organizations, and the agencies and operations of the federal government in U S WEST's region. The Consumer Division addresses the needs of residential customers, from local connect service and operator assistance to public, coin, and credit card-operated telephones.

The other side of U S WEST is the Diversified Group, which is made up of acquisitions and start-up companies that have emerged as logical outgrowths of the firm's core businesses. Among them are the U S WEST Data Systems Group and U S West Internal Operations. The former includes units that design software for financial services, provide enhanced information software and data-base products to telecommunications and scientific customers, market software for the

management of large internal corporate computer networks, publish telephone directories, sell and service mobile cellular telephone equipment, and offer full-service commercial real estate services.

A number of these U S WEST units also play an active role in the Twin Cities, including five-state regional centers for U S WEST Cellular, U S WEST Direct, and BetaWest Properties. U S WEST Cellular has been serving the Twin Cities since 1984—just nine months after the first mobile cellular telephone service was introduced in Chicago, and the first system to become operational west of the Mississippi River. In 1988 U S WEST Cellular opened the first of a growing network of personal communication centers—drive-in installation and service locations conveniently located in auto malls around the Twin Cities.

U S WEST Direct is the publishing arm of U S WEST. While widely recognized for the tele-

phone directories it publishes, it is perhaps less well known for the growing sophistication of its advertising support services. U S WEST Direct representatives help small businesses develop staged, multiple-year advertising programs designed to help their businesses grow. In-house artists serve clients by designing advertising that helps identify and position specific products and services. Meanwhile, directories are also taking on a more user-friendly configuration, generally as a result of U S WEST Direct's extensive research with the people who use its directories and the people who advertise in them.

BetaWest has become an active partner in Twin Cities real estate activities. BetaWest is a joint development partner with Opus Corporation in the 150 South Fifth building in downtown Minneapolis, home to many U S WEST operations. Encompassing a full block in the heart of the city, BetaWest's new development, LaSalle Plaza, is destined to become the pulse of Minneapolis. The new 28-story office tower and the historic downtown YMCA tower will anchor the development along LaSalle Avenue. The YMCA tower will be remodeled into new office space, and a new YMCA will be built on South Ninth Street. The celebrated State Theatre, built in the 1920s on Hennepin Avenue, will be renovated and reopened, featuring some of the finest live theater in Minneapolis. Connecting and complementing the office tower, YMCA, and theater will be an interior retail and entertainment plaza, with shops, restaurants, and cinemas. The development is a partnership between BetaWest and the Palmer Group of the Twin Cities.

The continuing theme that unites the various market units of U S WEST is technology, and Minneapolis is clearly a key center in the continuing growth and development of new and more versatile forms of telecommunications. Testimony to U S WEST's technology investment is the fact that the entire Twin Cities metropolitan area is served by electronic switching equipment and fiber optics. The continuing investment in state-of-the-art technology assures that U S WEST customers of every size and description, from large businesses to single-family homes, have access to the most modern and reliable communications support.

The traditions of the past continue in U S WEST's continuing commitment to the quality of the communities it serves. In the Twin Cities, U S WEST employees have organized themselves into 20 community service teams—there are another 11 teams based in outstate Minnesota communities—through which they can combine their efforts in meeting specific local needs. Activities range from the "I'm Okay" program that keeps in touch with seniors to Hug-A-Bears—teddy bears provided to police departments in Minnesota and North Dakota by the Telephone Pioneers for use in helping children deal with traumatic incidents ranging from traffic accidents to domestic abuse.

Education also is a continuing theme. At the college level, U S WEST funds two chairs: one at the University of Minnesota, the other at the College of St. Thomas. The U S WEST Foundation coordinates grants of more than $2 million annually to human services and the arts. U S WEST executives and workers are active in voluntary roles with a host of local organizations. Programs range from the U S WEST Outstanding Teacher of the Year Award, which recognizes outstanding classroom performers from kindergarten through grade 12, to the CHOICES program, which is designed to encourage eighth- and ninth-graders to stay in school—and, perhaps, consider careers in telecommunications.

In addition, U S WEST plays an active role in helping new businesses—which will be new customers—get themselves established. Under its economic development umbrella are contributions of time, talent, and physical facilities, often involving the kind of high-performance technology that can help a new business compete effectively. Through public-private partnerships with Minneapolis, Bloomington, Hennepin County, and other community and government organizations, U S WEST is helping to increase both jobs and economic value.

All that augments a continuing business investment in the 14-state service region created just five years ago. Since that time U S WEST has invested more than $7 billion to expand and modernize its telephone operations. That investment, backed by the traditions established close to customers at the local level throughout the West, positions U S WEST as a leader in the high-technology future of telecommunications.

Robert Caldwell, regional director of BetaWest Properties, Inc., stands in front of a BetaWest property in downtown Minneapolis.

STAR TRIBUNE

In recent years change has been one of the most visible stories at the *Star Tribune*. Since the merger of the afternoon *Star* and the morning *Tribune* in 1982, every part of the newspaper has been systematically improved. Sections from Marketplace to Sports to Variety have been enhanced, reorganized, and enlarged.

One of the results of those improvements has been steady circulation growth. With circulation exceeding 650,000, the *Star Tribune* is the largest Sunday newspaper between Chicago and the West Coast. Its daily circulation, more than 400,000, makes it the 18th-largest major metropolitan daily in the United States.

Because the *Star Tribune* is committed to comprehensive coverage of national and international events, as well as local and state-wide news, additional space has been devoted to these topics and another national correspondent added. The newspaper has opened a news bureau in New York City to complement existing bureaus in Washington, D.C., and in four regional locations.

Business coverage has grown

by 25 percent, accompanied by the hiring of reporters who are specialists in various areas of commerce and finance. The award-winning Sports pages boast visible increases in the coverage of not only professional competitions but also amateur and local sports activities. And editorial space devoted to commentary has doubled.

Perhaps one of the most visible changes has been the addition of color photographs and graphics. The front pages of daily and Sunday sections are filled with color, their brightness and clarity one of the results of the company's $110-million investment in a new printing plant that opened in 1987.

Heritage Center, the *Star Tribune's* new state-of-the-art production facility, is 16 blocks from the newspaper's news, advertising, circulation, and business offices on Portland Avenue.

Occupying two square blocks in Minneapolis' historic district north of downtown, the plant combines skilled and dedicated employees with high-quality offset printing, computerized bundle distribution, and advanced robotics to make each day's *Star Tribune* one of the best printed newspapers in the country. The 425,000-square-foot plant is a model produc-

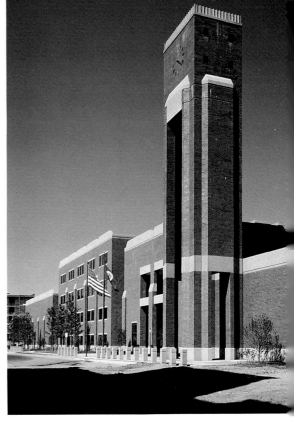

The exterior of the Star Tribune's *production facility was designed to reflect the heritage of the area's origins, using architectural elements that characterize turn-of-the-century warehouses.*

tion facility for the industry to follow for years to come.

The facility's exterior was designed to reflect the heritage of the area's origins, using architectural elements that characterized turn-of-the-century warehouses.

Heritage Center is connected to the Portland Avenue offices by fiber-optic cables. Every day each page of the paper is written, edited, typeset, and pasted up in the Portland facility; then it is fed by laser scanner, using these fiber-optic cables, directly to the plate-making department at Heritage Center.

As the metropolitan area has grown, the concerns and interests of the people who live and work in Minneapolis-St. Paul and the surrounding communities have become intertwined into a larger Twin Cities identity. Consequently, the most dramatic change came on August 31, 1987, when the paper adopted a new name: *Star Tribune, Newspaper of the Twin Cities,* and began publishing three distinct editions—one for the Minneapolis area, one for the St. Paul area, and one for greater Minnesota. World, national, and state news coverage is the same in the Minneapolis and St. Paul editions,

Heritage Center pressroom houses five Goss Headline offset presses.

The three editions of the Star Tribune — *Minneapolis, St. Paul, and State—reflect the increased use of high-quality color photos and artwork.*

and the year the *Minneapolis Tribune* was created through the merger of a pre-Civil War paper, the *State Atlas,* and the postwar *Minneapolis Chronicle.*

The *Minneapolis Star* first appeared in 1920 and was purchased by the Cowles family of Des Moines, Iowa, in 1935. Under the leadership of John Cowles, Sr., that paper thrived, and in 1941 the *Minneapolis Tribune* joined the Cowles family of publications. It has been a successful union. The *Star* and the *Tribune* have won four Pulitzers and more than 3,000 local and national awards.

The business principles established by the Cowles

issues, so our readers can form their judgments wisely."

The *Star Tribune* is the largest operating unit of Cowles Media Company, a diversified communications group headquartered in Minneapolis. Other Cowles publications include the *Great Falls Tribune* in Montana; the *Rapid City Journal* in South Dakota; *Scottsdale Progress* in Arizona; the Sentinal Publishing Company, which publishes weekly community newspapers in the Denver suburbs; Cowles Magazines, Inc., in Harrisburg, Pennsylvania, which publishes highly targeted consumer specialty magazines, including *Civil War Times, Country Journal, Early*

as are business, sports, and feature stories. Generally, the same local news is published in both editions, but the length or position of stories differ depending on their interest to Minneapolis or St. Paul area readers.

In a broader sense, a good newspaper not only covers events in its hometown but also takes an active and progressive role in the community. The *Star Tribune* is known for its long-standing commitment to corporate citizenship. The newspaper was one of the founding members of the Five Percent Club, whose members donate 5 percent of pretax earnings to charitable organizations each year. The *Star Tribune* and its parent corporation, Cowles Media Company, are major sponsors of literacy and literary arts programs, and, in addition, each year make substantial contributions to arts, cultural, and educational organizations as well as social services agencies.

The roots of the *Star Tribune* stretch back to 1867, the year that Minneapolis was granted a charter

A sampling of magazines and newspapers published by the other operating units of Cowles Media Company.

family in the 1930s continue to hold true today:

"We believe in presenting *all* of the news impartially in the news columns.

"We believe in expressing our own opinions as persuasively and forcefully as possible, but in confining those expressions to the editorial columns on the editorial pages.

"We believe in giving our readers also the opinions of other competent writers, representing all sides of important controversial

American Life, and *Fly Fisherman;* Hanson Publishing Group in Stamford, Connecticut, known for *Folio* magazine and conferences and other business magazines serving the print media; and Empire Press in Leesburg, Virginia, publishers of seven history magazines, including *Military History, World War II,* and *Vietnam.*

147

KMSP-TV

Over the past 10 years one of the top two independent stations in the country, as measured by the size of the viewing audience in its local broadcasting area, has been KMSP-TV, Channel 9, in the Twin Cities. Via its cable coverage its reach extends farther than any other television station in the Minneapolis/St. Paul area, including the network affiliates. KMSP's signal is carried to homes throughout the five-state area. From the eastern Dakotas to western Wisconsin and from the Iron Range to the Iowa border, KMSP delivers first-rate programming to its extensive viewing audience.

As recently as 10 years ago, there were just four commercial television stations serving the Twin Cities: three network affiliates and one independent. Today there are six commercial stations and cable systems that bring dozens more to the metro area. KMSP's market share is just as strong now as it was 10 years ago.

The station has been Channel 9 from the beginning, but not always KMSP. It was licensed to Morris T. Baker's Minnesota Tower Company on January 9, 1955, as KEYD-TV. A year and a half later Metro Goldwyn Mayer acquired a quarter-interest and changed the call letters to KMGM-TV. Channel 9 became KMSP in 1958, when National Television Associates acquired the interests of MGM and Minnesota Tower. National sold its interest to Twentieth Century Fox Film Corporation in October 1959. The station broadcast as an ABC affiliate from 1961 through March 1979, when it returned to the independent status it maintained in its first seven years of operation.

KMSP is now owned and operated by United Television, a publicly held company that is part of the Chris Craft corporate family. Chris Craft is one of the 10 largest broadcasting companies in the United States.

Broadcasters are licensed to operate in the public's interest, and Channel 9 has progressively strengthened that emphasis. One of the most visible aspects of its commitment to the community is the station's development of a

The weeknight anchor team for KMSP-TV's award-winning Prime Time News faithfully delivers the news to thousands of Twin Cities residents. Photo by Rick Bell

strong, independent news operation. A staff of more than 30 professional journalists and production specialists—one of the largest independent news staffs in the country—produce a complete, concise newscast, including local, national, and international news. Their efforts are supported by the national newsfeeds of CNN and Westinghouse. The station's independent status and the flexibility of the program's structure allows the staff the opportunity to adjust the newscast format to fit the story.

In 1988 KMSP's Prime Time News received regional and international recognition for its outstanding reporting of spot news, feature stories, and mini-documentaries. The Aviation/Space Writers Association presented its 1988 Award of Excellence to Channel 9's "Flying High" documentary and recognized the station for the overall excellence of its reporting in the area of general aviation and aerospace with the prestigious Earl D. Osborn Award.

In the spot news category of the Associated Press of Minnesota Awards, KMSP swept its network-

affiliated competition. The station received a first, second, and third place in the 1988 regional awards program. It also earned honors from the Minnesota Chapter of the Society of Professional Journalists, Sigma Delta Chi, and from the Northwest Broadcast News As-

BELOW: Much of KMSP's programming and national news feeds arrive at the station via satellite. Photo by Rick Bell

ABOVE: KMSP-TV uses remote vans for coverage of local news stories and production of live news segments. Photo by Rick Bell

sociation, including two NBNA Awards of Merit for feature and mini-documentary reporting. Also that year the readers of *City Pages* voted KMSP the best local news operation in the Twin Cities.

KMSP's "Senior Citizens Forum" received recognition in its own right in 1988: the red, white, and blue C-Flag, symbol of the president's Citation Program for Private Sector Initiatives. The flag, which bears the slogan "We Can—We Care," recognizes outstanding contributors to the American spirit of volunteerism and community action.

Originally created in 1972, "Senior Citizens Forum" is a unique public affairs program that informs older residents and other interested individuals in the Twin Cit-

ies about programs, services, and issues that have a direct bearing on the life-styles of older people. Each Saturday from October through June, host Abraham "Dutch" Kastenbaum interviews guests and examines issues of interest to seniors from public and private organizations whose services can be of benefit to the elderly. Kastenbaum, now in his eighties, came up with the idea for the show when he turned 65, and found a receptive home for it at KMSP.

Young viewers as well as old are important to Channel 9. Votemobile, a pilot voter-registration program developed by KMSP and the League of Women Voters of Minnesota, has become a model for national efforts designed to

encourage first-time voters in the 18- to 24-year-old age group. In the spring and fall of 1988, a 25-foot camper serving as a mobile voter-registration booth visited college campuses in the Twin Cities and beyond to register students and provide them with voting information.

The project grew out of widespread concern over a steady drop in voter participation rates nationwide, especially among young people eligible to vote for the first time. The league and KMSP recognized that voting habits start early and that those who register and vote as young adults are likely to continue to participate in the American political process.

The league registered more voters on its first day at the Minneapolis campus of the University of Minnesota than it had ever registered statewide in a single day. All total, the league registered more than 3,500 new voters. Another, perhaps more subtle, indication of the success of such community involvement was that in the 1988 presidential election Minnesota again led the nation in voter turnout.

From its commitment to public service and community involvement to its first-rate coverage of news, sports, and entertainment programming, KMSP continues to build a strong viewer following and remains as one of the leaders in Twin Cities television.

AT&T

Prior to the federally mandated divestiture of the local Bell telephone companies in 1984, the ambitious mission of AT&T was to provide universal telephone service, no matter how simple or involved, to virtually every business and residence in the United States.

Today AT&T designs, develops, manufactures, markets, and services a wide range of information movement and management products and services worldwide. It provides consumers with long-distance services and high-quality telephones and related products. It offers businesses and government agencies a range of voice- and data-transmission services, plus computer and data networking products and systems to connect widely dispersed and frequently incompatible computers into integrated networks. It supplies switching systems, transmission equipment, and operations support services to the telecommunications industry. And it designs and manufactures advanced electronic components for its own use and for sale to other high-technology firms.

In Minneapolis, AT&T will be the anchor tenant in the AT&T Tower, a new office tower in downtown Minneapolis, which will serve as the company's upper Midwest area headquarters. Ground was broken for the 34-story tower in the summer of 1989. When completed in 1991 as the third and final part of the International Centre complex, the AT&T Tower will allow about 1,000 AT&T employees to be consolidated in one downtown Minneapolis location from seven currently scattered

The AT&T Tower will serve as AT&T's Upper Midwest area headquarters. This photo shows a model of the tower at its future site on Ninth Street and Marquette Avenue in downtown Minneapolis.

This is how the AT&T Tower (far left) will look on the downtown Minneapolis skyline upon its completion in 1991. The Minneapolis based firms of Ryan Construction Company of Minnesota, Inc., and Walsh Bishop Associates, Inc., serve as developer/general contractor and architect, respectively.

locations.

Minneapolis is AT&T's area headquarters for a six-state region that includes Minnesota, Wisconsin, Nebraska, Iowa, North Dakota, and South Dakota. That presence includes a state-of-the-art long-distance switching center and a new, areawide customer service center established in 1988 to handle all customer maintenance and repair needs for the six-state region 24 hours a day.

Minneapolis is the focal point for a variety of business activities for the six-state region. Among them are sales efforts for products and services designed for business customers, as well as an area data

systems group responsible for the sales of AT&T's computer and data networking products.

The area servicing headquarters is there: Its responsibilities include the design, maintenance, and management of AT&T's Worldwide Intelligent Network in the six-state region as well as installation and maintenance of telephones, private telephone switches, and computer equipment and systems for large business customers. (The AT&T Worldwide Intelligent Network links virtually any point in the United States to 250 countries and territories worldwide through satellites, undersea cables, and high-speed electronics technology.) And areawide external affairs, including industry relations and regulatory activities, are centralized in Minneapolis.

The new AT&T Tower is by no means the only visible evidence of the company's presence in the Twin Cities. A major contribution by AT&T made possible the purchase of George Segal's *Walking Man* for the Minneapolis Sculpture Garden that opened in the fall of 1988. AT&T plans to remain an important part of the Twin Cities.

Photo by Greg Ryan/Sally Beyer

7

Manufacturing

Producing goods for individuals and industry, manufacturing firms provide employment for Minneapolis area residents.

Ambassador Sausage Corporation, 154   *Precision Associates, Inc., 156*

The Toro Company, 158   *Thermo King Corporation, 160*

Aeration Industries International, Inc., 162   *Juno Enterprises, 163*

Sandoz Nutrition, 164   *Jostens, 166*

Photo by Robert Friedman

AMBASSADOR SAUSAGE CORPORATION

In years gone by, when freshness meant food had to be prepared close to its consumers, almost 20 sausage and meat-packing plants operated in and around Minneapolis. Today only one survives: Ambassador Sausage. Its great-tasting products are found in meat cases at discount stores, supermarkets, delicatessens, and convenience stores—the continuation of an old-world family tradition that now spans more than a half-century.

thrive against the competition of large-scale food processors, primarily the result of the grit and determination of Ethel Arnold. She was by no means her husband's heir apparent—in keeping with the times her experience at Ambassador mostly involved her own years spent working in the plant and, later, as the company's bookkeeper. Her husband, a traditional German-born "wurst meister," seldom discussed the business with

Upholding the tradition begun by her late husband more than 50 years ago, Ethel Arnold and her daughter Shirley Severson have guided the thriving Ambassador Sausage Corporation to success despite competition from larger companies.

En route to a local parade, Ambassador's wiener car, driven by the founder's grandson Jim Koch, is sure to attract attention on the streets of Minneapolis.

Yet the Ambassador story is more than a tale of tradition. It is a family business with a modern twist—a company run by a pair of entrepreneurial women—Ethel Arnold, who took over operation of the company when her husband, Otto, passed away in 1958, and her daughter Shirley Severson. Another daughter, Dolores Balafas, is active in the business on a part-time basis; grandson Jim Koch represents the third generation of the family at Ambassador.

Ambassador survived the passing of its founder and chief sausage maker and continues to

her.

Otto founded the company on the recipes he brought with him from Blumenfeld, Germany, building the small sausage plant, Sanitary Sausage Company, to a regional producer of an array of high-quality sausage products. But his small, quality-conscious business was in increasing jeopardy as larger, more integrated food companies developed to serve the tastes of consumers willing to buy their food preprocessed and packaged in supermarkets rather than fresh from a mom-and-pop market.

For Ethel Arnold it came as a shock to learn at her husband's passing that the firm was in dire straits. Its markets were changing in the face of aggressive competition; packaging was changing; and

automation was clearly the way to go. In short order she took it upon herself to rectify this situation by adjusting prices to cover the costs involved in packaging, automating the plant, and updating sales and marketing practices to make Ambassador products competitive. Within three months the company was back on its feet, and in 18 months it was operating in the black.

Today Ambassador produces more than 48 varieties of fresh and prepackaged sausage products from its often-improved and upgraded plant on Northeast Harrison Street. Variety truly is the spice of life. Ambassador makes three different kinds of bratwurst and supplies specially spiced sausages for a growing number of restaurants. It also takes advantage of its small, close-to-the-customer scale of operations to produce seasonal specialties—bockwurst at Easter time, Swedish sausage, and Norwegian-style sylta (a combination of headcheese and spices) for the holidays—and special varieties treasured by ethnic customers ranging from Hispanic and black to Polish and Italian.

Two shifts of production workers—approximately 60 in all—grind, mix, pack, cure, and package the company's various products, from weiners, sausages, ring products, luncheon meat, and snack items to barbecue products. Some of those on the payroll today are the sons and daughters (and occasionally grandsons and granddaughters) of Ambassador workers. A sense of extended family pervades the plant.

Many Twin Cities professionals can look back on summers spent working at Ambassador, covering vacations for the plant's workers to earn money for books and tuition. Some worked side by side with Shirley Severson and Dolores Balafas (like their mother, who was working on a production crew when she first met her future husband); they learned the business first hand by working in the plant. And a number of former customers do more than remember the taste of Ambassador products; they have them shipped from Minneapolis to their new homes in locations that stretch from Arizona, California, and Washington, D.C., to Texas and Florida.

A network of 24 distributors, most of whom measure their service in terms of decades rather than years (and some of whom involve two or more generations of a family), service food and convenience stores throughout the Upper Midwest. From western Wisconsin to the Dakotas, they make sure that Ambassador products arrive fresh, often within hours of being produced.

Within the industry Ambassador is known as a "quality house," not a "price house." Its products are made with an eye toward constant quality control. There is no push to cut corners in the name of cost effectiveness or economies of scale. Many of the original recipes are still used, augmented by

others developed by Ethel. Individual spices are still blended specifically for each type of sausage, usually just hours before they are needed, in mostly all-natural casing.

While most sausage these days gets its smoked flavor from additives that often are sprayed on, Am-

Matheos Balafas removes a rack of wieners from the smokehouse. Most sausage processors apply sprayed-on additives to attain smoke flavor; Ambassador smokes its sausage the old-fashioned way.

bassador's plant in northeast Minneapolis boasts a number of old-fashioned 24-gravity smokehouses: Sausage, hung on racks, is placed in the smokehouse over low-banked wood fires, where the smoke can rise and gradually permeate the meat. The firm's old-fashioned style of smoking requires many hours.

The company's familiar ambassador was inspired by a character Ethel Arnold had seen in a parade on the northeast side many years ago of a hot dog man in a Scottish kilt. That led to a contest

among distributors to name him "The Ambassador" and change his dress to top hat and tails. It also led to the company's "wiener car," an 18-foot-long weiner mounted on a Volkswagen chassis. The car was one of three originally built as a stunt prop for the movie *Fooling Around*. One was broken up in the filming process, but the other two were acquired by Ambassador and repainted in the company's colors. The first turns up frequently at local events; the second can be seen on the roof of the Ambassador

plant on Northeast Harrison Street.

Ambassador Sausage Corporation's unwavering emphasis on quality traces back to Otto Arnold, but it may have been expressed best years ago when Ethel Arnold told former newspaper columnist Oliver Towne, "I wouldn't sell what I wouldn't enjoy eating or let my children enjoy eating."

On May 10, 1989, Ethel Arnold was named Small Businessperson of the Year by the Greater Minneapolis Chamber of Commerce at a luncheon held in her honor.

PRECISION ASSOCIATES, INC.

Over the middle years of the twentieth century Minneapolis developed a national reputation as a place where larger-scale manufacturers could come to find detail-conscious specialty firms to design and produce the hundreds of pieces, parts, components, and tooling needed for more complex and integrated processes. At Precision Associates, the specialty of the house is molded rubber products.

In one year as many as one billion separate parts come out of the molding machines at Precision Associates. O-rings, U-Cup rings, and Back-Up rings account for some 60 percent of the company's production. The other 40 percent involves custom products manufactured to a client's often exacting specifications. More than half are sold through independent distributors, the balance direct to the end users.

In 1954 Wells Horvereid, an alumnus of Minnesota Rubber Co., was seeking "grub stake" funding for the forming of a new rubber

company. He learned about Arnold Kadue through an executive search agency. He then persuaded Kadue and his wife to risk almost their entire lifetime savings in this new molding enterprise. As the former production manager of a valve and faucet factory in Ohio, Kadue had been impressed by the savings being accomplished by the use of O-rings as replacements

LEFT: President Arnold Kadue presents some of Precision Associates' numerous array of rubber parts utilized in the country's space program.

BELOW: About 95 percent of the factory equipment is American-made. One exception is this new German molding machine being inspected by Maintenance Department supervisor Brian Messerschmidt.

BELOW, RIGHT: Rubber quality is evaluated by as many as 35 different parameters. Checking a new inspection instrument is Les Kehn, quality assurance manager.

BELOW: High magnification helps determine final part dimension detail accuracy. Quality assurance inspector Michelle Peterson is shown measuring a shadow imprint.

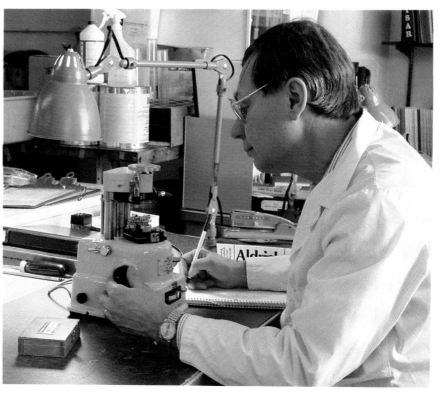

The voices of 16 cheerful operators respond to customers and prospects who call to inquire or make orders. At Precision Associates, "the customer is the boss."

ABOVE: In "The Chapel," one of four molding rooms, presses are reserved for vulcanizates in silicone rubber compounds and other pastel or white materials.

BELOW: Shipping Department associate Julie Earley determines individual item gram weight for a customer.

for braided packing seals.

In 1955 and early 1956 Kadue took part in the new business only by writing some selling solicitations and visiting a few Twin Cities prospective customers. He still recalls vividly a visit with a purchasing executive at Minneapolis Honeywell's Fourth Avenue headquarters. Bluntly he was told that it was "silly" to even think about starting another rubber company in Minnesota since there were already many such firms active in the state. The only possible niche would be for a company that could specialize in super-high-quality vulcanizates.

Probably unknowingly, that Honeywell executive established the guiding star for this fledgling firm. The corporate name of "Precision Associates" already had been selected from a Connecticut undertaking organized by Kadue 12 years ago. Only two other firms named Precision were listed in the Minneapolis telephone book. (Today there are 55.) Cofounder Kadue wanted the business philosophy to be different from the old "boss and employee" and "management and labor" makeup. The new company

should be a group of achievement-minded people, cordially and enthusiastically "associated" together to produce top-quality products with dependable deliveries at competitive prices. Annual employee profit sharing has been in effect for decades.

In the happy "Nordeast" part of town, more than 150 associates work cooperatively in an economical six-story concrete structure at 740 North Washington, utilizing four floors. Another dozen operate in another location, manufacturing the high-precision steel molds needed to turn out quality moldings. That department also produces molds for other firms in the rubber business when such compa-

nies are in need of extremely high-quality tooling.

The father of three sons, Kadue has had all of them busily laboring in his factory throughout all their high school and college weekends and summers. Two left the rubber business for the profession of medicine or law, but Paul, an engineering major, is active as the executive vice-president of Precision Associates, Inc.

THE TORO COMPANY

It began as the Toro Motor Company, a subsidiary of the Bull Tractor Company (hence the name, the Spanish word for "bull"), charged with building engines for the parent company's line of farm equipment. Over the years it developed a reputation for quality and innovation in products as diverse as large golf course turf maintenance equipment and small snowblowers and lawn mowers.

The faces have changed, but the Pride in Excellence remains: Toro's first work force, then known as "craftsmen" (left) and The Toro Company today (above).

Though it encountered its share of bears in the early 1980s, Toro celebrated its 75th anniversary in 1989 in a decidedly bullish mood. Through an action-oriented philosophy known internally as Pride In Excellence, Toro is poised to enter the 1990s as a world-class manufacturer of commercial, consumer, and irrigation products—the nation's leading independent manufacturer and marketer of consumer lawn-care and snow-removal products, turf-maintenance products, and irrigation systems.

Toro operates in three basic market areas: consumer products, commercial products, and irrigation products. The consumer products area represents a little more than 60 percent of the company's annual sales volume. It includes gas- and electric-powered walk lawn mowers, snowthrowers for home owners and commercial use, trimmers, and debris management equipment as well as riding mowers, lawn and garden tractors, and low-voltage outdoor lighting.

Toro has played a leadership role in the lawn care, maintenance, and beautification industry for more than 40 years—since 1939, when it produced its first power mower for the home owner—and on an international level as well as in the United States. The firm is a leading marketer of consumer lawn and garden products in Europe, and the familiar bright red Toro color

scheme can be found from Canada to Australia.

Toro's record of product innovations spans decades. Its famous "wind tunnel" lawn mower housing revolutionized the rotary mower. It was the first to build a consumer lawn mower with an electric starter system, the first to include a bagging attachment with each mower, and the first to stand behind the reliability of its product with its Guaranteed to Start offer, which offers a money-back warranty if a Toro mower fails to start on the first two pulls.

The 1986 acquisition of Wheel Horse Products, Inc., a highly regarded manufacturer and marketer of upscale lawn and garden tractors, and the introduction of a continuing series of new products, particularly in the decorative outdoor lighting category and in do-it-yourself home improvement products, has made the Toro name an increasingly visible one in consumer markets nationwide.

The company also continues to pride itself on its industry leadership in snow-removal products. The Toro line spans the spectrum from small, single-stage, hand-held power shovels to large, two-stage, walk-behind snowthrowers. Among many product innovations, Toro was the first to introduce a swing-axle two-stage snowthrower, the Power Shift, a design that gives greater traction and better maneuverability than ever before.

In the commercial products sector, Toro serves the golf course, commercial, and municipal markets with riding and walk-behind mowers and tractors used to maintain country clubs, parks, school grounds, municipal greenbelts, large estates, and other highly landscaped areas. For nearly 70 years Toro has been setting the pace in grounds maintenance—and again that leadership has grown to the international level with the firm's increasing penetration of European markets.

While consumer products today represent a larger proportional share of Toro's sales, those lines clearly benefit from the heritage of superior engineering and safety designed into equipment for the large institution-size market. From 21-inch, walk-behind rotary mowers to giant grounds maintenance machines that can mow more than 10 acres per hour, Toro defines the state of the art in commercial turf management.

Irrigation products include components and systems for underground automatic irrigation of home lawns, golf courses, and other large turf areas. Whether the installation is in a residential setting, a school or park, a golf course, or another area where water management is an important concern, Toro systems have established themselves as pacesetters in both operating reliability and conservation of energy and water resources.

According to *Golf Digest* magazine's annual list of the country's top golf courses, Toro irrigation systems are used on 70 of the top 100 courses in the United States, including Augusta National, home of the Masters, and Pebble Beach along the scenic California coast at Monterey. The firm is also keeping the greens green and the fairways

lush from Hong Kong to Sweden to the Middle East.

Products don't make a company successful, however. People do. In 1986 Toro created the Circle of Excellence to recognize and honor employees whose on-the-job dedication to quality, innovation, and productivity goes above and beyond. The Circle of Excellence features a limited-edition bronze sculpture of an American Eagle poised for flight within a circle symbolic of family commitment and strength in unity.

Employees may earn the award either individually or for team effort in four categories: performance, customer service, leadership, and profit improvement/cost savings. Nominations are submitted by their peers, making the recognition doubly significant.

Toro people contribute off the job as well, playing active roles in community activities such as the Twin Cities Paint-a-Thon and industry initiatives designed to focus attention on the need for effective water conservation the world over. In 1988 Toro's directors approved the creation of The Toro Foundation to assure community support despite the inevitable cyclical variations of the firm's business.

The company poised to enter the 1990s is a far different organization than the one that struggled

for its very survival in the early years of the 1980s. In 1980 and 1981, after several heady years of rapid growth, a variety of conditions and events conspired to push the firm's balance sheet into the red. For one thing, it didn't snow. Even worse, the United States was mired in a recession with 20-percent interest rates that depressed markets worldwide.

Eight years later the Toro story has a more upbeat tone. It didn't happen overnight, and it didn't happen easily, but the company's refocused attention on Pride in Excellence has paid visible dividends. In 1987, for the first time ever, Toro moved onto the elite register of corporate stature, the *Fortune* 500 (entering the list at number 469 based on sales—but 226 when measured by return to stockholders). The record level of sales and earnings culminated the turnaround of the 1980s that has seen Toro record eight consecutive years of earnings growth.

By all indications, The Toro Company is indeed poised to enter the 1990s as a leader in the lawn, garden, and turf maintenance and beautification industry.

The Toro Company is headquartered at 8111 Lyndale Avenue South in Minneapolis.

THERMO KING CORPORATION

Fifty years ago a Minneapolis company was formed to pioneer a new idea: instead of ice, use mechanical means of refrigeration to keep perishables fresh while they are being transported. A half-century later Thermo King—since 1961 a wholly owned subsidiary of Westinghouse Electric Corporation—is a world leader in mobile temperature control.

Thermo King was responsible for developing the first successful transport refrigeration unit in 1938, making it possible to refrigerate and transport food, medicines, and delicate cargo such as flowers safely and reliably to people worldwide.

Today Thermo King manufactures transport refrigeration equipment for trucks, trailers, and ship containers, as well as bus air conditioners. The company has a well-earned reputation for quality and excellence in products that meet customer needs for precise temperature control.

Headquartered in Bloomington, Minnesota, Thermo King has 3,000 employees with 11 manufacturing facilities (three in the United States, three in the Caribbean, four in Europe, and one in South America).

The company's fully automated Service Center is located in Minneapolis and has satellite facilities in Ireland, Brazil, and Hong Kong.

Thermo King sets the world standard for quality in transport refrigeration equipment for trucks, trailers, and ship containers, as well as bus air conditioners.

The company is renowned for providing customer satisfaction with a network of almost 400 dealerships worldwide offering products and services 24 hours a day, seven days a week.

Thermo King prides itself on developing the most advanced mobile temperature control applications through careful research, design, and testing techniques. Product development begins at Thermo King's Engineering Research and Test Center in Minneapolis, where the design process includes testing equipment in cells that duplicate the harshest environmental conditions. From sub-zero Arctic temperatures to the heat, dust, and pounding of the unpaved roads of the Australian outback, reliability is checked and rechecked. That proven reliability is ensured during the manufacturing process with state-of-the-art quality control methods.

Thermo King's commitment to customer satisfaction is reflected in its training and education program, which was established in 1948 for Thermo King dealers and technicians worldwide. More than 17,000 have completed the company's training courses since the program's inception. Training is available at the corporate headquarters Training Center in Minneapolis, which features laboratories,

test cells, and the latest in diagnostic equipment. Programs are also conducted at multiple domestic and international locations to make certain that Thermo King technicians have the skills and knowledge to service increasingly sophisticated temperature control systems.

Minneapolis is home to the company's fully automated Service Parts Distribution Center, backed by satellite parts facilities in Ireland, Brazil, and Hong Kong. Because Thermo King units are built for longevity, the same exacting manufacturing standards apply to replacement parts as to original equipment.

The modern application of trans-

During the research and testing process, Thermo King tests its products using equipment that duplicates the harshest conditions possible.

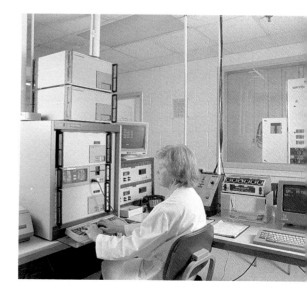

port refrigeration is a far cry from the first system rigged up by founder Joseph A. Numero and little-known Minnesota inventor Frederick McKinley Jones in 1938 "to keep a truckload of chickens from spoiling." Numero was an entrepreneur whose interests ranged from hotels to sound systems, and Jones was a self-educated black engineering genius. Their relationship spanned 30 years. Jones eventually held 25 patents for transport refrigeration equipment, designs that Numero brought to the world through Thermo King.

The business challenge that led to the creation of Thermo King had been given to Numero by a golf partner who had just lost an entire shipment of poultry when the ice melted on a truck en route to Chicago. The solution Jones devised involved designing and building a mechanical system that could replace the barrels of ice, salt, and dry ice that, up to that point in time, was the only method available to transport perishable cargo, and only for short distances.

The first unit, dubbed a Model A, was mounted on the underside of the trailer. It was bulky and heavy, but it worked. Trucking companies that for years had been unable to transport perishables found that lack of refrigeration no longer was an insurmountable barrier to their businesses. The words "out of season" began to be replaced by "fresh food" and later "frozen food." Before long the original ungainly design had been refined into a lightweight, low-profile configuration that could be mounted on the front of trucks and trailers.

Through the years Thermo King developed a variety of applications for mobile temperature control. The Defense Department chose Thermo King during World War II to build portable refrigeration units for use in the field to get food and medicine to the

Thermo King's manufacturing process features state-of-the-art quality-control methods and ensures the reliability and high performance of the company's transport refrigeration units.

troops throughout Europe and the South Pacific. Another application was the preservation of plasma. In addition, Thermo King devices cooled planes to transport wounded soldiers from the field to hospitals.

Thermo King's dedication to expand the use of transport refrigeration technology continued. In 1956, responding to the interest of getting fresh food to troops stationed in Alaska, Thermo King developed the world's first oceangoing container refrigeration unit. In the process it launched a whole new industry—now the mass distribution of perishable commodities could span the oceans to link nations worldwide.

Now, some 30 years later, Thermo King continues to manufacture both standard and customized container refrigeration unit systems, capable of meeting precise temperature control requirements in harsh operating environments. For seagoing customers authorized service dealerships span the ports of the six major continents. The goal continues to

be getting perishable goods to market in prime selling condition—ensuring that no matter what kind of cargo is shipped, it will be as good on arrival as it was when it was first loaded.

Thermo King continues its efforts in research and development to meet customer needs for precise temperature control in a variety of applications with such advances as multitemperature control units that can keep ice cream frozen in one section of a trailer, while preserving delicate lettuce and other fresh produce in another compartment. The company remains the leading domestic supplier of high-performance air-conditioning systems for buses, with customized units designed for municipal railways and other rapid transit systems.

Product quality, innovation, and a dedication to service is what Jones and Numero worked to achieve 50 years ago. Today's management, employees, and dealers have carried on that tradition. Thermo King Corporation, the pioneer of transport refrigeration, continues to set the world standard for quality products and services.

AERATION INDUSTRIES INTERNATIONAL, INC.

The technology of *aeration* involves drawing fresh air from the atmosphere and injecting it below the surface of water. Its primary application is to renew the supply of oxygen that sustains and can increase biological activity in rivers, lakes, bays and estuaries, and the ponds used in the increasingly important fields of aquaculture and wastewater management. Aeration Industries International, Inc., of Chaska is the worldwide leader in the development of that advanced technology.

Founded in 1974 by Joseph Durda and his son, Daniel—now chief executive officer and president, respectively—Aeration Indus-

Joseph Durda, chairman of the board.

Daniel Durda, president.

The AIRE-O₂ aeration system injects air below the water surface, dramatically increasing oxygen content in a body of water.

tries focuses its efforts on the health of the earth's waters. While more than two-thirds of the planet is water, all but 3 percent of that total is salt water. And more than two-thirds of the fresh water is locked away in icebergs and glaciers. Less than one percent of the planet's water is readily available—and life as we know it is constantly using and reusing (and wasting and polluting) it.

The health of our freshwater resources is a vital concern. Both the public and the private sectors

are realizing the importance of reclaiming the world's stagnant and polluted waterways and finding better ways to solve water treatment problems. Aeration Industries got its start as a supplier of systems to reduce winter fish kills in Minnesota lakes. It enjoyed its first commercial successes when it applied those systems to wastewater treatment. But the technology at its product line's heart has applications on a much larger scale.

The company's principal product is the AIRE-O₂ aeration system, a surface-mounted aerator that induces atmospheric air into the water and then distributes it evenly through strong horizontal mixing, increasing the water's ability to support life—including a high, active population of bacteria, the important agent in speeding the breakdown of organic wastes. The AIRE-O₂ aerator's mixing action helps keep water surfaces free of ice in even extremely cold temperatures and can operate year round in virtually any climate.

In 15 short years advanced aeration technology has found plenty of applications: treatment of municipal and industrial wastewater

(industrial users include manufacturers of food products, textiles, chemicals and petrochemicals, pulp and paper, and refineries; restoration of the vitality and water quality of lakes, rivers, and harbors); decorative ponds; and fish farms in developing nations, where protein is in great demand, but industrial resources are slim.

Aeration Industries has been extending the technology to new applications. In lakes and rivers, AIRE-O₂ systems have reduced or reversed the effects of winter and summer kills of fish due to extremes of cold and heat. When the Mississippi River fell to record lows during the 1988 drought, trapping pollutants in harbors and encouraging the growth of damaging algae, the Lake City Marina used the company's equipment to literally turn the tide and restore the basin's vitality. And in the months immediately leading up to the 1986 Asian Games and the 1988 Winter Olympics in Seoul, Korea, Aeration Industries played a major role in cleaning up and restoring fish and plant life in the heavily polluted Suyong River and Pusan Harbor.

More than a product line, Aeration Industries International, Inc., offers an advanced technology with a growing range of problem-solving aplications the world over.

JUNO ENTERPRISES

Beckwith "Beck" Horton christened his high-technology enterprise Juno because his first choice, Gemini, was already registered in Minnesota, and he wanted a name with a similar flavor. In fewer than 15 years Juno Enterprises has turned in some suitably Olympian results. That Juno is a black-owned enterprise with a strong sense of commitment to the community is impressive—but of less interest to the marketplace than its commitment to quality and close cooperation with its customers.

Juno is a Minneapolis-based designer and manufacturer of custom components for the computer and automotive industries. Juno was established in 1975 to help a line printer manufacturer solve a problem with a component that kept failing under heat stress. Horton suggested a transfer molding process he had observed in use at IBM. Although the name of the business has changed—from Customer Engineered Products—the customer focus has remained.

Horton was originally transferred to Minneapolis in 1962 as an electrical engineer at Honeywell. He acquired sales experience while gravitating to smaller organizations where his entrepreneurial instincts could enjoy freer rein. When he went into business for himself in 1975, he was working out of his house in Golden Valley. He landed his first order before he even had a place to produce it.

Today a growing product line includes the design and manufacture of impact printheads for use in dot-matrix printers, voice coils, precision custom coils, and transformers.

Production is based in a modern plant in Coon Rapids, but more than 80 percent of Juno's products are sold to computer equipment manufacturers outside the state of Minnesota, most in California's Silicon Valley, the Eastern Seaboard, and internationally in France and Germany. Juno compo-

Ensuring Juno's position as a leading manufacturer of electronic components are (from left): Mike Johnson, Raul Cantu, Rick Orgon, Beck Horton, Eric Mahmoud, and Keith Horton.

nents are found in the printers and computers of many major computer manufacturers, including IBM, Unisys, and Hewlett-Packard.

Juno specializes in transfer molding techniques—a process in which electrical coils are encapsulated in an epoxy resin that can conduct heat—sophisticated computer-controlled testing, and precision grinding and lapping. Precision injection-molding and wave-soldering operations are also done in-house. An on-site CAD system produces and updates technical drawings to customer specifications.

The quality of Juno's designs and workmanship has helped a "bootstrap" business grow to annual sales of nearly $10 million and employ more than 100 people. Horton's son, Keith, started at the plant when he was 14 years old, and now, MBA in hand, is Juno's sales manager; daughter Pamela is business manager for Juno Technical Services, a subsidiary based in Hayward, California.

In September 1988 Juno added a second enterprise: Microtron, a joint venture with Lectron Products of Rochester, Michigan, a manufacturer of mechanical, elec-

President and owner Beck Horton and vice-president John Goss chart Juno's course into the 1990s.

tromechanical, and electronic components for the automotive industry. Microtron produces electronic chime modules for the Ford Tempo, Topaz, Mustang, and Escort, plus many of the company's pickups and four-wheel-drive vehicles.

A former Control Data plant in north Minneapolis has been converted into Microtron's new home. Initially the business will provide some 70 jobs, and as many as 170 by the early 1990s. Ford is counting on Juno's and Lectron's combined experience in precision manufacturing to provide high-quality components.

SANDOZ NUTRITION

Sandoz Nutrition was created on January 1, 1984, when three U.S. subsidiaries of the Swiss-based international giant, Sandoz Limited, were merged into one entity. Ovaltine Products and Chicago Dietetic Supply had been headquartered in the Chicago area. With the merger, their operations were consolidated into the home offices and high-tech manufacturing and laboratory facilities of the third organization, The Delmark Company, based in the Minneapolis suburb of St. Louis Park.

Crispbread are familiar names on supermarket shelves coast to coast. The best-known is undoubtedly Ovaltine®, the world's most popular vitamin-and-mineral-fortified milk flavoring since it was created in 1904 by Dr. George Wander of Berne, Switzerland. For 85 years Ovaltine®—now sold in a variety of flavors and blends—has remained a leading nutritional beverage product.

Featherweight® dietetic products are also pioneers in the twentieth-century field of nutrition-

The control of particle size, density, and other characteristics is maintained at Sandoz' highly computerized spray-dry center.

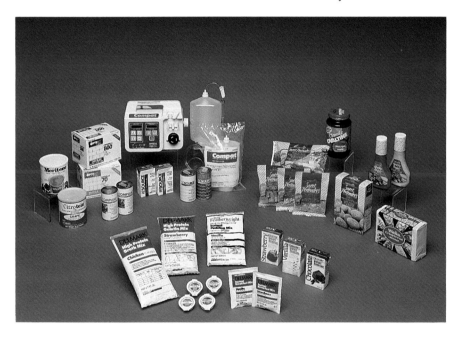

Sandoz Nutrition products range from familiar consumer favorites, such as Ovaltine®, to clinical and food-service lines designed to meet the nutritional needs of health-care patients.

As a result, Minneapolis is today the home of one of the world's most dynamic forces in the promising field of food and nutrition. Sandoz Nutrition produces and markets more than 300 nutritionally beneficial food products for consumer, clinical, foodservice, and industrial customers. Some help correct nutritional deficiencies and improve physical and psychological well-being. Others serve general menu needs. More than 90 percent of them are manufactured in Minneapolis.

Sandoz products are produced for three distinct markets. In the Consumer Products Division, Ovaltine® Beverages, Featherweight® Special Dietary Foods, and Wasa®

ally restricted food products. Since they were introduced in 1919 as the world's first broad line of dietetic foods, Featherweight® products have been recognized as the leaders in meeting the nutritional needs of consumers placed on medically directed diets due to health problems such as heart and coronary artery diseases, stroke, hypertension, diabetes, and obesity.

The Foodservice and Industrial Products Division targets its products to America's growing foodservice establishments. The

division supplies low-calorie and low-sodium foods and condiments as well as nutritionally fortified beverages, desserts, and entrees to meet specialized health-care needs.

Sandoz Nutrition's third market group, the Clinical Products Division, specializes in the areas of clinical nutrition and slimming. In the former, its lines range from general supplements to products created to provide complete nutrition for people with disease- or trauma-specific needs arising from conditions such as burns and cancer. Notable brands include Meritene®, Isotein HN®, Citrotein®, and Compleat-B® and Compleat Modified®.

For the latter area, Sandoz Nutrition offers the Optifast® Program for medically supervised weight reduction in health-care centers. More than 500 leading medical institutions use the Optifast® program to treat massively obese patients on a medically sound yet cost-effective outpatient basis.

The company's manufacturing facilities in St. Louis Park and Lincoln, Nebraska, are as diverse as its multiple, market-driven product lines. In addition to aseptic liquids, they include state-of-the-art retort and hot-fill liquids as well as a wide array of dry-powder-based options—basic dry mixes, spray dry processes, and a variety of agglomeration systems.

In the Twin Cities, Sandoz Nutrition's production facilities feature the latest in advanced spray-drying and agglomeration technologies crucial to the preparation of custom ingredients for the industrial market. By making optimum use of these advanced technologies, the company is able to provide customers a choice of unique functional properties that improve both the manufacturing process and the quality of finished food products and ingredients. The St. Louis Park facility offers both a modern physical plant and the potential for expansion and upgrading as technology continues to advance.

Since the consolidation of operations, Sandoz Nutrition has commissioned numerous expansions to plant and production process capabilities, reflecting both sustained growth in its existing product businesses and forward-looking investments in new manufacturing technology to support the development and introduction of new product concepts. The most recent addition, completed in 1988, is a sophisticated aseptic liquid processing facility. Sandoz Nutrition is the first to apply this new technology to high-quality convenience liquids used in professional nutrition products for clinical and food-service markets.

The professional health-care applications of many Sandoz Nutrition products require diligent

quality-assurance and quality-control programs throughout all phases of the manufacturing operation. Rigorous sanitation standards are designed into both manufacturing equipment and management systems. Uncompromising, carefully monitored procedures govern all stages of production, from ingredient selection and specifications, through actual manufacturing and regulatory compliance, to validating finished product quality and maintaining trace records on all products.

Equally important as sales to the organization's Twin Cities operations are continuing research and development activities into products designed to satisfy the world's changing nutrition needs and life-style demands. Since 1958 Sandoz Nutrition researchers have developed more than 200 new products, many of them setting new industry standards for both market success and nutritional value.

Behind Sandoz Nutrition are the resources of Sandoz Limited, a worldwide leader in the fields of nu-

The company's St. Louis Park manufacturing facility incorporates nearly 300,000 square feet of operations on a 25-acre site.

trition, pharmaceuticals, chemicals, agribusiness, and seed genetics: 44,000 people, operations in 50 countries, and annual sales in excess of $6 billion. Under the Sandoz banner, science and technology combine to fulfill an ambitious mission for people the world over: "To improve health and quality of life through better nutrition."

That's the same essential mission that in the 1950s led to the founding of Delmark, the first company to market oral supplements to meet the needs of professional health care providers and food-service operations. It is that combination of manufacturing for current markets and development of new products and formulations for changing needs and emerging markets that has made Sandoz Nutrition a leader in its highly specialized and demanding areas of business.

JOSTENS

Jostens started in Owatonna, Minnesota, in 1897 as a small jewelry and watch repair shop upstairs from the local opera house. By the time it moved its headquarters to Minneapolis in 1969, 10 years after going public, it was known nationwide and beyond—but not for fixing watches. Just three years after launching the business, Otto Josten had branched out into

Jostens has produced numerous sports awards, including the 1984 Summer Olympics and 1988 Winter Olympics medals, as well as Rose Bowl, Super Bowl, and World Series rings.

making emblems and awards for schools in southern Minnesota. By 1906, the year he incorporated the business as Jostens Manufacturing Company, he had started making class rings as well.

Those new business ventures turned out to be rewarding ones. Today Jostens is a leading provider of products and services for the youth, education, sports award, and recognition markets. A member of the *Fortune* 500 since 1985, it has grown into a diversified, service-oriented organization with eight operating divisions, 42 plants and offices, more than 8,000

employees and 1,500 independent sales representatives across the United States and Canada.

Its list of products, many of them custom designed and produced for events ranging from graduation ceremonies to professional sports championships, is extensive and constantly expanding: class rings, yearbooks, and graduation products; customized sales and service awards; custom-imprinted clothing designed for athletics and other active uses; student photography packages; sports awards; customized products for university alumni; and computer-based educational products and services.

The Jostens family includes eight market-focused operating divisions, two of which—Scholastic and Printing & Publishing—are based in the company's headquarters, built in Minnesota in 1975.

Scholastic specializes in high school and college class rings, graduation announcements and diplomas, trophies and awards, and graduation caps and gowns. This division has eight plants nationwide, including facilities in Owatonna (where the first Jostens manufacturing plant was built back in 1930)

Jostens yearbooks have helped generations of students preserve school memories. Today's yearbook combines innovative design with the latest in printing techniques.

and Red Wing.

Printing & Publishing concentrates on the production of high school and college yearbooks and also handles commercial publications. Jostens not only supplies the printing resources, it also supports young journalists with microcomputer software that helps them write, edit, and design their publications. Printing & Publishing is the largest producer of yearbooks in the world.

Jostens Canada Ltd. is the leading supplier of class rings, yearbooks, school photography, and recognition awards to customers in Canada.

The company's Education Division provides customized computer-based learning labs plus computer software and hardware for classroom instruction. Through its Jostens Learning Corporation, the firm operates more than 3,500 learning labs in schools across the United States.

The Recognition Division works with business and sports organizations that realize the value of honoring their employees for service, productivity, safety, sales, and career accomplishments. Its product lines include custom-designed rings and jewelry; silver, crystal, and other gift products; and plaques and certificates.

Artex licenses popular designs, logos, and cartoon characters for custom imprinting on activewear for people of all ages. Among its most popular lines are those featuring Disney characters, Charles Schulz' Snoopy, and National Football League logos.

Wayneco specializes in the direct marketing of customized products to university alumni and other special groups, and School Pictures develops, prints, finishes, and sells school pictures and senior graduation portraits.

Some of Jostens' products are truly special editions. The company made the first Super Bowl rings in 1967 (for the Green Bay

Jostens Learning Corporation has established more than 3,500 computer-based learning laboratories in schools nationwide.

Jostens Canada Ltd. is the industry leader in school photography in Canada.

Packers), and has made the rings for 14 of the 22 subsequent Super Bowl winners. The size 23 ring made in 1986 for the Chicago Bears' William "The Refrigerator" Perry is still the largest ring the firm has ever produced.

Jostens also created the 1987 World Series rings for the Minnesota Twins and provided the medals for the 1984 Summer Olympics in Los Angeles, the 1987 Summer Special Olympic Games (for which Jostens designed and donated

nearly 6,000 medals), and the 1988 Winter Olympics in Calgary.

For 32 consecutive years, dating back to 1958, Jostens has recorded continuous growth in sales, earnings, and earnings per share. Although Jostens was listed number 450 on the 1989 *Fortune* 500, its return on shareholders' equity and 11-year growth rate for earnings per share rank the firm among the top 20 percent of the businesses on that prestigious index.

Jostens has embarked on a long-term process that has affected every employee, every independent sales representative, every aspect of every job at every level of the company. Known as QIP—the Quality Involvement Process—the initiative emphasizes the kind of teamwork, problem solving, and focus on customer satisfaction that will energize the company for years to come. The process of quality awareness and training, which relies heavily on problem-solving teams reflecting the full spectrum of the organization, has become a basic part of Jostens' corporate culture.

Community service—both personal and corporate—is an ingrained value with a long history at Jostens. Since its creation in 1976, The Jostens Foundation has served as an important element of

that corporate commitment. Reflecting the company's business emphasis on youth and education, the foundation's activities are focused to support programs and organizations that principally benefit young people between the ages of 12 and 24.

As it nears its 100th anniversary, Jostens maintains a reputation for quality recognized by everyone from high school students planning their yearbook to the sports officials who commission championship medals and rings. In March 1988 the firm adopted a mission statement that summarizes its strengths and rededicates the company to building on that foundation as it nears its centennial.

One of the statement's four tenets says that "The corporate culture will encourage and support participative management, open communication, the Quality Involvement Process, and community service." Though the business he founded almost a century ago has changed and grown remarkably over the years, Otto Josten would recognize and fully agree with that statement.

Business and Professions

Minneapolis' business and professional community brings a wealth of service, ability, and insight into the area.

Norwest Corporation, 170

The Dolphin Corporations, 174

Greater Minneapolis Chamber of Commerce, 176

E.W. Blanch Co., 178

Piper, Jaffray & Hopwood Incorporated, 179

Miller, Johnson & Kuehn, Incorporated, 180

Arthur Andersen & Co., 182

Ernst & Whinney, 184

Merchant & Gould, 186

First Bank System, 188

Marquette Bank Minneapolis, 189

Lutheran Brotherhood, 190

Photo by Robert Friedman

Popham, Haik,
Schnobrich &
Kaufman, Ltd., 191

Doherty, Rumble &
Butler, Professional
Association, 192

Carlson Companies,
Inc., 194

169

NORWEST CORPORATION

Norwest Corporation is in high spirits as it prepares to enter the new decade of the 1990s. While the company has been gaining praise for its record-breaking financial performance, its new world headquarters in downtown Minneapolis is winning acclaim as an architectural triumph, a jewel in the heart of the city.

When Norwest Center, a 57-story office tower designed by Cesar Pelli, officially opened its doors in January 1989, Norwest had just completed its sixth consecutive quarter of record earnings and celebrated 1988 as the most profitable year in its 60-year history with $211 million in earnings.

This major player in the financial services industry is experiencing a resurgence that has seemed to parallel the progress of construction of its new home and continued as the company settled into its new surroundings.

Not all of the 1980s were kind to Norwest. A disastrous fire on Thanksgiving Day 1982 destroyed

The visionary leadership of Lloyd P. Johnson (right), chairman and chief executive officer, and Richard M. Kovacevich, president and chief operating officer, has played a pivotal role in the renaissance of Norwest Corporation.

the corporate headquarters and the home of its largest bank. But the fire did not extinguish the Norwest spirit. That spirit is evident today in Norwest Center and throughout the Norwest organization, which operates more than 1,000 offices in 47 states and internationally.

As Norwest enters the 1990s with renewed financial strength and stability, it is expanding and extending its tradition of helping the communities it serves to grow and prosper.

While striving to be the premier financial services company in all of its markets, Norwest is stepping up its commitment to community development and annually provides millions of dollars in contributions to charitable, social, and educational causes.

As a highly diversified financial services organization, Norwest offers broad-ranging, sophisticated resources to meet the needs of businesses and consumers virtually nationwide. This breadth of services enables Norwest customers to use one source to meet all their financial needs.

While gaining customers, the company also gained added respect as a responsible and caring corporate citizen. Its contribution of Norwest Center to the Minneapolis downtown ranks high among its efforts to fulfill its corporate responsibilities.

Norwest Center is a magnificent addition to the increasingly imposing skyline of Minneapolis. In the words of Lloyd P. Johnson, Norwest chairman and chief executive officer, "Norwest Center looks to the future while remembering the past. We felt that Norwest Center should project an image of our public responsibility. We wanted it to be a companion to our neighbors, but at the same time to set standards for future buildings. We wanted Norwest Center to make us and the entire community proud. Cesar Pelli has achieved in

The elegant Norwest Center rises 57 stories in the heart of Minneapolis. Designed by world-renowned architect Cesar Pelli, the building is clad in reflective glass and the rosey beige color of native Minnesota stone.

tangible form what we could only dream about."

Norwest Center, he said, was designed to project the vitality of the Upper Midwest and the dignity and warmth of its people. It is imposing, yet inviting— remarkable for its size, but functional for the people who do business in it.

The organization and design of the public space of Norwest Center harks back to the original bank building that occupied the site. Visual links between old and new abound. Bronze chandeliers, bronze and plaster medallions, and cast-iron railings that once graced the old bank building were painstakingly salvaged and restored. Together with Norwest's extensive collection of Modernist art they reflect traditions of excellence fostered over the years and blend with and complement Pelli's archi-

A skylight and expansive windows make Norwest's rotunda interior a luminous and glowing space. Six 10-foot-high chandeliers were salvaged from the old bank. Atrium walls are finished in soft red marble.

tecture.

Norwest Center provides a renewed focal point for customers and employees of Norwest Corporation. The majority of Norwest's 5,400 Twin Cities-based employees work either in the new headquarters or in the Norwest Operations Center five blocks away, giving Norwest a strong presence in the heart of downtown. Both structures are visual evidence of the company's ongoing commitment to the community.

Today Norwest Corporation is a national leader in the financial services industry, of which banking is just one part. Yet, as Norwest enters the 1990s, it remains a company sensitive to local banking needs, a tradition that traces back to Norwest's deep roots in America's heartland.

In 1929, as the nation slid into a financial crisis, Norwest began to take shape with the organization of Northwest Bancorporation (the name was changed to Norwest Corporation in 1983). The initial confederation consisted of three independent banking companies in three states: Northwestern

National Bank of Minneapolis; First National Bank and Trust Company of Fargo, North Dakota; and First National Bank of Mason City, Iowa.

The first issue of *Fortune* magazine carried a feature about the new bank holding company and its visionary plan to assure better and more reliable service to customers by bringing strong community banks together for mutual support. Although the concept of a bank holding company had been tested earlier in other locations, it got its most impressive start in Minnesota with the funding of Norwest.

This was an era when modern business connections like the telephone were still in their infancy and everyday customer conveniences such as personalized checking accounts and installment credit were still unproven products.

The three founding banks were joined by nearly 90 others in the company's first 12 months in business. Together they went on to help customers weather the Depression and to play a vital role in the regional recovery that followed.

In its first 30 years Norwest grew in total assets to $2 billion. In the ensuing 30 years it surpassed the $20-billion mark, rank-

ing it today among the 35 largest banking organizations in the United States.

In the 1970s and 1980s, as deregulation changed the shape and diffused the focus of traditional financial services, Norwest's original loose-knit confederation has become more closely linked. The evolving structure of regional networks has given Norwest's banks access to centralized support services while allowing each to stay close to its customers and the specific needs of their hometowns.

Norwest today represents the best of two worlds, in banking and in specialized financial services.

With more than a half-century of banking service behind it, it draws on a depth of local and regional experience that reaches back to the first major stirrings of growth and development. Today the Norwest banking presence extends to more than 300 locations throughout a seven-state banking area in the Upper Midwest, including Minnesota, Wisconsin, North Dakota, South Dakota, Montana, Iowa, and Nebraska. And, with a recent expansion to Arizona, Norwest's banking services have been extended to the growing Sun Belt region as well.

In recent years changing state

With more than 50 locations across the Twin Cities, Norwest Bank Minnesota offers retail customers a full range of banking and banking-related services at more locations than any other financial organization.

171

The lacey steel grillwork surrounding the rotunda's teller area was salvaged from the old bank. For added convenience, teller facilities are located on the skyway level and at ground level.

banking regulations have made it possible for Norwest to improve services by combining the activities of previously separately chartered banks. Legislative changes in South Dakota (1984), Nebraska (1985), and North Dakota (1987) allowed Norwest banks in those states to merge into statewide systems.

In Minnesota, Norwest has reorganized more than 90 locations into 10 regional banks, most with multiple branch offices for the convenience of their customers. The largest is Norwest Bank Minnesota, the result of combining Twin Cities banks into one organization with more than 50 locations. Norwest Bank Minnesota gives Norwest customers access to the Twin Cities' largest financial network.

Through branch offices large and small, Norwest customers have access to a full range of banking and related services, including funds management, brokerage, and investment services such as mutual funds, retirement planning, trust services, and insurance. True full-service banking enables customers to rely on Norwest for 100 per-

cent of their financial services needs.

But the Norwest of the 1990s is far more than a regional banking organization. Its family of banking and specialized financial services companies operates through more than 1,000 offices in 45 states. The groups of specialized financial companies provide consumer loans, mortgages, venture capital, leasing, and other financial services.

Many other financial institutions, including independent banks, savings and loan associations, and credit unions, turn to Norwest for essential support services.

The Norwest Banking Group manages trust and investment services and a network of insurance agencies. Its capital markets companies offer specialized expertise and services to corporations, municipalities, institutional clients, and high-net-worth customers.

Businesses large and small find a dependable source of expertise and support at Norwest for their operations outside the United States in Norwest's growing international banking department, which has offices in the United States, Mexico, Argentina, Brazil, Chile, and Hong Kong.

Corporate banking customers find Norwest banks are vital resources in everything from cash management and trusteeships to data-processing services, retail dealer financing, equipment leasing, bond underwriting, and the facilitating of transactions in global markets.

The integration of merchant banking and corporate banking activities in recent years has provided an ever-widening variety of services to meet the evolving needs of businesses in Norwest's markets. As one of the outgrowths of this process, Norwest has become the Upper Midwest's largest corporate stock servicing agent.

In the area of cash management, a 1988 national survey recognized Norwest as a leader in quality of service, ranking the organization among the top banks nationwide for the quality of its lockbox, disbursement, and information reporting services.

In addition, through Norwest's unique BankTIES® service, a growing number of corporate customers can electronically access their

Creative promotional programs at Norwest help generate interest in products such as the Startline™ checking account for youth and the Norwest Classic™ accounts for mature citizens.

Norwest bank account at any Norwest bank for information, transaction or balances reporting, and transaction initiation.

Norwest's group of specialized financial companies includes Norwest Financial, Norwest Mortgage, and Norwest Venture Capital. These firms provide consumer finance, mortgage banking, leasing, asset-based lending, venture capital investments, and other services, and enable Norwest to serve financial services markets nationwide. Norwest Financial, Norwest Mortgage, and Norwest Venture Capital have more than 780 offices in 45 states.

The largest of Norwest's specialized financial companies, Norwest Financial, was founded in 1897 in Des Moines, Iowa. Norwest Financial provides consumer and commercial finance services such as direct installment loans, equipment leasing, and credit insurance. Acquired by Norwest in 1982, it has grown to a network of more than 600 offices in 45 states.

Norwest Mortgage generates residential mortgages through more than 125 offices in 30 states. Norwest Venture Capital, with four locations, helps young and promising enterprises build into successful businesses. It provides start-up funds for new businesses,

Visitors to Norwest Center can view an extensive collection of Modernist art that ranks as one of the finest in the country. This art nouveau punch bowl was crafted in Germany at the Wurtemburgische Metalwarren Fabrik around 1900.

Architect Cesar Pelli (right) and local artist Siah Armajani discuss a model of Norwest's skybridge, which they co-designed. To Pelli the skybridge system is a "celebratory arch . . . filled with color and light . . ."

additional funds for continued growth, and funds to finance leveraged buyouts.

In the course of Norwest growth and expansion, there have been many milestones and major innovations. For example, Norwest's excellence in technology is visible throughout the organization. Sophisticated computer systems are in place at each Norwest Bank teller location, whether the banking office is in downtown Minneapolis or in a small town in the Dakotas, to provide instant access to each customer's complete banking records. For those who prefer electronic banking, Norwest's Instant Cash system handles the largest number of automated teller machines (ATM) transactions in the Upper Midwest.

Norwest is one of the top two organizations in the country in volume of automated clearinghouse transactions, a vital service for corporations and public agencies as well as other banks and financial organizations. And Norwest Financial supplies data-processing services to a large segment of the consumer finance industry.

To further its leadership role in financial technology, Norwest is working with Electronic Data Systems Corporation and Banc One Corporation to pioneer a deposit, loan, and management information

system for retail banking.

As a corporate citizen, Norwest has invested its people as well as its capital in the communities it serves. The annual Twin Cities Paint-a-thon, which puts volunteers and their paint brushes at the service of the elderly and those who need assistance with home upkeep, typically finds hundreds of Norwest people at work.

Another program, the GED (high school equivalency) program, sponsored with the City of Minneapolis and quartered in Norwest's banking facility at Seventh and Olson Highway, has helped hundreds of men and women earn high school diplomas.

In addition to human resources, Norwest provides grants and special funding through Norwest Foundation, which annually disburses more than $5 million to nonprofit social action organizations and community activities, especially in the areas of education and economic development. It is all in keeping with Norwest Corporation's commitment to enhance quality of life wherever it serves.

THE DOLPHIN CORPORATIONS

Founder and chairman Dorothy Dolphin (seated) with the Dolphin management team: Greg (left), Kathy (center), and Tom Dolphin.

The Dolphin Corporations are an expanding group of business enterprises controlled by the Dolphin family of Minneapolis.

The growing list of operations includes more than a dozen Burger King franchises located throughout the Twin Cities metropolitan area, as well as the central part of West Germany; three automobile dealerships in Blaine and Cambridge, Minnesota; a rapidly expanding bank holding company, and finally, Dolphin Temporary Help Services, Inc., the flagship of the Dolphin Corporations, Inc. Dolphin Temporary Help Services has long been a major force in shaping the temporary help industry in Minnesota and is recognized as the largest independently owned temporary help service in the state.

From its corporate headquarters in downtown Minneapolis, Dolphin Temporary Help Services, Inc., serves a prominent majority of the *Fortune* 500 corporations based in Minnesota, and well over 1,000 small to mid-size companies stretching across the metro area.

With the incorporation of computer technology in 1982, a highly sophisticated Data General computer system now automates many of the operational functions within the company.

This innovative computer aids in guiding the complex management systems associated with the annual assignment of more than 20,000 clerical and light industrial temporary employees.

The computer system has clearly placed Dolphin Temporary Help Services, Inc., in a position of strength in the competitive Twin Cities' temporary help market. It has become the perfect complement to the firm's hallmark reputation for quality and outstanding customer service.

The Dolphin Group entered into the banking industry in 1976 through the purchase of the Farmers State Bank of Cedar, a $3.5-million bank in Northern Anoka County. Today that bank has $50 million in total resources. This growth was largely accomplished through the establishment of two branch offices, one in Blaine, at the corner of highways 65 and 242, and the other in St. Francis, Minnesota. Additionally, the bank's main office and charter was moved from Cedar to Ham Lake, Minnesota, at the corner of Highway 65 and Crosstown Boulevard. Being located on Crosstown Boulevard and serving as one of the anchors of the Crosstown Shopping Center, it was only fitting that the name of the bank be changed to the Crosstown State Bank of Ham Lake. Lately the Crosstown Bank has received area wide publicity for its use of celebrity Ed McMahon of the "Tonight Show" as its spokesman.

The Dolphin Group also owns a 50-percent stake in the First State Bank of Isanti, an $18-million bank in the city of Isanti near Highway 65, just south of Cambridge. The two banks, Crosstown and

Greg Dolphin, president of Dolphin Temporary Help Services and Dolphin Fast Food, Inc.

Isanti, have been aggressive lenders, deposit seekers, and high-performance banks over the years of Dolphin Group involvement.

Another business venture mentioned above as part of the Dolphin Group is the automobile dealerships group. This group includes Blaine Dodge, located at 9999 Highway 65 in Blaine, Minnesota, and Cambridge Chrysler-Plymouth-Dodge and Cambridge Ford-Mercury, both located on Highway 65 in Cambridge. Blaine Dodge was honored by Chrysler Motors as the number one volume retail Dodge dealer for the 1988 model year, largely by selling the most retail Dodge Caravans and Dodge Dakotas in 1988. Cambridge Ford-Mercury and Cambridge Chrysler-Plymouth-Dodge offer a full selection of Ford and Chrysler products all under one roof on Highway 65 in Cambridge, 40 miles north of Minneapolis.

While the temporary service, banking companies, and automobile dealerships follow a steady growth track, the Dolphin Group's restaurant arm, Dolphin Fast Food, continues to capture a significant share of the fast-food operations

Tom Dolphin, chief executive officer of Dolphin Corporation.

market in both the Twin Cities as well as overseas.

Beginning in 1979 with the purchase of the first Burger King franchise in Blaine, Dolphin Fast Food, Inc., had by 1988 successfully acquired or developed eight Burger King franchises in the Minneapolis/ St. Paul metro area.

Expansion efforts have also included franchises in West Germany. Dolphin Fast Food, Inc., currently operates four Burger King franchises in the Rhein-Main area of West Germany with full territorial rights to expand in the German states of Hesse and Rhineland-Pfalz, including the cities of Frank-

furt and Wiesbaden. Plans call for as many as 15 locations to be developed in Germany in the 1990s.

While there are larger Burger King franchise organizations, few have the Dolphin family's penchant for quality service. In a four-month evaluation of 90 Burger King restaurants in the Twin Cities area, eight Dolphin locations included in the area were all ranked in the top 20, and four ranked in the top five.

The many achievements attained by the Dolphin family in just the past two decades have earned them the respect and admiration of the Twin Cities business community. In fact, the state's premier business periodical, *Corporate Report Minnesota,* featured the Dolphin family in a cover story detailing their rapid rise to prominence.

As the Dolphin Group and its network of companies continue to flourish, the family vision for further conquests remains strong. Whatever business ventures lie in pursuit, one thing is certain: The Dolphin family will travel every avenue necessary in their drive to ensure full and unequivocal success.

Kathy Dolphin, senior vice-president of Dolphin Temporary Help Services.

GREATER MINNEAPOLIS CHAMBER OF COMMERCE

The 1990s promise change and growth for the city of Minneapolis and the surrounding seven-county Twin Cities metropolitan area. For the Greater Minneapolis Chamber of Commerce, that prospect offers both challenges and opportunities.

To meet them, the chamber itself has been changing and growing:

—There's a new external focus: Much more than in the past, the chamber is organizing its efforts around specific legislative, civic, and membership priorities.

—There's a new internal watchword: "Value" is the standard against which each new and existing initiative is measured.

—There's a new home for the organization: The Young Quinlan Building, one of the city's most distinctive links between the past and the future, gives the chamber a window on Nicollet Mall, one of the city's most vital arteries.

—There's a new look: A redesigned organizational logo and comprehensive identity program is helping people throughout the community gain a clearer perspective on what the chamber is and does.

—There's a new hand on the helm: Former state house representative Connie M. Levi became the chamber's president in 1988.

As befits its name the Greater Minneapolis Chamber of Commerce operates across a broad spectrum. Its activities fall into three major categories: economic development, community development, and public affairs. Increasingly, the chamber is working to develop the interrelationships among those three energizing concerns.

On the economic development front, for example, it has placed a priority on youth employment programs such as the Minneapolis Youth Internship and Jobs Training Partnership Act (JTPA) programs. While those activities have an obvious impact on the local job market, they also carry over to the

health and vitality of the community at large by developing job skills and self-esteem for young people seeking to build their own personal futures.

Public affairs priorities include the area's relatively high rate of commercial/industrial taxation—not only because of the effect on business vitality, but also because one reason for higher business taxation is the need to offset blighted community areas where the property tax base has eroded. If costs are simply shifted, the root problem of urban decay goes unaddressed, with consequences for the entire community, including its businesses.

Increasingly, the chamber is developing an active role in the educational process—part of a philosophy that holds that education is one of the key forces that drives economic development and underlies a healthy, growing regional economy. In the 1990s businesses will need to work smarter than ever before. Trend-watchers see a growing imperative for regions to anticipate changing needs for well-educated, well-trained workers. Those that can augment a strong educational base with the resources to upgrade the skills of people already in the work force will be able to retain businesses already in place and nurture locally based start-ups while attracting others from more educationally impoverished areas.

The chamber's evolving educational priorities focus on three areas. At the traditional kindergarten to grade-12 level, its members support the state's renowned commitment to quality education. In training and retraining, the chamber's ground-breaking research into the employee-skill needs of local businesses has discovered a missing link—and a new opportunity. Many businesses report unfilled needs for skilled, semi-skilled, and unskilled workers. Yet many workers who might, with

some additional training, fit those needs are unable to find those companies. In the 1990s the chamber may be able to provide or support that connection between prospective employer and employee.

The chamber also is exploring ways to nurture new initiatives in postsecondary education. At stake is finding ways to provide the kind of training that could be used as a recruiting tool to bring people and businesses alike into the region.

Internally, the chamber has turned to zero-based budgeting as part of its overall commitment to more businesslike principles. With a staff and budget larger than some of its members, the organization has determined to plan in greater detail, operate in line with more specifically defined priorities, and spend its member-contributed funds smarter.

As Levi (whose desk features a conspicuous "Value" sign) notes, "Not for profit does not mean not for accountability. The intent of our efforts is to maximize the tangible value of membership dollars to our members and the community, ensuring that the maximum effort of those membership dollars goes to programs of value."

The chamber's energy becomes visible to the community in a number of ways:

The annual Minnesota Keystone Awards spotlight companies in the forefront of Minnesota's nationally renowned five-percent and two-percent movements—companies that commit themselves to reinvesting a percentage of their pretax earnings in meeting the community's needs.

Leadership Minneapolis provides valuable mid-career training designed to groom potential leaders for the city and its businesses while adding new levels and layers to the city's fabled business networks.

For small business, the chamber provides a growing sched-

Connie M. Levi, president of the Greater Minneapolis Chamber of Commerce. Courtesy, Sue Kyllonen

ule of affordable seminars and programs—many of them made possible through the involvement of the organization's larger members.

For members large and small, the chamber's efforts are designed to help executives and entrepreneurs find expertise and knowledge in key areas such as law, accounting, taxation and finance, advertising, public relations, human resources, and business development.

In recent years cooperation

has become the norm between the chamber and its crosstown counterpoint, the Saint Paul Area Chamber of Commerce. The Minnesota Keystone Awards begun by the Greater Minneapolis Chamber of Commerce are now presented jointly. Working groups help plan common strategies in areas of mutual interest. And the two organizations work together on a common agenda to make their legislative approaches both more efficient and more effective.

Founded in 1881 to serve the interests of the city's grain merchants, the Greater Minneapolis Chamber of Commerce enters the 1990s as the common bond between more than 2,000 business members—and an increasingly involved participant in the development of the region's future.

E.W. BLANCH CO.

Founded in 1957, E.W. Blanch Co. is today the nation's largest private and employee-owned reinsurance intermediary and the second-largest company in the industry. Its payroll has expanded to more than 200 locally and nearly 300 worldwide. It is headquartered in Bloomington, with domestic branch offices in Chicago, Hartford, New York, and San Francisco; and international locations in London and Copenhagen.

The basis of the business, reinsurance, is a business through which insurance companies share the risk of the policies they write

Account team members Pat Dowd and Sandra Engel review reinsurer program participation.

with reinsurance companies. As a reinsurance intermediary, Blanch is an organization of professionals similar to an accounting, legal, or investment-banking firm providing specialized service to its insurance company clients. Using knowledge of the financial and risk management needs of its clients, Blanch professionals negotiate with reinsurers to create a mutually beneficial financial transaction.

Reinsurance—sometimes referred to as "insurance for insurance companies"—has three main functions. It helps insurance companies assume more or larger risks by spreading the potential loss from any one incident among a number of partners. It is especially

useful in protecting against natural catastrophes such as earthquakes, tornadoes, and hurricanes. And it provides stability to the industry, especially when underwriting unusual risks for which there is no actuarial history, such as the Metrodome.

In this sophisticated business, an individual's skill and expertise are key elements. Beyond this skill and expertise, Blanch insists on unquestionable integrity and commitment in its people. These qualities are critical due to the long term nature of reinsurance relationships. As a result of these high standards, Blanch has been growing steadily and is a leading developer of new talent in the industry.

This growth is also in part a result of Blanch's Fundamentals-Plus approach. It provides the fundamental services expected of a premier intermediary and also offers specialized services not commonly available from other reinsurance sources, including actuarial support, reinsurer financial information services, and catastrophe reinsurance analysis. Blanch actuaries provide pricing and exposure analysis for difficult lines of business, and market security analysts counsel clients on the strength of potential reinsurance partners. Blanch's CATA-

Senior brokers confer with London and Copenhagen counterparts on coverage terms. Left to right: Leo Heifetz, Tony Fox, Frank Wilkinson, and Morton Helge.

E.W. Blanch, Jr., chief executive officer and partner.

LYST windstorm and earthquake computer models analyze an insurance company's potential exposure to hurricane, tornado, and earthquake losses. Blanch also has specialized departments in such areas as life, professional liability, and retrocession (reinsurance for reinsurance companies).

The E.W. Blanch Co. has earned an industrywide reputation for its people, many of them recruited from universities and colleges in the Twin Cities area. The firm highlighted its commitment to local education in 1987 with a million-dollar endowment to the College of St. Thomas for expanded business programs in insurance.

PIPER, JAFFRAY & HOPWOOD INCORPORATED

Pillsbury, 3M, and Cray Research are just three among the many Upper Midwest-based companies that were helped along their road to success by the investment firm of Piper, Jaffray & Hopwood Incorporated.

Piper Jaffray traces its history to 1895, when it was known as George B. Lane's Investment Co., a three-person operation. In 1913 H.C. Piper, Sr., and C. Palmer Jaffray, who had graduated from college together, started the partnership of Piper, Jaffray and Co. Their partnership joined forces with Lane's firm in 1917. They merged with Robert G. Hopwood's company in 1932 to form Piper, Jaffray & Hopwood, the name familiar to investors in Minneapolis, its corporate headquarters, and throughout the firm's 16-state sales region that extends from Wisconsin to Washington.

Today Piper Jaffray offers individual, corporate, and municipal clients a full array of financial services. In addition, Piper Capital Management Incorporated, a subsidiary of parent company Piper Jaffray Incorporated, offers asset management services, 10 mutual funds, and two closed-end funds. The new Piper Jaffray Trust Company provides varied trust services with an emphasis on personalized, managed investment accounts. Through the Premier Acceptance Corporation subsidiary, Piper Jaffray sponsors and syndicates mortgaged-backed bonds.

As Piper Jaffray looks forward to its 100th anniversary in 1995, the firm is proud to build on is traditional strengths of serving individual investors, corporations, and public finance clients.

Piper Jaffray retail investors are served by the firm's sales force of nearly 800 investment executives in more than 60 locations. Clients receive the benefit of the Piper Pipeline, a unique electronic information and communication system that provides individual client information and portfolio valuation reports, as well as up-to-the-minute price quotes on stocks, bonds, options, and futures, and data on more than 4,000 companies.

In addition, Piper Jaffray helps its individual and institutional investor clients make sound investment choices by supplying them with original research. Its research analysts closely follow more than 200 companies and industries, primarily in the firm's sales region.

The capital markets group at Piper Jaffray services corporate clients, both emerging and established companies, from the initial public offering through the aftermarket operations and future financing needs. Institutional sales operations in Minneapolis, New York, and London follow through with market support, bringing Piper's research on those companies to the attention of banks and other investment managers worldwide.

Piper Jaffray also continues to play a significant role as a public finance originator. The firm has managed municipality financing for projects as diverse as the Hubert H. Humphrey Metrodome and Saint Paul's district heating program, the largest water heating system in the country.

Etched in Piper Jaffray's Mission Statement is its long-standing commitment to contribute to the communities in which it is located. The firm was a founding member of the Five Percent Club, comprised of corporations that pledge to contribute 5 percent of their pretax earnings to charitable and civic organizations. Piper, Jaffray & Hopwood Incorporated upholds this commitment through both corporate contributions and its active employees who volunteer their time and expertise to numerous local organizations.

The city lights of Minneapolis provide a dramatic backdrop for the Piper Jaffray Tower at dusk.

MILLER, JOHNSON & KUEHN, INCORPORATED

In March 1981 the economy—both nationally and in Minnesota—was sputtering, and America's oil-induced recession was well under way. "Many municipal issues slumped 13 to 19 percent last year," wrote economic columnist Jane Bryant Quinn in a *Newsweek* article titled, "Can Bonds Be Saved?"

Nevertheless, Eldon Miller decided the time was right to strike out on his own and establish his own business (Miller Securities, Incorporated) as a broker-dealer specializing in municipal securities. The first office out on Highway 100 had five employees, all of whom had worked with Miller during his years with another Twin Cities brokerage firm, Miller (no relation) & Schroeder. Four of them are still there. The business is still at the same address.

The original small suite has been expanded several times, and the first handful of employees has

Miller, Johnson & Kuehn's Minneapolis Trading Department is hard at work to maintain the firm's reputation for excellence among Twin Cities investors.

since been joined by 90 others.

Miller's fledgling firm, founded in such unpromising circumstances, is now one of the Twin Cities' largest broker-dealers in municipal securities and has grown to include branch offices in Scottsdale, Arizona; San Diego, California; and Sarasota, Florida.

In July 1989 Miller Securities, Incorporated, acquired certain aspects of McClees Investments, Incorporated, of Minneapolis, including its most important asset—15 investment brokers. The firm also changed its name to Miller, Johnson & Kuehn, Incorporated.

Today two-thirds of the team at Miller, Johnson & Kuehn is made up of investment brokers who specialize in fixed-income investments. The emphasis continues to be municipal bonds, but corporate bonds, certificates of deposit (CDs), and U.S. Treasury and agency bonds are also significant parts of the mix. But with its recent acquisition, the firm can now offer full stock brokerage services. The client list is heavily oriented

to individuals, especially those in their fifties who, with children grown and homes paid for, are now thinking seriously about their financial future and retirement.

The emphasis on municipals, or "munis" as they are sometimes called, is no coincidence. The Twin Cities area—and, indeed, Minnesota in general—has long been a major center of municipal finance, in part because of the attractions of tax-exempt securities to people seeking economic value and protection from the state's high personal income tax rates. As Miller, Johnson & Kuehn has grown, it has reached out to serve investors in outstate communities and cities throughout a multistate region that now stretches throughout the Midwest.

The branch office network in Florida, California, and Arizona grew out of customer satisfaction. As Miller, Johnson & Kuehn customers have retired and moved to warmer climates, they have faced the need to change doctors, banks, churches, and other comfortable parts of their Minnesota life-styles. Consequently, in 1986 Miller, Johnson & Kuehn opted to locate offices near its customers as they migrate to the Sunbelt.

The company's regional emphasis and close-to-the-customer scale of operations has not limited its activities, however. Miller, Johnson & Kuehn has the resources to back an active research program focused on its clients' specific needs. At the same time, it has the capability to take on limited or unique offerings that might not fit a huge national firm.

Tax exemption and stability are the two primary attractions of municipal bonds, but flexibility and marketability also are important considerations. The business thrives on the relatively low risk and high yield of municipal bonds, and investors further benefit from the independent organizations in the industry that rate

those customer/broker relationships, including placing a strong emphasis on growing people from within.

Through the turbulent 1980s the bond market has gone through a succession of changes. Revisions of the federal tax code have limited some new types of bonds. Some familiar names have left the business. Through it all, Miller, Johnson & Kuehn has grown and flourished based on its ability to stay close to its customers and emphasize attentive, responsive service for a range of safe and reliable investment products.

In that regard, its smaller size and regional orientation have paid off in greater flexibility and an abil-

Serving an increasing national client base, Miller, Johnson & Kuehn counts among its service areas Scottsdale, Arizona (below), and Sarasota, Florida (left).

bonds for their credit-worthiness.

In contrast to brokerage businesses focused on the trading floors of major stock exchanges, Miller, Johnson & Kuehn usually works from an inventory position. First it researches and buys bonds and other securities issues it considers promising and reliable investment products, then it makes those securities available to its customers. On the other hand, it also has the resources to respond to customer requests and specific needs by finding securities on the market that match an investor's criteria.

The counseling role is particularly germane because while bonds have a maturity date ranging from one to 30 years, they need not be held to maturity to yield benefits to investors. Market fluctuations are generally smaller and less intense, but taking advantage of them requires a combination of good research and good timing. Based on an individual investor's needs, securities can be held, sold, or exchanged to maxi-

mize returns.

The key to Miller, Johnson & Kuehn's growth has been the firm's high retention rate, both of investment brokers and their clients. In the securities business, customers and their counselors tend to develop very strong relationships. Miller, Johnson & Kuehn has worked to further strengthen

ity to respond faster and more personally to changing market conditions and customer needs. Decisions that might involve weeks and a policy blessing from a New York headquarters in a large national firm can be made simply and in a matter of hours at Miller, Johnson & Kuehn. It's a difference customers can see—and value.

ARTHUR ANDERSEN & CO.

The largest public accounting and consulting firm in Minneapolis and one of the largest worldwide is actually the youngest of the fabled Big 8. Arthur Andersen & Co.—founded in 1913 by a college professor—opened an office in Minneapolis in 1940 and expanded to St. Paul in 1974. Today more than 500 accounting and audit, tax, and consulting professionals serve many large and small businesses in Minnesota, the Dakotas, and other parts of the Ninth Federal Reserve District from offices in Minneapolis' Plaza VII complex and St. Paul's World Trade Center.

The traditional strengths of Arthur Andersen are in the accounting and audit and tax practices. Rigorous auditing of prominent, large corporate clients' financial statements drives the audit practice—the firm has earned a worldwide reputation for the thoroughness and efficiency with which it examines company records, analyzes procedures, and expresses an independent report on a company's

The Minneapolis office library features a display of Arthur Andersen & Co. publications, a wide selection of general business periodicals, and specific audit, tax, and consulting information.

financial condition. Its professionals become thoroughly familiar with each organization it audits and the industry conditions in which that organization must compete. Arthur Andersen's accounting and audit professionals also offer supporting services that include profit improvement evaluations, merger and acquisition assistance, purchase investigations, bankruptcy and reorganization counseling, litigation support, reviews of internal control systems and procedures, small systems consulting, and general business advisory services.

Back in the 1930s Arthur Andersen was the first to establish a specialized small-business practice. It has helped thousands of firms emerge and grow by combining the problem-solving abilities of a large accounting firm with the personalized attention customarily associated with a smaller organization. The Twin Cities offices of Arthur Andersen reflect this commitment to small businesses by serving numerous closely held and emerging businesses and entrepreneurs.

In addition to its large accounting and audit practice, Arthur

The open doors welcoming clients to the main reception area of the Minneapolis office of Arthur Andersen & Co. are a trademark of the firm. The Minneapolis office moved into its new home in Plaza VII in 1987.

Andersen also fields the largest tax team in the Upper Midwest—more than 130 professionals dedicated to a constantly changing field that demands specialization. The majority of the firm's tax work involves planning and consulting—helping clients identify objectives, evaluate alternatives, and obtain desired tax results. Arthur Andersen tax professionals work with their clients on selecting or changing accounting methods, reviewing tax strategies, structuring corporate reorganizations and acquisitions, and evaluating and implementing incentive compensation plans. The firm also specializes in such areas as tax planning for owners of closely held businesses, personal tax and financial planning for corporate executives, and appraisal services.

While the accounting and audit and tax practices of Arthur Andersen & Co. provide the firm's foundation and its traditional strengths, the consulting practice is the most rapidly growing ele-

ment of the organization. In 1954 Arthur Andersen completed the first successful application of an electronic computer to a business application. Today Arthur Andersen ranks as one of the largest consulting groups in the world and is the leading systems integrator. To better communicate its leadership role in this area, Andersen Consulting became a separate business unit of the firm in 1988.

In the area of information technology, Andersen Consulting provides assistance to businesses seeking to use technology to their competitive advantage through effective planning, systems implementation, and change management consulting.

The core practice of Andersen Consulting continues to be its systems integration practice. Experienced professionals, automated development tools, and the most tested and proven methodologies in existence assure all of its clients of efficient implementation of new technology to solve business problems. Its strong industry focus enables Andersen Consulting to provide tailored solutions required by the current and future leaders of American businesses.

The strategic services consulting practice provides front-end assistance through strategy development and execution, and change management services focus on the human organizational dimension of improving performance in a business organization. The combined talents of Andersen Consulting professionals, from strategy development and systems planning through systems implementation and organizational change, provide an unparalleled integrated resource to businesses throughout the Twin Cities.

One reason for Arthur Andersen's rapid growth in Minneapolis/St. Paul and elsewhere is the continuing investment it makes in developing the skills of its people. It established the ac-

counting profession's first training school and is the only public accounting and consulting firm to have a major campus facility for continuous professional education. The Center for Professional Education in St. Charles, Illinois, is where Arthur Andersen's almost 46,000 employees worldwide receive ongoing training during their careers. The 145-acre center can accommodate more than 1,800 students at one time. In excess of $120 million is invested annually in training and development.

Among Arthur Andersen's more than 225 offices worldwide, the Minneapolis/St. Paul practice ranks in the top 15. Since 1974 Twin Cities operations have been under the direction of managing partner Jay H. Wein. His predecessor, University of Minnesota graduate Duane R. Kullberg, was Arthur Andersen's worldwide chief executive officer from 1980 through 1989. Jackson L. Wilson, Jr., has headed the Andersen Consulting aspect of the Twin Cities practice since 1988.

The Twin Cities offices of Arthur Andersen also set the pace in volunteerism. AACAP, the employee-managed Arthur Andersen & Co. Community Ac-

tion Program, was created in 1986 by Minneapolis and St. Paul personnel to promote "the common good and general welfare of the people of the community." Its wide range of activities include helping local organizations, such as Minnesota Food Share and the Twin Cities Metro Paint-A-Thon, and fund raising for the March of Dimes, the Red Cross, and Junior Achievement. Many partners and managers are active in numerous other civic and charitable organizations.

As the leading public accounting, tax, and consulting firm in the Upper Midwest, Arthur Andersen & Co. offers the depth of resources needed to handle engagements of any size quickly and efficiently. The firm takes pride in the people, the competence, and the experience it has for serving its clients. These ingredients—often called the Arthur Andersen Advantage—are the right mix for its success.

The Center for Professional Education in St. Charles, Illinois, is where Arthur Andersen & Co. personnel from around the world receive ongoing training throughout their careers. An expansion program, to be completed in 1990, means that the 145-acre center will be able to accommodate more than 1,800 students at a time.

ERNST & WHINNEY

Managing partner Ed Finn confers with new employee Robert Doty, who interned with Ernst & Whinney as part of the INROADS program to identify talented minority students.

As American business on both the local and the world level continues to change, expertise has come to be an increasingly important part of the accounting equation. In the Information Age it is the quality of information that provides competitive advantage for companies of virtually every size and description. The continuing evolution of the profession is reflected in the Minneapolis practice of Ernst & Whinney, one of the country's largest Big 8 accounting firms.

Ernst & Whinney Twin Cities has more than doubled in the 1980s. A staff exceeding 300 now serves locally based—in many cases internationally active—business clients from the firm's downtown Minneapolis office in the Pillsbury Center and the St. Paul office in the Minnesota World Trade Center.

Ernst & Whinney has grown with the companies it serves. Its growth is visible in the pacesetting orientation toward industry and market specialization. It is visible in the meticulous approach to recruiting that assures that trained

and qualified people will be in place before they are needed—and will stay in place to provide continuing service based on extensive knowledge of their clients' changing needs. The firm's culture emphasizes involvement in the Twin Cities community as well as the profession; it holds that the quality of service provided is more important than the growth of the firm's own practice.

The combination of this emphasis on quality and a bias toward the future is visible in the significant growth of Ernst & Whinney/Minneapolis' management consulting services through the 1980s. The firm's expertise in the area of MIS (management information systems) has been a valuable resource for companies wrestling with the effective use of the computer. Specialized orientation in the areas of manufacturing, retail-

ing, health care, and financial services has helped existing clients to grow and attract new clients. Ernst & Whinney's commitment to assisting businesses in the knotty area of employee compensation and benefits has made it a valued resource for both established and emerging companies.

In 1918 Minneapolis became the 10th office established by Ernst & Ernst (in 1979 the practice combined with the English firm Whinney, Murray & Co. to form the current Ernst & Whinney international network). Building on its roots in the headquarters city of the Ninth Federal Reserve District, Ernst & Whinney/Twin Cities continues to rank among the firm's top 12 offices nationally in size of operations. Yet it remains a practice where individuals and working groups can stay close to customers and their co-workers—large enough to provide wide-ranging resources, small enough to offer a comfortable and familiar scale of operations. In recent years the Twin Cities practice has been under the direction of more than two dozen partners, headed by managing partner Edward L. Finn.

In the areas of audit and tax, the Twin Cities practice has developed a diverse client base, with several strong clusters of specialization: manufacturing; retailing; financial services and insurance; high technology, especially emerging businesses in medical technology and electronics; transportation; communications; food processing; and agribusiness. Whether the need is for timely assistance with ever-changing federal and state tax regulations or the stock offerings and other financial transactions, Ernst & Whinney's local office provides on-staff expertise backed by the larger resources of a worldwide leader in the accounting field.

To harness the power of the computer to clients' needs, experienced specialists are available with expertise ranging from large-scale MIS applications to small-scale personal computer networks. Ernst & Whinney supports them with in-depth training and nearly two dozen customized software packages. Within the Ernst & Whinney family, the Minneapolis office was the first to introduce microcomputers.

Ernst & Whinney is one of the few major accounting firms to maintain its own national training operation, the award-winning Richard T. Baker Education Center. There, more than 175 company-specific courses are provided to meet the continuing education needs of its professional staff.

Over the years the local practice has set high standards for itself—and for the profession. To this day the Minnesota Society of CPAs presents the Harold C. Utley Award (named for the managing partner who headed Ernst & Whinney's Minneapolis office from 1929 through 1960) to the highest scorers on the state's CPA exam. And if the name of the current co-chairman has a familiar ring to business people in the Twin Cities, there is a good reason: from 1975 through 1981 Robert J. Kelly

served as the managing partner in Ernst & Whinney's Minneapolis office.

That is in keeping with the philosophy of founder A.C. Ernst, who maintained that the firm's success "depends wholly upon the

Tax senior manager Mark Sellner (right) served as a loaned executive for the the Greater Minneapolis United Way. In this picture he meets with a local businessman as part of that effort.

character, the ability, and the industry of the men and women who make up the organization." Ernst's vision of client service did much to define the modern accounting and consulting practice. In an era when accountants generally confined themselves to the numbers, Ernst recognized the value of using the insights gained during the auditing procedure to advise his clients on better ways to do business. That focus on service quality was uncommon in 1903; today it is the basis of the modern field of accounting.

These days Ernst & Whinney has almost 120 U.S. offices and more than 470 in nearly 86 countries worldwide. It is the solid reputation for quality, accountability, and attention to client service that has come to characterize Ernst & Whinney's Twin Cities activities.

MERCHANT & GOULD

In 1896 a young graduate of the University of Minnesota Law School started a law practice in Minneapolis specializing in patent law. The late Frank D. Merchant soon became the man to see about patents. Merchant formed a partnership in the 1930s, when his sons, Ralph and Harvey, joined him in the practice of patent law. In the early 1950s John D. Gould, a litigation specialist, joined the firm that became known as Merchant & Gould. Over the years the firm continued to grow, and new attorneys joined to help broaden the firm's resources and range of expertise.

Today the firm Frank Merchant started almost a century ago is the largest of its kind in the region and one of the largest intellectual property firms in the country. Merchant & Gould now has offices in Minneapolis, St. Paul, and Los Angeles, and is engaged exclusively in the practice of intellectual property law, including patent, trademark, copyright, unfair competition, and trade secret matters.

The firm has more than 50 attorneys, each with strong legal and

Merchant & Gould is a leader in the growing field of computer law.

The attorneys of Merchant & Gould blend legal ability with scientific expertise to serve clients in an increasingly technical world.

scientific abilities. The firm's attorneys have degrees in electrical engineering, mechanical engineering, chemistry, molecular biology, physics, or other technical fields, and a number of its attorneys have Ph.D. degrees. They are registered to practice as members of the Patent Bar, one of the legal profession's only recognized and credentialed specialties.

Through the years, as Merchant & Gould's reputation and expertise have grown, its clientele has grown as well. Today the firm represents individuals and organizations in virtually every area of business and industry, including

chemical, computer, medical, manufacturing, and consumer products. The firm's dual expertise in technology and law makes its attorneys a proven resource for businesses seeking to expand their markets, license new technology, or protect a potentially breakthrough product.

Traditionally, patent law firms have served primarily to obtain patents, trademarks, and copyrights for their clients. Merchant & Gould goes far beyond this traditional focus. In addition to offering full representation of its clients before the United States Patent, Trademark, and Copyright Offices, Merchant & Gould handles all forms of complex intellectual property litigation and licensing matters. The firm's litigation expertise includes licensing, unfair competition, trade secret, and computer law, as well as patent, trademark, and copyright matters. Clients see it as a full-service firm for counsel, registration assistance, licensing, and litigation, regardless of what technology or form of intellectual property may be involved.

Merchant & Gould attorneys

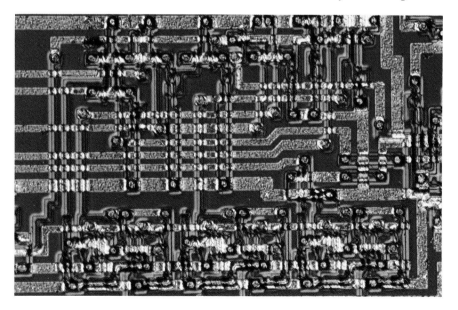

serve hundreds of companies throughout the five-state region that includes Minnesota, Wisconsin, Iowa, and the Dakotas. Its reputation in intellectual property law has also propelled it into a national and international practice.

Merchant & Gould has a long tradition of active involvement in academic and civic affairs. The specialized nature of the firm's practice results in many of its lawyers being involved in teaching, writing for legal publications, and speaking at legal and continuing education functions. Merchant & Gould attorneys serve on the faculties of the University of Minnesota Law School and William Mitchell College of Law. They also conduct periodic courses on the protection of intellectual property for corporations and business and legal associations.

The firm supports a number of cultural and civic organizations, including the Guthrie Theatre, Minnesota Orchestra, Minnesota Opera, St. Paul Chamber Orchestra, Walker Art Center, and the Science Museum of Minnesota. For years programming on public television and radio has been supported in part by contributions from Merchant & Gould.

The demand for the firm's legal services has more than doubled Merchant & Gould's size in the 1980s. In 1988, after almost 20 years in the Midwest Federal Building in downtown Minneapolis, Merchant & Gould moved its main office to the new Norwest Building. To better serve its clients near their places of business, Merchant & Gould has long had an office in St. Paul. Another branch office was recently opened in Los Angeles, California.

TOP: Minneapolis

MIDDLE: St. Paul

BOTTOM: Los Angeles

FIRST BANK SYSTEM

Minneapolis is the largest financial center between Chicago and the West Coast. It is the region's pacesetter in banking, insurance, investment services, and corporate and consumer finance. And the largest bank holding company in the region's largest financial center is First Bank System (FBS).

First Bank System includes 44 banks and trust companies in Minnesota, Colorado, Wisconsin, North Dakota, South Dakota, Montana, and Washington, plus offices from London to Los Angeles.

First Bank System is a regional bank holding company headquartered in the Upper Midwest with assets of $21.9 billion. The company provides complete financial services to individuals and institutions through more than 140 domestic and international subsidiary offices. These services include trust, commercial banking, consumer banking, cash management, credit card, capital markets, investment management, insurance brokerage, leasing, mortgage banking, brokerage services, and international banking. FBS Insurance is the largest insurance operation in the nation to be owned and operated by a financial institution; First Trust is the Upper Midwest's largest trust company.

FBS provides capital funds as required and assists its subsidiaries in asset and liability management, portfolio management, property planning and development, business development, corporate communications, human resource management, accounting, tax, and legal services.

FBS operates the FASTBANK network of automated teller machines, making electronic banking transactions available 24 hours a day both locally and, through Plus System, on a nationwide basis. It was the first financial organization in the Upper Midwest to provide 24-hour foreign exchange trading.

First Bank System and its people have earned a remarkable repu-

Adding color and dimension to downtown Minneapolis are the First Bank System corporate headquarters in the Pillsbury Center (left) and First Bank Place West.

tation for community involvement, including the 1988 President's Award for Volunteerism, presented by the White House in recognition of the approximately 585,000 hours invested annually in community activities by the people of the organization. Through the First Bank Foundation, established in 1976, FBS and its affiliates have awarded grants totaling almost $50 million in the areas of human services, arts and culture, education, and community development.

It all began in 1929 with the formation of First Bank Stock Investment Company, an organization launched by two of the Twin Cities' oldest and most respected banks—First National Bank of Minneapolis and First National Bank of Saint Paul—to help smaller banks in the region survive the financial turmoil of the times. From those beginnings came the organization's lead bank, now known as First Bank, which serves individuals and institutions through a net-

The First Bank System Capital Markets Group trading floor was first in the Upper Midwest to offer 24-hour foreign exchange trading.

work of 37 locations throughout the Twin Cities. In 1968 the holding company's name was officially changed to First Bank System.

More than 10,000 people work for First Bank System today, roughly two-thirds in and around Minneapolis. Most work downtown, where First Bank System has traditionally maintained a strong and highly visible presence.

MARQUETTE BANK MINNEAPOLIS

The business of banking is one in which careful attention to every detail is important. From spelling the name on the account correctly to handling funds and providing records in a timely and accurate manner, professionalism can be defined as getting it right the first time, all the time. One Minneapolis bank, Marquette, offers Performance Guarantee, a program that pays five dollars any time the bank makes a mistake on an individual's account or transaction.

The Marquette Banks make the guarantee as visible evidence of their commitment to providing sound, prudent, and uncompromisingly professional banking services to their customers. The Marquette Bank Minneapolis family totals 14 locations—Marquette Bank Columbia Heights (with an office in Fridley, too), Marquette Bank Eden Prairie, Marquette Bank Edina, Marquette Bank Lake (near Lake Street and Chicago Avenue), Marquette Bank Northeast, and Marquette Bank University (offices in Stadium Village and Dinkytown)— including three downtown offices and three in nontraditional locations: Abbott-Northwestern Hospital, the Park Center Retirement Apartments near downtown Minneapolis, and the Jerry's Foods retail complex in Edina.

Marquette traces its roots in Minneapolis to the earliest days of the city. Its forerunner companies were Marquette National Bank of Minneapolis (which began in 1889 as the Guarantee Savings & Loan Company and became Marquette in 1922) and the Farmers & Mechanics Savings Bank (founded in 1874 and known for generations in the Twin Cities as "F&M"). The two institutions became one in 1982, retaining F&M's distinctive downtown home at Sixth Street and Marquette Avenue and the leadership of the man who became Marquette's president in 1955—Carl Pohlad.

Marquette has since become an assertive force in banking in the Twin Cities and beyond. Its customer orientation is reflected in a relationship banking profile with both business and consumer accounts and a willingness to find imaginative ways to help businesses grow and consumer customers meet their financial objectives. Its services are carefully tailored to specific needs; the company is organized by customer markets rather than products, allowing Marquette to respond quickly to emerging demands and opportunities.

Marquette's approach to banking has created and maintained a safe and secure banking environment. Its emphasis is on continuing to serve loyal, long-term customers. Privately held, it concentrates on close involvement with its customers, preferring to put its capital to work close to home and eschewing forays into risky international markets.

Marquette Bank Minneapolis prides itself on providing the best of both worlds: a close-to-the-customer scale of operations in which businesses and individuals receive personal attention, yet with the capital resources and financial sophistication needed by the larger and growing businesses active in the Twin Cities.

Marquette Bank Minneapolis is owned by Bank Shares Incorporated, the third-largest bank holding company in the Ninth Federal Reserve District. Bank Shares banks also include Marquette Bank Rochester (three offices in Rochester, one in Stewartville), plus Marquette Bank Apple Valley, Marquette Bank Brookdale (two offices in Brooklyn Center), and Marquette Bank Lakeville (offices in downtown Lakeville and Orchard Lake). Through its subsidiaries, Marquette Insurance Group and Marquette Lease Services, the Bank Shares family of banks offer a wide range of financial services.

From its headquarters at Sixth and Marquette in downtown Minneapolis, Marquette Bank provides innovative banking to serve the needs of both its business and consumer customers. Photo by Phil Prowse

LUTHERAN BROTHERHOOD

Looked at as a business, Lutheran Brotherhood is a large and successful one. With $24 billion of life insurance in force and more than $7 billion in assets under management (including investments in mutual funds), it ranks in the top 5 percent of U.S. life insurance companies and is one of the nation's largest financial services organizations. It is the second-largest fraternal benefit society in the country.

But the best light in which to evaluate Lutheran Brotherhood is as a force for good works. It provides financial security through life and health insurance, annuities, mutual funds, and other products and services. A portion of the society's assets are distributed as fraternal assistance for its nearly one million members, its branches (local volunteer units) and their communities, and the Lutheran church. Some examples include scholarships, matching gifts to Lutheran schools and colleges, church loans, and support for numerous local causes throughout the county. In 1988 the organization allocated $32 million to fraternal activities and resources, continuing a far-reaching impact that began more than 70 years ago.

Lutheran Brotherhood's distinctive, eight-story, green-and-glass-walled headquarters building, opened in 1956 at the corner of Second Avenue South and South Eighth Street (now the home of Minnegasco), marked the first significant new office construction in

downtown Minneapolis since the Foshay Tower was erected in the late 1920s. One of the first buildings in the Midwest to make use of curtain-wall construction and be totally air-conditioned, its opening and the vote of confidence it represented marked the beginning of today's busy, gleaming downtown business and commercial core.

Twenty-five years later, as growth required, Lutheran Brotherhood reaffirmed its commitment to downtown Minneapolis by building the eye-catching, 17-story headquarters that today fronts Fourth Avenue South across from the Hennepin County Government Center. The organization decided to stay in the heart of Minneapolis for several reasons, including the society's historic location, cultural interaction, business activity, large Lutheran population, and employee preference.

The building has multiple dimensions. Its primary purpose is to provide an efficient and attractive facility for home office employees; but it also represents a sensible and prudent business investment, provides public places—a spacious art gallery, a large auditorium, five private meeting/dining rooms, and retail

Featuring an art gallery, an auditorium, meeting/dining rooms, and retail space, in addition to office space, the Lutheran Brotherhood headquarters on Fourth Avenue South adds 17 stories of beauty and style to the Minneapolis skyline.

President and chief executive officer Robert P. Gandrud (standing) and chairman of the board Clair E. Strommen are committed to the financial security of each member of Lutheran Brotherhood.

services—that are available for civic and community needs, and contributes to the overall architectural quality of downtown Minneapolis.

Lutheran Brotherhood grew out of the 1917 merger of three Norwegian church bodies. Two delegates, J.A.O. Preuss and Herman L. Ekern, proposed forming an "aid society" for members of the newly formed Norwegian Lutheran Church of America. Originally called Luther Union, the organization quickly joined forces with Lutheran Brotherhood of America, a World War I organization created to serve the spiritual needs of Lutheran servicemen and women.

The modern Lutheran Brotherhood, under the guidance of leaders such as chairman emeritus Arley R. Bjella, current chairman Clair E. Strommen, and president and chief executive officer Robert P. Gandrud, is a not-for-profit organization operating solely for the mutual benefit of its members and their beneficiaries. Almost 1,500 district representatives counsel members on their insurance and financial needs and serve as consultants to local branches. Some 900 people work in the society's home office, administering Lutheran Brotherhood's corporate, fraternal, and insurance operations.

POPHAM, HAIK, SCHNOBRICH & KAUFMAN, LTD.

One of the first areas in which the firm began to develop a reputation was commercial litigation.

LEFT: From left to right are partners Wayne G. Popham, Raymond A. Haik, Roger W. Schnobrich, and Denver Kaufman.

ABOVE: The Minneapolis office of Popham, Haik, Schnobrich & Kaufman, Ltd. Photo by Chas. McGrath

Few legal firms have made their mark faster than Popham, Haik, Schnobrich & Kaufman, Ltd. Founded in Minneapolis in 1958, it grew slowly but steadily at first as it established its expertise in business and administrative law and litigation. In the 1980s it hit full stride as a major national firm, doubling in size to a staff of more than 120 attorneys in less than five years and growing out from its Minneapolis roots to establish offices in Washington, D.C., and Denver.

Popham Haik's administrative law practice is national in scope—its attorneys have represented clients on regulatory matters in more than 25 states plus the District of Columbia and Puerto Rico. Its business department includes an international group to assure that the firm can meet the needs of clients ranging from major corporations to sole proprietors, no matter where in the world they might require legal services. In matters that go to litigation, Popham Haik's attorneys provide expertise in areas ranging from antitrust and environmental matters to real estate and securities law.

Today its expertise includes specialties in product liability, securities and commodities, antitrust, employment discrimination, hazardous waste, medical device and drug liability, environmental law, government liability, construction law, professional liability (representing architects, engineers, real estate agents, and other attorneys), and white-collar crime.

Popham Haik also has distinguished itself through participation in the public process. It counsels municipalities, development authorities, and regional commissions. It represents clients before local, state, and federal regulatory and legislative bodies. It serves as a resource in matters involving regulated industries, environmental regulations, land use, and commercial development.

Its attorneys are of service to both owners and their organizations, whether closely held or publicly traded. That includes estate and financial planning, real estate transactions, bankruptcy, franchising, and product distribution, as well as legal support on matters involving corporate and individual tax planning, public offerings, private placements, mergers, acquisitions, and SEC compliance.

In addition, Popham Haik has demonstrated an ability in labor law, immigration matters, election and campaign finance, libel, computer law, trademark and patent law, and trade secret protection. The firm is developing a national reputation in the area of preventive law, a specialty that focuses on helping businesses and individuals minimize the risk of future legal liability by identifying potential problems.

Popham Haik has represented hardship and political asylum cases and has worked with the Minneapolis Housing and Development Authority. Its attorneys do volunteer work in social services and involve themselves in legal education activities.

As it celebrates its 30th anniversary in 1989—from offices in the Piper Jaffray Tower that have won national accolades from *Interior Design* magazine—Popham, Haik, Schnobrich & Kaufman, Ltd., looks back over a record of achievement. In just three decades it has become one of the 10 largest law firms in the Twin Cities—one of the 250 largest in the country. It has a young, aggressive outlook. At Popham Haik the strength of the practice is the strength of each of its people.

DOHERTY, RUMBLE & BUTLER, PROFESSIONAL ASSOCIATION

Doherty, Rumble & Butler, Professional Association, is Minnesota's oldest law firm. Established in 1859—just one year after the state was admitted to the Union—it has grown to become a broad-based professional association with a number of well-developed specialties in all major areas of business law. With offices in the IDS Center in downtown Minneapolis, the World Trade Center in St. Paul, and the Magruder Building in Washington, D.C., Doherty, Rumble &

Doherty, Rumble & Butler attorneys Larry McIntyre and Dean Edstrom (left and center, respectively), supply legal counsel to such prominent Minneapolis clients as The Toro Company. With the two counselors is Toro's Vernon A. Johnson.

Butler today numbers more than 175 attorneys, paralegals, and professional support personnel.

When the firm began, the population of Minneapolis and St. Paul was only 15,000. One of the firm's founders had to supplement his income by teaching. As the region grew, so too did Doherty, Rumble & Butler, P.A. Over the years its professionals made their mark, not only in private practice but in pub-

lic service. Among the firm's distinguished alumni are a U.S. Supreme Court Justice (Pierce Butler, from 1922 to 1939), a solicitor general of the United States (William Mitchell, who later founded the law school in St. Paul that bears his name), a chief justice and associate justice of the Minnesota Supreme Court, and many others who have held important positions in government and industry.

Throughout its 130-year existence the firm has prided itself on a record of innovation. In 1917 and through the 1920s, it was Doherty, Rumble & Butler, P.A., that helped establish the crucial agricultural exception to antitrust laws that enabled cooperatives such as Land O' Lakes to be formed. In that same era principals of the firm played a major role in convincing the Ford Motor Company to locate a production plant in the Twin Cities.

In more recent decades the firm's combination of financial and legal expertise played an important role in helping a significant number of entrepreneurs to creatively find ways to finance their new businesses and realize their personal and organizational objectives. Prominent among them were the beginnings of Northwest Airlines and Cray Research, Inc.

Today the firm's attorneys concentrate on serving the legal needs of businesses of all sizes and descriptions. The expertise at Doherty, Rumble & Butler, P.A., includes corporate and securities law, tax law, agricultural cooperative law, labor and employment law, international and immigration law, real estate law, banking law, environmental law, estate and financial planning law, employee benefits law, and both commercial and noncommercial litigation.

In recent years the firm has played an important role in the founding and growth of companies involved in high-technology

Serving Minneapolis' corporate real estate needs are attorneys (standing, left to right): Sara Rosenbloom, Dean Edstrom, James Wittenberg, Ron McFall, and Rob Beattie. Seated (from left) are Jon Scoll, Maggie Madden, and Steve Braun.

markets such as genetic engineering, medical and electronic devices, supercomputer and other computer hardware, pharmaceuticals, computer software, and advanced materials. It also works with a broad spectrum of "low-tech" (but no less legally exacting) businesses: venture capital companies, banks, developers and real estate firms, breweries, motion picture production companies, and businesses engaged in the design and development of various types of new machinery and equipment.

Doherty, Rumble & Butler's role often begins with creatively assisting business founders as they organize their new ventures and arrange their financial affairs. Legal efforts in this regard can range from structuring traditional private placements and public offerings of equity and debt securities—both initial public offerings (IPOs) and other issues—to assisting with term and revolving credit arrangements that provide continuing financial stability.

Doherty, Rumble & Butler often applies its legal expertise to the establishment of research and development partnerships and the orderly conduct of leveraged buyouts. It handles transactions involving industrial revenue bonds, leveraged leases, and debt restructuring. It offers strong credentials on international legal matters, from sophisticated licensing and joint-venture agreements to the fine points of immigration law. It provides the full range of legal support that may be needed to meet the challenges of growth: trade secret protection, employee benefits law, franchising, technology licensing, and the establishment of clearly defined distribution channels and sales representative arrangements.

Technological innovator Cray Research is among the firms that benefit from the specialized legal expertise of Doherty, Rumble & Butler. Pictured from left are attorney James Wittenberg, David Dyson of Cray Research, and attorneys Rob Beattie and Ron McFall.

In the area of cooperative law, Doherty, Rumble & Butler has worked to extend the organizational advantages of the traditional agricultural cooperative to newer ventures ranging from cable television systems to marinas. This expertise extends back to the 1920s, when cooperatives were fighting for the right to exist and evolving from small rural associations to more diversified and economically

viable competitive organizations. Other law firms frequently turn to Doherty, Rumble & Butler, P.A., for timely and innovative support for their cooperative clients.

While many law firms provide counsel on tax matters, Doherty, Rumble & Butler is one of the few firms in the country equipped to do tax litigation work in the United States Tax Court. This capability stems from the creation of the first national tax code, and it goes hand in hand with business development efforts, which include expertise in labor and employment law, an emerging area of business concern. In this area of service, the firm's role ranges from counsel in employment policy development and labor negotiations to litigation of employment issues such as wrongful termination and age discrimination.

Another continuously evolving specialty area is health care law. Throughout the region Doherty, Rumble & Butler, P.A., has played a significant role in working with hospitals, health maintenance organizations (HMOs), insurance companies, and various provider organizations. It has helped hospitals consolidate and reorganize their operations in a more streamlined and economically competitive manner, handled real estate transactions and financial restructurings, and helped improve negotiations between hospitals and

Deborah Hilke (left), Gary Hansen (seated), Peter Hintz, and Jack McGirl help keep Doherty, Rumble & Butler on the leading edge of employment law and litigation.

physician groups.

Through its professionals and a culture that fosters personal involvement and initiative, the firm has always taken an active part in community affairs as well as legal matters. Doherty, Rumble & Butler, P.A., is a strong benefactor of the arts community in the Twin Cities. Through the voluntary assistance of its people, it has helped strengthen nationally renowned organizations ranging from the Walker Art Center, the Saint Paul Chamber Orchestra, the Guthrie Theater, and Minnesota Public Radio to many smaller groups, including a number of new groups whose challenges parallel the needs addressed by the firm's involvement with starting businesses.

Doherty, Rumble & Butler, P.A., has grown and succeeded along with the growth and success of the region's economy. Its expertise extends from agriculture to high technology. Its service area includes not only the Twin Cities and Minnesota, but the full five-state region of the Upper Midwest, the nation, and several foreign countries. Its professionals reflect a firm with both a sense of heritage and a tradition of innovation.

CARLSON COMPANIES, INC.

Even before he had created a business empire, Curtis L. Carlson set goals. In 1938, as a soap salesman for Procter & Gamble, he left notes in his pockets reminding himself to earn $100 per week. A year later he quit his job and took a gamble on a new enterprise—transferring the promotional concept of trading stamps from department stores to grocery stores. More than ever, he continued the practice of setting concrete goals.

He called his new firm the Gold Bond Stamp Company ("gold" for value, "bond" for safety), and the goals now came as slogans. "There's Gold to Mine in '49," for example, was succeeded by "It Shall be Done in '51"—which was realized when Gold Bond Stamp Company made a planned $200,000 profit. The following year Carlson's ambitions leaped because the Super Valu company signed up as the first supermarket chain to offer the stamps. The trading stamp boom was on, and Carlson and his growing business rode it into Canada, Europe, Japan, and the Caribbean.

Carlson's beautiful new world headquarters brings the firm into the next century. It anchors the expansive 325-acre Carlson Center, located on the western outskirts of Minneapolis.

A larger market was at his fingertips and he found new ways to penetrate it. Following his own belief that "nothing happens here until we sell it," Carlson took on new challenges. He invested in hotel operations, beginning with the downtown Minneapolis landmark Radisson Hotel named for seventeenth-century French explorer Pierre Esprit Radisson, believed to have been the first white man to explore Minnesota. He ventured into marketing, motivational, and promotional services. He added assorted retail product lines, real estate investment, and travel services. And with each success he continued to set ever more ambitious goals.

In 1977, to motivate all the divisions of what was now called Carlson Companies, Inc., Carlson offered a trip around the world to his top executives if they could boost annual revenues to the billion-dollar mark within the next three years. When the dramatic new goal was met—well ahead of schedule—Carlson happily made good on his promise. Half the group went east, the other half headed west, and they all met in Tokyo—where Carlson announced plans to open the first Radisson hotel operation in Mainland China.

Today Carlson Companies is

Curtis L. Carlson, a graduate of the University of Minnesota, recently donated $25 million to his alma mater, exemplifying his commitment to private philanthropy. Carlson, pictured here at the university's Northrop Auditorium, has helped to raise $365 million for the school in recent years. Photo by Arnold Newman

one of the nation's largest privately held corporations. Though it has experienced dramatic growth through the years, it still reflects the aggressive and optimistic personality of Curt Carlson. But it also reflects the collaborative vision of a staff—now numbering more than 55,000 worldwide—that has taken all Carlson's goal setting to heart.

Three operating groups make up the Carlson Companies as it enters the 1990s. Each group builds on an aspect of the founder's own interests.

Motivation of his own employees led Carlson to establish the Carlson Marketing Group, which today is the largest marketing, motivation, communications, and training organization in the world. James Pfleider, corporate executive vice-president/marketing, heads this group, which also encompasses the Carlson Promotion Group. Building on the heritage of Gold Bond stamps, it provides

Curtis Carlson (right) with son-in-law and heir apparent Edwin C. "Skip" Gage III, who now serves as Carlson Companies' president and chief operating officer.

both consumers and corporate clients with hundreds of different merchandise, rebate, sweepstakes, and catalog programs.

The Carlson Hospitality Group reflects Carlson's wise decision to diversify into hotel ownership with his investment in the Minneapolis Radisson Hotel in 1960. Headed by Juergen Bartels, corporate executive vice-president/hospitality, Carlson's hospitality operations encompass more than 200 properties worldwide, including today's Radisson Hotels International, the fastest-growing upscale hotel company in North America.

The Carlson Travel Group, headed by James F. Calvano, corporate executive vice-president/travel, is North America's largest retail travel organization. Its operations include Ask Mr. Foster Travel Service, P. Lawson Travel of Canada, Neiman-Marcus Travel, and a number of wholesale travel operations.

Both Carlson's travel and hospitality operations have set new standards of quality and innovation in their respective industries, and are poised to play leading roles in the burgeoning global economy in the

years to come.

Carlson's commitment to the ongoing globalization of his synergistically related enterprises is manifested by the dramatic new Carlson Companies' world headquarters, located 10 minutes west of downtown Minneapolis in Minnetonka, Minnesota, where employees, formerly spread among a number of office complexes, took up residence in the summer of 1989.

Carlson has an office there, as does his heir apparent, president and chief operating officer Edwin C. "Skip" Gage, the son-in-law who was persuaded to join the firm back in 1968. While he has no plans to retire completely, these days Carlson, "The Ultra-Entrepreneur," devotes a little more time to his other interests, which include his Scandinavian-American heritage and personal and corporate philanthropy.

Community involvement is nothing new for Carlson Companies. It was a founding member of the Minnesota Five Percent Club, now the Keystone Club, which set a new national standard of corporate responsibility and involvement in public service causes. Gifts from The Carlson Foundation have benefited arts and scientific activities worldwide. In honor of his philanthropy, *Town & Country* magazine gave Carlson its Generous American Award for 1987-1988.

More recently, Carlson has given generously to the University of Minnesota, his alma mater. He played a key role in the creation of the Hubert H. Humphrey Institute of Public Affairs, established the Carlson Lecture Series at the university, gave the school $25 million, and then headed a campaign to raise $365 million—a record for public universities. Out of gratitude for this and other efforts, the university in 1986 renamed its business school the Curtis L. Carlson School of Management.

The Carlson Companies threw Minnesota's biggest corporate bash in July 1988, when 4,000 employees gathered for a sit-down 50th Anniversary dinner at the St. Paul Civic Center. It was a perfect moment to combine showmanship with hospitality, motivational inspiration with corporate unity, and travel logistics with the opportunity to learn from one another.

Because the preparations for this feast were nothing more than what the various Carlson Companies already do in a normal day's work, it should have been no sur-

Comedian Bob Hope (left) saluted Arleen and Curtis Carlson with his theme song, "Thanks for the Memories," before an audience of 7,000 employees and friends gathered at the St. Paul Civic Center in 1988 for the culmination of Carlson Companies' week-long 50th anniversary extravaganza.

prise to the guests that the dinner ended almost 20 minutes ahead of schedule. The extra time just left more room for the humor of guest emcee Bob Hope and the high-stepping of dozens of dancers, who dazzled the 7,000 employees and friends assembled for the after-dinner show staged to celebrate the corporation's 50 consecutive years of success in business.

The company's most recent slogan is "$9.2 Billion in 1992," and no one working for Curtis L. Carlson doubts that this newest goal will be achieved.

Photo by Ed Bock

ERECTED IN THE
YEAR 1941

Photo by Greg Ryan/Sally Beyer

Chapter 9

Building Greater Minneapolis

From concept to completion, Minneapolis' building industry shapes tomorrow's skyline.

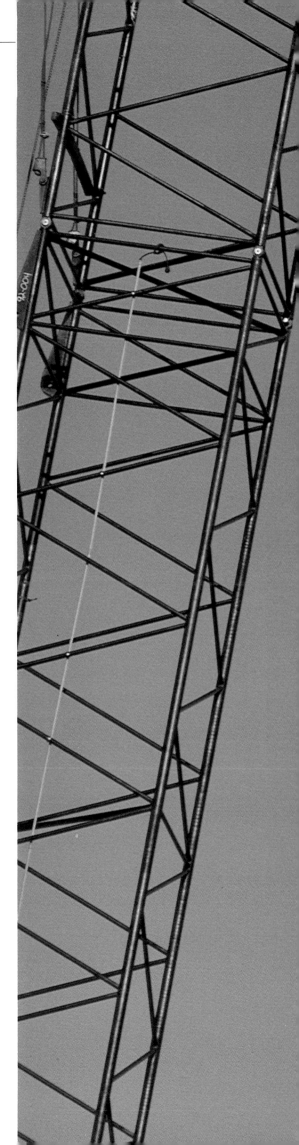

Hammel Green and Abrahamson, Inc., 200

Whitney Mill Quarter by CitySide Development, 201

BCE Development Properties Inc., 202

Opus Corporation, 204

The Kerr Organization, 206

Eberhardt Company, 209

Photo by Thomas K. Perry

HAMMEL GREEN AND ABRAHAMSON, INC.

Successful architecture is a collaborative effort. It results from the vision of skilled architects, the technical sophistication of engineers, and the rigorous sensitivity of interior designers. When the design carries the notation "HGA" on it, successful integration of these disciplines is no accident.

Since its founding in 1953 HGA has earned a reputation as Minnesota's leading design firm, setting an example for high-quality architectural design and responsible client service. Today HGA has a staff of 225, including architects, engineers, interior designers, landscape architects, lighting designers, and support professionals.

The firm operates with a market-driven focus, creating and deploying project teams with expertise in a variety of building types. Each team includes a principal who remains involved with the client throughout the project. Other specialists, such as planners, designers, engineers, CADD operators, and project managers, are added as the work progresses.

Architecturally, HGA's expertise encompasses programming, fea-

The award-winning design of the law offices of Frederikson & Byron presents an image of professional tradition in a contemporary framework. The HGA design received an award from the American Bar Association Journal. Photo by Phillip Macmillan James

sibility studies, master planning, interior design, and working with community and governmental agencies to secure the necessary project approvals. As an engineering firm, HGA provides mechanical, electrical, civil, and structural engineering, as well as computer-assisted specifications, cost estimating, and project management.

HGA's earliest work was in education—a specialty ideally suited to the baby boom years of the 1950s. From traditional schools to open schools to flexible modular schools, HGA has set the direction for educational architecture. That work continues today with such award-winning projects as the Deerwood Elementary School in Eagan, the Electrical Engineering/Computer Science Building at the University of Minnesota, and the Mayo Great Hall Student Center in Rochester, Minnesota.

In downtown Minneapolis, HGA's work is most clearly visible in the 42-story Piper Jaffray Tower, the dramatic blue glass skyscraper that anchors the southern edge of the city's core. The Piper Tower provides not only the high-profile image demanded by corporate clients, but also the technical sophistication of a "smart" building. Integrated engineering systems offer extensive telecommunications and computer access capabilities, energy management

The graceful 42-story Piper Jaffray Tower was designed by HGA to provide a distinctive, high-profile image for the company while offering interior flexibility for tenants. The building was 60-percent leased 18 months prior to its completion. Photo by Shin Koyama

systems, electronic temperature control, closed-circuit television, and security systems—all in one flexible and affordable package.

At the other edge of downtown, HGA designed the much-needed Hennepin County Health Services Center. Developed with the assistance of the firm's computer-aided design system, this building will allow the client to expand and reorganize the space as needed over the coming years.

Although best known for its office buildings and educational facilities, HGA has developed a significant practice in the design of fine arts projects. Locally, clients include the Minneapolis Institute of Arts, the Walker Art Center, the Guthrie Theatre, the Science Museum of Minnesota, and the soon-to-be-constructed Minnesota History Center.

As Hammel Green and Abrahamson, Inc., moves into its fourth decade of growth, the future promises a continuation of quality design and uncompromising client service. From the beginning, a commitment to design excellence has been the foundation of HGA's practice, and with more than 50 architectural and engineering awards, it is clear that this commitment has led to success. The tradition will continue.

WHITNEY MILL QUARTER BY CITYSIDE DEVELOPMENT

Once the Mississippi riverfront was the focus of commerce and business activity in Minneapolis. The great mills and elevators along the river below the Falls of St. Anthony were served by busy rail lines connecting the city to waiting markets to the east, south, and west. Then business life of the city spread away from the river, and the riverfront became an urban backwater. Now a new spirit of revitalization is visible along the west bank of the Mississippi. Between the lower end of Nicollet Mall and the city's new Technology Corridor a new bridge is being put in place: Whitney Mill Quarter.

In the shell of the Crown Roller Mill, built in 1879 and gutted by a devastating fire in 1983, almost 95,000 square feet of new, high-amenity office space is attracting designers and other professional firms to the riverfront. Connected to it by a spacious plaza, the Ceresota Elevator, originally constructed in 1908, has been reborn as a companion office building with almost 105,000 square feet of space. In the former boiler house for the Crown Roller Mill, another 25,000 square feet of space rounds out the office complex. And across a second large open plaza, the 97-room Whitney Hotel—created in what was once the old Standard Mill—offers modern business travelers European-

style luxury just a short walk from the city's commercial center.

All four buildings' exteriors are registered with the National Register of Historic Buildings. While their exteriors were reconstructed according to guidelines that preserve their architectural integrity, the interiors use the finest quality materials and mechanical systems to create a traditional elegance in a modern business environment. They represent a $54-million investment.

The four landmark buildings and their plazas are bordered by Washington Avenue South, West River Parkway, Portland Avenue, and Fifth Avenue. Their rebirth is the work of CitySide Development, a closely held, Minneapolis-based real estate development company dedicated to bringing new life to the banks of the river where it touches the downtown.

The Whitney Hotel was the first to open its doors, in March 1987. A member of Preferred Hotels and Small Luxury Hotels, its service is a given—more than 130 staff members are on hand for just 97 guest rooms, including the luxurious penthouse and 40 expansive bi-level suites with dramatic spiral staircases. Amenities include plush terry towels and robes, 24-hour room service, and free parking. The Whitney Grille serves classic American cuisine in a warm, intimate setting. The outdoor Whitney Garden Plaza offers casual

The brick and limestone facade of The Whitney Hotel overlooks the plaza that forms part of Whitney Mill Quarter. Diners at The Whitney Grille can enjoy lunch and cocktails amid the ambience of the Quarter's four historic buildings.

Water cascades from an overhanging ledge of Dark Emperador marble and then rises in a lighted fountain at the Crown Roller Mill office building.

dining on Whitney Mill Quarter's spacious lower plaza, with a dramatic view of the historic Stone Arch Bridge at St. Anthony Falls.

Opening in 1988, the Crown Roller Mill's distinctive copper mansard roof has been restored. The Ceresota's famous flower girl sign has been lovingly restored and stands high above the Quarter as a landmark. Both the Crown and Ceresota buildings offer open, skylit atriums, large fountains, and marble and brass furnishings. The lower plaza, terraced in rose-colored cement, features a central fountain surrounded by park benches and almost 2,000 plants, shrubs, and trees. The upper plaza is the showcase for a life-size chess board with chess pieces designed and sculpted by a Twin Cities artisan.

The Mississippi rolls by, accessible along the city's Great River Parkway. The parkway will eventually hug the river from Plymouth Avenue on the north to the West Bank Campus of the University of Minnesota—making the Whitney Mill Quarter the midpoint in a new urban jewel.

BCE DEVELOPMENT PROPERTIES INC.

Webster's definition of "common" as something "belonging to or serving the community" is an appropriate description of Gaviidae Common, the newest retail gem along Nicollet Mall.

Gaviidae Common offers 75 specialty shops and restaurants anchored by Saks Fifth Avenue. The shopping complex creates a Minnesota environment that features a

five-story indoor cascade of pools and waterfalls and a golden loon seemingly taking flight from the third level. Escalators in the atrium move shoppers between levels while a beautiful, translucent glass stairway, lit from below, sweeps from ground to skyway level.

Gaviidae Common's name has been carefully chosen. "Gaviidae" is the Latin family name of the four species of loons. "Common" not only refers to Minnesota's state bird, the Common Loon—the only one of the four loon species that nests in the state—but also describes the new complex' role as an open public area in the heart of the downtown. Skyways connect Gaviidae Common to the IDS Center, City Center, and the Norwest Tower.

The unusual company behind Gaviidae Common is BCE Development Properties Inc. (BCED), the U.S. development arm for Vancouver-based BCE Development Corporation. The parent company is in turn part of BCE Inc., one of Canada's largest corporations. Among its many other subsidiaries are Bell Canada, Northern

The Minnesota World Trade Center, St. Paul Center, North Central Life and Meritor Towers are all managed by BCED, and enhance the working and shopping environment in St. Paul.

Telecom Limited, and TransCanada Pipeline.

While Gaviidae Common represents the first major new development in the city for BCED, it is the third corner on Seventh and Nicollet to be owned and/or managed by the company.

Since its entry into the Twin Cities real estate market in April 1986, BCED has become a major force in the continuing process of renewal in downtown Minneapolis. It now owns and manages more than 2.5 million square feet of rentable office space and nearly one million square feet of retail space in the city's downtown—and there's more to come.

BCED came to the Twin Cities in 1986 through the purchase of the former holdings of Oxford Properties, which included the site of the Minnesota World Trade Center, St. Paul Center Complex, the North Central Life and Meritor Towers, the IDS Center, and Minneapolis City Center. Four of the state's 17 *Fortune* 500 companies make their homes in BCED-managed Minneapolis properties.

The quality and reputations of those properties is indicative of the business strategy employed by BCED. The company's primary objective is to expand its leadership role in the acquisition, development, leasing, and management of prime commercial properties throughout North America. Typically, those properties are located in the commercial heart of the city they serve. They tend to offer mixed uses—retail and office space—working together to provide a high-quality commercial environment that adds to the vitality of the city's downtown. The properties almost always display a unique visual identity that enhances the images of the companies that choose them as their

In Minnesota, Gaviidae Common means the most exciting collection of retail shops ever assembled in one stunning shopping environment.

own corporate address.

Such is the case in Minneapolis, where the IDS Center has long been the prestige address for businesses, and where City Center has become synonymous with the rebirth of quality retailing along Nicollet Mall. Yet each has another personality. The IDS includes three levels of retail shops and restaurants, the 19-story Vista Marquette hotel, and parking for 640 cars. The City Center complex is home to three levels of retail shops and restaurants, Multifoods Tower, the Minneapolis Marriott, and provides parking for 680 cars.

IDS Center came first, in 1972. Occupying the entire block bordered by Nicollet Mall and Marquette between Seventh and Eighth streets, it gave the downtown a visual focal point: a gleaming, eight-sided, 52-story tower with more than one million square feet of office space. It also gave the downtown a ground-level crossroads by linking the tower to the rest of the complex with the now nationally renowned Crystal Court, a central indoor common enclosed under a canopy of glass, steel, and plastic pyramids that soars 120 feet from the second-story level of the skyway system to the eighth-story level of the tower.

Designed by world-renowned architect Phillip Johnson, IDS Center was the first high rise of architectural note in Minneapolis and is still the most distinctive building on the city's skyline.

City Center, which opened in 1983, features a bustling, three-level indoor shopping and dining complex under a six-story skylit atrium.

Office space is also a key element. The Multifoods Tower, which connects to City Center's retail atrium, offers more than one million square feet of office space in a 50-story structure located in the heart of the city's retail, financial, and entertainment district. Up on the roof, the Multifoods Tower is home to a different kind of tenant: Peregrine Falcons that once made their homes all along the upper reaches of the Mississippi River now maintain an aerie with a truly commanding view of the river. In addition, Minneapolis City Center connects to the 32-story, 605-room Marriott Hotel, which features some of the city's finest restaurants.

Construction is now under way on a new multi-use project on Nicollet Mall, between Fifth and Sixth streets, right across from Gaviidae Common, which will be the future site of Minnesota's first Neiman Marcus store, joined by 50 specialty shops, and a 35-story office tower that will be the corporate headquarters for one of the city's largest regional brokerage companies, Dain Bosworth. It is planned to be opened in the fall of 1991.

In all, BCED now has more than $2 billion in real estate holdings in the Twin Cities, Chicago, Denver, Seattle, Phoenix, and Irvine, California, with an additional $500 million in new development planned or under way. It owns and manages more than 12 million square feet of prime commercial space. Its skills range from market and feasibility analysis to marketing and property management, including land acquisition and assembly, zoning and servicing, financial structuring, design and construction, leasing, and continuing property management.

Though relatively new to the Minneapolis business scene, BCED has already become an important part in the development and management of the city's premier office and retail complexes.

LEFT: BCED's City Center graces downtown Minneapolis with three levels of retail shops, restaurants, and a food court under a skylit atrium. The shopping complex is also connected to the Marriott Hotel, offering further convenience to shoppers and visitors.

BELOW: Containing within its glass walls three levels of retail shops and restaurants and the completely renovated Vista Marquette hotel, the IDS Center has long been the prestige address for Minneapolis businesses.

OPUS CORPORATION

In Latin the word "opus" means "a creative work." In Minneapolis—and in an increasing number of cities from coast to coast—Opus has come to mean creative solutions for commercial and industrial buildings. The connotations of achievement and lasting quality are equally appropriate for this full-service architectural, engineering, development, construction, leasing, and management firm.

The enterprise began in 1953 as the Rauenhorst Construction Company and reflected Gerald Rauenhorst's desire to create a business around a combined design/build capability. The typical commercial building process involves mutiple and sometimes conflicting lines of authority among a number of specialized companies and subcontractors. Rauenhorst envisioned a form of single-source capability that would link architects, engineers, project management,

The waterfront Opus Center is the cornerstone building of the 550-acre Opus 2 office/industrial park, which is occupied by about 7,500 employees who work at more than 100 businesses.

real estate specialists, field construction services, and property management into an integrated and smoothly functioning team.

More than 1,000 buildings later, the strengths of such integration are obvious. With all the necessary specialties under one roof, Opus can focus its many resources on the client's specific space and financing needs. The organization's edge comes through in quality, cost, and schedule control.

As one of the largest development companies in the nation, Opus can draw on deep resources in experienced personnel and financing. With more than 70 architects, engineers, and design professionals on staff, Opus is among the largest architectural firms in the Upper Midwest. The construction staff is made up of more than 32 project managers, all degreed professionals.

Opus' real estate development staff maintains professionals with local real estate market experience and professionals in governmental affairs, finance, asset management,

and, through its affiliate, Normandale Properties, Inc., property management.

Opus can operate within time constraints that would be unattainable if the efforts of several different companies had to be coordinated. Opus project managers can tap resources and expertise anywhere in the organization to keep their projects on schedule and within budget.

High-rise office buildings that create a signature on the skyline, efficient office-warehouse complexes, corporate headquarters, and retail shopping centers all fall within Opus' area of expertise. To date Opus companies have built projects in more than 23 states. Among those close to home are:

—Opus 2, A mature, 550-acre office/industrial park featuring essential business services in a carefully preserved natural environment just 10 miles southwest of downtown Minneapolis. The park is headquarters for American Medical Systems, Data Card Corporation, Molecular Genetics, Ford, Eastman Kodak, General Elec-

Developed jointly by Opus and BetaWest Properties, Inc., the 35-story office building at 150 South Fifth has nearly one million square feet of space and is home to many prominent Minneapolis area firms.

tric, American Hardware Insurance Group, and the UMAGA Merchandising Mart, as well as more than 100 other businesses. Opus has designed the development with an eye toward preserving the area's natural beauty and ecology while providing high-quality office and industrial facilities for technology and service clients. One of Opus 2's recent buildings is the 16-story, 320-room Marriott Hotel constructed for Interstate Hotels Corpo-

ration.

—American Medical Systems offers a good illustration of the advantages of Opus' design/build capabilities. During the construction of that firm's office/manufacturing headquarters in Minnetonka, Minnesota, Opus had to completely redesign the mechanical systems to accommodate a clean room that was added. Despite the extensive changes, the project was completed on time and within budget.

—150 and 100 South Fifth, twin office towers (36 and 25 stories, respectively) that were Opus' first ventures in downtown Minneapolis. The tower at 150 South Fifth was developed in partnership with BetaWest Properties, Inc., the real estate development subsidiary of U S West. The towers offer attractive office space on the skyway system in the hub of downtown Minneapolis to a variety of law, accounting, finance, and investment firms, as well as serving as the regional headquarters for U S West. The first phase, 100 South Fifth, was fully leased within 12 months of completion. The freestanding towers are linked by a two-story atrium, while an outdoor waterwall wraps around the corner of Second Avenue and Fifth Street. The four-season water display creates patterns of falling water in the summer months and special ice and frost patterns during the winter. It is surrounded by a plaza, complete with trees and plantings for public enjoyment.

Opus' latest downtown project is First Bank Place, created with IBM as its development partner. Opus will be constructing the new office center at the corner of Second Avenue and Sixth Street, in the heart of the Minneapolis financial district. The complex, designed by the world-renowned architects I.M. Pei & Partners, will be anchored by First Bank System, the Upper Midwest's largest bank holding company. IBM will also be a major tenant. Opus, in addition

to being a partner and the general contractor, will also be the leasing agent and property manager. The new complex will feature a 50-plus-story office tower and a companion 18-story building linked by a circular atrium. It will include more than 1.3 million square feet of office space, plus retail shops and restaurants. Initial occupancy is scheduled for mid-1991.

As Opus continues to grow, the firm continues to look for new opportunities to apply its experience and creative abilities. An example of this is the current development of the corporate campus for ConAgra, Inc., in Omaha, Nebraska. The campus is part of a 105-acre redevelopment in downtown Omaha. Opus did the master plan and is developing, designing, and constructing the campus, which will include a series of buildings for various product groups, consistent with ConAgra's corporate philosophy of independent operating companies.

Rauenhorst and Opus (the latter name was officially adopted in 1982) have more than proven the benefits of the total capability concept. Opus has developed a range of vertically integrated capabilities that enables it to complete a project faster than traditional methods and respond to the changing needs of its clients.

One result of that track record has been Opus' growth. A satisfied Twin Cities business client planning new facilities in another part of the country will frequently bring in Opus to take on the new location. In areas where growth and development are proceeding at a rapid pace, Opus has set up full-service offices. Today Opus Corporation has affiliated companies in Minneapolis, Milwaukee, the Chicago suburb of Rosemont, Tampa, Pensacola, Phoenix, and Carlsbad, California. Serving them all is the Minneapolis-based property management affiliate, Normandale Properties, Inc.

THE KERR ORGANIZATION

Norman J. Kerr, president of The Kerr Organization.

Every city has its landmark buildings, and Minneapolis is no exception. Some are modern, gleaming architectural triumphs that have risen in recent years and some are older, distinctive buildings of charm and character with their roots in the city's past.

A surprising number of the buildings bear the imprint of a Minneapolis entrepreneur with an eye for creating value through quality real estate projects. The Kerr Organization, established 10 years ago by Norman Kerr, has become an important force in the continuing rebirth of the downtown and the well-planned growth of its surrounding suburban communities.

And now, the biggest, and probably its most exciting project of all—one that could change the skyline of Minneapolis—may be just around the corner.

It all began in the late 1970s, when Kerr was in the midst of a sig-

nificant career change. As a successful advertising executive with some of America's largest agencies, such as Ted Bates in New York City, Campbell-Mithun, and Grey Advertising, Kerr and his wife, Carol, dabbled in small real estate projects and enjoyed some success at it. The creation of his own company, in 1979, marked his transition from the creativity of the advertising world to the creativity of real estate deal making.

One of Kerr's first major successes, a project that caught the eye of the public, was the purchase and restoration of the historic Times Building, located on the famous "newspaper row," now called the Marquette Building in downtown Minneapolis. Kerr purchased the building in 1979,

brought in a general contractor as a partner, and renovated it from top to bottom. He quickly leased it and then sold it to a large financial institution a short time later for a substantial gain. Throughout the next 10 years the Commercial Building, The Omni Building, The Lincoln Norwest Bank Building, The Produce Bank Building, The Metropolitan Mansion, The Pick-Nicollet Hotel, The Curtis Hotel, and the CPT Building have all benefited from Kerr's talents, some simply because he proved to be a catalyst for making things happen by merely being associated with the property. Kerr was doing deals and buying buildings on the fringe areas of downtown and on Hennepin Avenue and First Avenue North before it became the "in thing to do."

Over the years Kerr has experimented with different styles and uses: The Metropolitan Mansion involved the renovation of a large, stately, century-old brownstone, New York-style mansion into first-class office space. A vacant parcel of land covered with weeds became the classy, high-amenity office complex known as The Edina Executive Plaza, overlooking a plush country club.

Commercial activities were not the only focus of The Kerr Organization. Its projects also included residential developments, which began with a series of apartment buildings in the University of Minnesota area. His residential operations quickly grew to more than 1,000 apartment units, in several buildings, which he owned and managed.

Then, in the mid 1980s, Kerr entered the new home market with the creation of a number of highly regarded residential complexes in the Minneapolis suburbs. This included the award-winning Village Greens, an attractive 127-unit development on a golf course in Eden Prairie. Others quickly followed: Scenic Heights, a California-style land development of single-family homes; Hidden Valley, with 250 single-family sites; and PineGate, a unique mixture of 125 single- and multi-family style homes.

The residential complexes, developed under the aegis of New American Homes, became noted for their unique combination of condominium and townhouse configuration mixed with traditional single-family residential styles while avoiding the "complex feel" too often typical of multi-family buildings.

New American Homes soon established itself as an important developer in the Twin Cities, where it has sold 700 new homes and lots over a four-year period. Kerr explains that phase of his business operation is over. "Home building is definitely not worth the effort to us. We prefer to concentrate our money and energy in more rewarding projects."

A completely different kind of living space has also been a business specialty of Kerr's through the years: hotels. In 1979 Kerr purchased a major interest in the 900-room Curtis Hotel, a famous landmark, spreading over one and one-half blocks in downtown Minneapolis. Faced with this new challenge, Kerr soon had the place filled with activity and excitement but later sold his interest, after a friendly difference of opinion with his partner on the future direction of the hotel. However, he retained his interest in the hotel industry. Kerr made a substantial investment in the then "hot" Sunbelt market, with a touch of perfect timing, as he purchased several hotels in Dallas, Austin, Corpus Christi, and Albuquerque. He transformed the hotels into an operation of small, luxury properties that Kerr's hotel company managed. As the Sunbelt market boomed, Kerr's properties increased in popularity and were soon pursued by several groups of investors. He eventually sold each of the properties. These

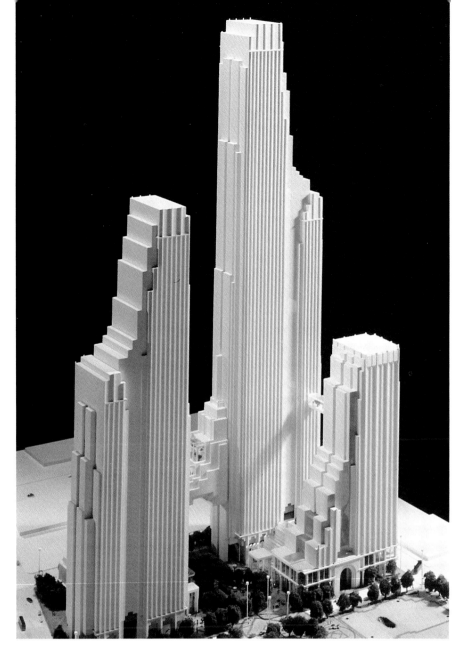

This 72-story tower and office complex, shown here in an architectural model, is sure to change the face of downtown Minneapolis. Jointly developed by Kerr and an Atlanta, Georgia-based company, the building will grace the city at the site of the Ritz Hotel block.

transactions brought him a substantial profit and also the reputation of being an astute deal maker. Kerr's luck, or incredible sense of timing, was perfect. Shortly after his sale, the price of oil plummeted while Kerr was negotiating deals in Minneapolis and other parts of the country.

One property Kerr had his eye on was an old hotel building, in downtown Minneapolis, which had been sitting empty for several years. His gut instinct told him that the property was definitely undervalued. He purchased the property and quickly flipped it to another company, which made plans to renovate it into luxurious new apartments. Kerr walked away knowing that, once again, he made something happen that would benefit the city by bringing new life to an area that had been lying dormant.

Although Kerr has renovated, built, bought, and sold hundreds of thousands of square feet of space, the biggest and most exciting project of all may lay just around the corner. And, if it all comes together as planned, it could become one of the most spectacular projects in America while changing the entire skyline of Minneapolis.

It began in 1987 with the purchase of the former Sheraton Ritz hotel, which local real estate experts now regard as one of the shrewdest acquisitions Minneapolis has seen in recent years. The purchase included a classy, 300-room hotel, a 250-car parking ramp, and one full block of land near the business center of downtown Minneapolis. When the smoke cleared, Kerr owned the entire project for less than one-half of the market value.

One key to Kerr's success has been his ability to get choice properties for ridiculously low prices, often before others knew they were on the market.

Kerr started with an offer several million dollars below the asking price, only to be turned down. He waited patiently while other investors toyed with the acquisition. He suddenly pounced with a similar low offer, but all cash. After several long negotiating sessions, Kerr's offer was accepted. But he then went back and renegotiated for terms, keeping the price the same. His persistence and patience paid off, and he won the deal.

After closing the transaction, Kerr went in and operated the hotel for more than a year, but he had much bigger plans in mind for the site. He knew that the real value was worth millions more, not only as a hotel operation but as a major office complex. In fact, he envisioned the biggest building in the city with potential for future development of three surrounding blocks.

Local real estate experts shook their heads in amazement, but Kerr ignored skeptics and charged ahead with his office development plans. He wanted to line up a major development partner with national expertise and experience, close the hotel, and begin to market the development to major prospects.

After meeting with several potential partners, all highly regarded, national developers, Kerr selected The Landmarks Group, based in Atlanta, Georgia, to help make the project a reality. Kerr selected The Landmarks Group because of the national expertise in major office projects and because

he considered their organization a perfect match with the people in Minneapolis.

News articles and rumors have it that a major tenant, one of the area's largest and most important businesses, is considering relocating its entire operation to the firm's spectacular new tower— which could be as high as 72 stories. If all goes as planned, Kerr's acquisition could soon be transformed into a spectacular complex of new office buildings, adding a "gem" while dominating the Minneapolis skyline.

Local real estate, city, and business leaders give Kerr credit for creating a project that will change the very face and personality of the city, while competing against some of the nation's biggest and most highly respected developers. They credit it to a combination of factors: an eye for value, tenacity, aggressiveness, and his ability to deal with a large number of personalities with a unique combination of charm and emotion that could bring his dreams to a reality.

Kerr quickly dismisses that type of talk saying, "It was not a dream; it was a business objective." He adds that if it all happens, it simply is because "we worked very hard and were lucky. If it doesn't, I'll be satisfied in knowing that we did our best. We'll just go on to the next deal," Kerr says. "I like making deals. That's my business and my hobby. The bigger, the better."

Kerr believes "Thinking big is fine, but the real secret is 'acting big.' Knowledge without action is useless. Action is what gets results!"

So, what's next? The answer is: Kerr will continue to do deals. "We're in the process of negotiating on another large office building in Minneapolis and are making plans. If we get it, we may upgrade it, keep it, or sell it." One thing is certain: Whatever Kerr decides, the building will never

again be the same because when he does a deal, things happen!

Kerr is also involved in projects outside Minneapolis in Washington, D.C., and Chicago. Even so, Minneapolis is home. "It is a unique mixture of people and environment. It is absolutely beautiful most of the year. If the weather gets too cold, the airport is just 20 minutes away."

When asked about his business and financial success, Kerr says, "Compared to real heavy weights around here, it is miniscule. Without a doubt, my biggest asset and real secret to the only success I've had is my longtime partner and wife, Carol. We have been married for 25 years, and she hardly even looks 25 years old! People are starting to find out that she is smarter than I am and a lot nicer to deal with. Lately she's been doing some deals on her own and that has me worried. There is enough competition out there already.

"Our core staff has also worked together for many years, which is very beneficial to the entire business operation," Kerr says. There are only two types of people who work with Kerr: Lifers and the Gone Quicks. "If you are good, you sense this is the place to be," says Pamala Wilson, a long-term executive vice-president. "The future looks very promising. The best words to describe our operation are action and results," says Wilson.

A man of many reputations, ranging from the super promoter to tough negotiator, Norman Kerr apparently has what it takes to succeed, combining a fast-paced business operation with the role of husband and father to his three children.

Although Kerr has other business interests, real estate is his major focus and likely always will be. It has been good to Norman Kerr, the deal maker, and Norman Kerr has been good for Minneapolis.

EBERHARDT COMPANY

For more than 50 years Eberhardt Company has been an active participant in the Twin Cities and national real estate markets. Under the leadership of the Nelson family—Walter, the company's former chairman, and his son, Jim, its current president and chairman— the shape of that participation has changed with business conditions.

Today the firm concentrates its efforts in brokerage (both sales and leasing), consulting, finance (commercial mortgages, joint ventures, and loan servicing), and property management. With a professional staff of more than 60 in the Twin Cities, a new home base in the heart of downtown Minneapolis, and a growing joint venture in Arizona, Eberhardt enters the 1990s as a full-service provider of market-sensitive commercial real estate services.

Even though Eberhardt currently concentrates on commercial and investment real estate, it was once more widely known in the Twin Cities for its residential activities. From the 1950s through the mid-1980s the firm built a productive, successful sales organization with more than a dozen local real estate offices staffed by almost 500 brokers. But as industry conditions changed, Eberhardt emphasized its commercial real estate activities that had continued to grow, albeit less visibly, through the years.

The company has long played an active role behind the scenes of many Twin Cities commercial real estate developments. As president of the Downtown Council, Walter Nelson was a key figure in the creation of Nicollet Mall. Eberhardt represented Dayton Hudson in the acquisition of the site that would become Ridgedale Center. It acquired the land for the Minneapolis Institute of Arts, the "new town" of Jonathan, and numerous downtown projects. Recent transactions include acquisition of the property that is now Lincoln Cen-

Eberhardt Company founder and former chairman Walter Nelson (left), with his son James, who currently serves as president and chairman.

ter and The Conservatory complex—as well as a significant role in leasing and financing placement for the Conservatory Partnership that developed the new retail center—as well as the sale of 1221 Nicollet Mall.

The firm's commercial real estate expertise has evolved into a vigorous real estate consulting practice. More than property sales and acquisition, Eberhardt's Consulting Services Division serves clients whose needs include assistance in leasing, investment, development, and marketing. It has played an active role in everything from the preservation and revitalization of the Young Quinlan Building to the redevelopment planning for Block E on Hennepin Avenue.

Today the Real Estate Finance Division structures every manner of transactions: joint ventures, participation loans, land sale/lease-backs, equity purchases, presales, traditional debt instruments, forward commitments, tax-exempt financing, and the sale of contracts

for deed. Its clients include life insurance companies, savings and loan associations, commercial banks, and pension funds.

As a property management firm, Eberhardt represents institutional and individual clients as the manager of their investment properties. Office, retail, industrial, and apartment facilities are all represented in Eberhardt's management portfolio. In a competitive market Eberhardt's role as manager of property involves not only the traditional roles of financial reporting and property maintenance, but also marketing and value enhancement for the real estate asset.

With the creation of Morken-Eberhardt Commercial Real Estate, which has offices in Phoenix and Tucson, the Eberhardt Company has extended its service territory to include the southwestern states of Arizona and New Mexico.

10
Quality
of Life

Medical institutions contribute to the quality of life of Minneapolis residents.

LifeSpan, Inc., 212

Metropolitan-Mount Sinai Medical Center, 213

Minneapolis Heart Institute, 214

Photo by Greg Ryan/Sally Beyer

LIFESPAN, INC.

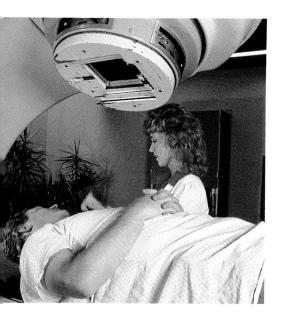

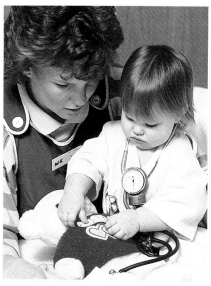

Founded in 1982, LifeSpan is a comprehensive regional health care system that includes primary and tertiary-level hospitals and numerous health care businesses and organizations as its members. In keeping with the emerging need for health care with an emphasis on both quality care and cost effectiveness, LifeSpan represents a regional network through which independent member institutions can coordinate strategic planning, marketing, financial planning, and management direction while continuing to develop their own specialties.

Three LifeSpan hospitals are located in the metropolitan area. Just south of downtown, Abbott Northwestern Hospital, Sister Kenny Institute, and Minneapolis Children's Medical Center provide one of the largest concentrations of health care services in the area. In nearby St. Louis Park, Methodist Hospital reaches out to patients in west Minneapolis and suburbs to the south, west, and north.

Abbott Northwestern, the largest private hospital in the Twin Cities, is a comprehensive health care provider that serves more than 60,000 patients each year—some 30 percent of them from beyond the seven-county metropolitan

area. Its 1,200 physicians and 5,200 employees are known for their expertise in heart care (including heart and heart-lung transplantation), perinatal services (including high- and low-risk obstetrics, gynecology, and WomenCare), as well as behavioral health services, cancer care, the neurosciences (neurology and neurosurgery), and low back care. The adjacent Sister Kenny Institute has earned a national reputation for its inpatient and outpatient brain injury, stroke, spinal cord, and chronic pain rehabilitation programs.

Minneapolis Children's Medical Center is the region's largest freestanding pediatric specialty facility. Its medical staff of more than 650 and some 1,350 employees provide care for children from premature newborns to adolescents. More than half of its 130 beds are designated for critical care services. Minneapolis Children's offers comprehensive ambulatory medical and mental health programs and services. The medical center cares for nearly 5,200 patients each year and has more than 116,000 outpatient visits annually.

Methodist Hospital is both one of the oldest hospitals in Minneapolis (founded in 1892) and one of the newest (the first in the city's growing suburbs when it moved to St. Louis Park in 1959). More than 750 physicians and 2,200 employees provide care to the Twin

ABOVE: State-of-the-art, nonsurgical heart care is saving more than lives at Abbott Northwestern Hospital; procedures performed in the institution's $1.2-million heart catheterization lab are less painful and less dangerous than traditional surgery for patients who can be helped by these procedures—and for those paying the bill, the costs are greatly decreased. Photo by Jeffrey Grosscup

FAR LEFT: At Methodist Hospital in St. Louis Park, radiation therapy is one of a wide range of cancer therapies patients receive. The hospital offers one of Minnesota's largest and most comprehensive cancer centers.

LEFT: Minneapolis Children's Medical Center has become the region's largest freestanding pediatric specialty facility by concentrating its efforts on creating a specialized health care environment that responds soley to the needs of children at every age, from infancy to adolescence. Photo by Mark Luinenberg

Cities and outstate communities through such programs as one of the state's most active cancer centers, a cardiology program that has pioneered the use of arterial lasers, an accredited rehabilitation center, an area trauma center, a comprehensive senior program, and one of the state's largest maternity centers.

LifeSpan's other acute care hospitals are located in Cambridge, Hutchinson, and Morris. Other LifeSpan members include Select Care, a preferred provider organization, and other health care organizations specializing in home health services, clinic management, and other charitable foundations.

LifeSpan is also a founding member of Voluntary Hospitals of America (VHA), a network of more than 800 of the nation's most respected health care providers.

METROPOLITAN-MOUNT SINAI MEDICAL CENTER

In 1988 Metropolitan Medical Center (MMC) and Mount Sinai Hospital merged to become Metropolitan-Mount Sinai Medical Center. The merger united two health care institutions whose roots extend as far back as the 1870s and as recently as the 1950s. Today Metropolitan-Mount Sinai combines the strengths of the former MMC and former Mount Sinai, and continues the strong commitment to high-quality medical care as one organization, located on two campuses. The downtown campus (formerly MMC) is located at 900 South Eighth Street in downtown Minneapolis. The Phillips Campus (formerly Mount Sinai) is just one mile south of the downtown facility at 2215 Park Avenue.

Metropolitan-Mount Sinai serves more than 17,000 patients each year in such specialty areas as Behavioral Health Services, Cancer Care Services, Phillips Eye Institute, Orthopedic Services, Knapp Rehabilitation Center, and Cardiology.

The Phillips Eye Institute is the Upper Midwest's leading center for the diagnosis and treatment of eye problems. The institute's network of ophthalmologists and its highly skilled support staff are dedicated to one mission: preserving human vision.

Metropolitan-Mount Sinai's Cancer Care Services have been certified by the American College of Surgeons since 1960. Cancer services include the Colon Cancer Center, as well as cancer research, radiation therapy, chemotherapy, counseling for patients and families, nutrition services, and hospice care.

Orthopedic Services range from the newest procedures for joint-replacement surgery and treatment of conditions affecting the lower back, to the comprehensive Arthritis Care Program. In cooperation with Hennepin County Medical Center, Metropolitan-Mount Sinai operates the only full-scale orthopedic biomechanics laboratory in the Twin Cities.

In Behavioral Health Services, Metropolitan-Mount Sinai offers a variety of settings for treatment that are flexible and responsive to each individual's needs. Behavioral Health Services include Chemical Dependency, Mental Health, and Employee Assistance Programs.

The Cardiac Center at Metropolitan-Mount Sinai has long been a pioneer in the field. Cardiac Services range from prevention and education to open-heart surgeries, cardiac catheterizations, and laser angioplasties.

Knapp Rehabilitation Center provides inpatient and outpatient rehabilitation services for adults and older children with a wide

Metropolitan-Mount Sinai Medical Center operates two campuses in Minneapolis—the Downtown Campus at 900 South Eighth Street (left), and the Phillips Campus at 2215 Park Avenue (below).

range of diagnoses: strokes, head injuries, spinal cord injuries, joint replacements, amputations, and more. The center is known for its leadership role in physical medicine and rehabilitation.

The former MMC traces its roots to two of the city's first hospitals: St. Barnabas, originally Cottage Hospital, founded in 1871, and The Swedish Hospital, which opened in 1898. In 1970 the two hospitals consolidated to form MMC. One year later MMC and Hennepin County Medical Center, located across the street, became the first private and public hospitals in the United States to share certain facilities and services, a national model of cooperation that continues to this day.

The former Mount Sinai Hospital was founded in 1951 by members of the Jewish faith as a gift to the city of Minneapolis. Patients of all race and creeds were treated there. Mount Sinai became the first private hospital to have a major affiliation with the University of Minnesota Medical School, becoming especially well known for its clinical and research studies in cardiology and internal medicine.

Metropolitan-Mount Sinai offers the talents and services of more than 1,100 physicians, 2,000 employees, and 2,500 volunteers, auxilians, and service guild members working together to provide comprehensive health care services to the Upper Midwest.

MINNEAPOLIS HEART INSTITUTE

The Minneapolis Heart Institute (MHI) is an organization of cardiovascular physicians devoted to providing quality medical care to persons with heart disease in the United States and abroad.

Established in 1981 by several groups of independent heart specialists, the Minneapolis Heart Institute offers state-of-the-art, personalized, comprehensive cardiovascular care. The institute's mission is to address the full range of heart health needs for people of all ages: heart disease prevention, diagnosis, interventional therapy, surgery, heart and lung replacement, rehabilitation, and cardiac research.

Still in its first decade, the Minneapolis Heart Institute is already at the forefront of the world's heart institutes, with an internationally renowned group of more than 45 distinguished physicians. These physicians are supported by more than 100 health care professionals, including cardiac nurses, technologists, heart health educators, researchers, rehabilitation specialists, dieticians, and administrators.

The institute has a unique team approach to its personalized patient care. Physicians and other health care professionals work closely together with the patient and family to provide the most comprehensive care possible, for the institute believes that such involvement, support, understanding, and education are vital to successful recovery and rehabilitation.

Located on the campus of Abbott Northwestern Hospital in Minneapolis, the institute's new and advanced facility serves more than 10,000 patients per year, one-half of whom come from locations far beyond the Twin Cities metropolitan area. This highly specialized state-of-the-art institution provides sophisticated, noninvasive diagnostic technologies along with corrective surgical procedures, for which it has unexcelled success rates—from open-heart surgery to pace-

ABOVE: Ten thousand patients each year are treated at the state-of-the-art facilities of the Minneapolis Heart Institute.

RIGHT: MHI uses several types of scans of the heart to identify abnormal blood flow and to measure heart muscle efficiency.

maker implantation and heart and lung replacement. The Minneapolis Heart Institute leads in the development and application of a unique variety of advanced technologies such as its pioneering work in laser applications, valve debridement, and the use of mechanical devices as a bridge to transplant.

MHI offers a unique and comprehensive program in heart disease prevention that includes early detection and intervention along with risk-factor modification for both adults and children. In addition, it provides extensive programs in cardiac rehabilitation and follow-up care.

The Minneapolis Heart Institute Foundation is a separate nonprofit organization, whose 20-member board of directors is made up of MHI physicians and representatives from the community at large. The foundation participates in a number of wide-ranging heart research efforts in conjunction with both local and national centers including the National Institutes of Health. MHIF also implements specialized educational initiatives and seeks to provide financial assistance for patients in need.

The Minneapolis Heart Institute and Foundation are committed to sharing their resources, expertise, and knowledge. As a result, MHI has taken an active role in the training of cardiac specialists worldwide, establishing fellowships in interventional cardiology and cardiovascular surgery. Training efforts include nurses and technicians as well as physicians.

The Minneapolis Heart Institute and Foundation are strongly responsive to the needs of their community. Throughout the Upper Midwest region, MHI's community education efforts—from seminar and workshops to the traveling Heartfair program—have become familiar and valued heart health teaching aids.

As the Minneapolis Heart Institute continues to grow, it remains dedicated to its goals of providing personalized quality patient care and to the advancement of medical science in the prevention and treatment of heart disease.

Photo by Steve Schneider

11
The
Marketplace

Minneapolis' retail establishments, theater, and service industries are enjoyed by residents and visitors alike.

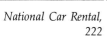

Photo by Ed Bock

MURRAY'S

"Silver Butter Knife Award—steak"

For many Twin Citians—as well as for many regular visitors to Minneapolis—that is all the information necessary to describe the restaurant with the reputation for the best food in town. Since the 1930s three generations of the Murray family have made dining out in Minneapolis a pleasure.

The late Arthur and Marie Murray's first restaurant, originally located on Penn at Broadway, later on Fourth Street, was called the Red Feather. Marie was the company's president, serving as host-

pened inside the restaurant as well: Murray's closed for six weeks for a complete renovation.

The enduring commitment to quality was never in need of refurbishment. Murray's succeeds because its staff of almost 100 has remained dedicated to doing what they do as well as it can be done. High standards are the rule in both food and service quality— nothing is left to chance. To assure that its trademark steaks are tender and done to a turn, Murray's has developed its own aging process, built special ovens, and em-

Murray's owner and president Patrick J. Murray (left), with his son Tim, who serves as the restaurant's vice-president and general manager.

The best steak in town is served nightly in Murray's elegantly appointed dining room. Diners are likewise treated to the soft music of a small string ensemble.

ess and taking charge of the menu; Arthur was the vice-president and handled the business details. Since 1946, when the restaurant moved to 26 South Sixth Street, the name for fine dining in downtown Minneapolis has been simply Murray's. Since 1983 the Murray behind Murray's has been the founders' son, Patrick.

Yet while the restaurant has spent the past 40 years in the same place, it has not been standing still. From the heart of downtown Minneapolis, Murray's has watched and been part of the rebirth of the city's center—City Center, in fact, is right across the street. In 1984 a rebirth of sorts hap-

ploys its own butcher. An on-premise bakery is operated by a master baker. All dressings, special seasonings, and the garlic toast are private family recipes.

Mid-afternoon is tea time at Murray's, a chance for people in the decidedly American Twin Cities to experience the civilizing tradition of England. Exotic teas from around the world are brewed up, and there are trays of scones, pastries, and finger sandwiches from which to choose. Late at night Murray's menu turns "Late & Light"—simple fare ranging from omelettes to burgers and an array of homemade desserts, all in a quiet, elegant setting only a few steps away from the night life of the city.

Patrick Murray directs the business. Following in his rise through

the ranks, son Tim serves as vice-president. Joyce Murray, Patrick's wife, has played a major role in the redecorating and updating of the restaurant in the 1980s. Most nights, two of the Murrays' daughters, Tina and Jill, can be found serving customers in the dining room. A third daughter, Megan, is at college studying hotel and restaurant management—the field Tim also earned his degree in—and the youngest son, James, may soon augment his family education in the restaurant business with a formal one.

Arthur Murray was elected to the Restaurant Hall of Fame for his contributions of creativity and innovation to the industry. Author and world traveler Maurice Dreicer's *The Diner's Companion* originally conferred the Silver Butter Knife Award for the excellence of Murray's steaks. Author C. Paul Luongo cited Murray's for the best steak in the country in his book, *America's Best 100!* Local publications such as *Twin Cities* and *Mpls/St. Paul* regularly highlight the restaurant for its continuing excellence.

In an industry dominated by huge chains, Murray's remains a one-of-a-kind success. Murray's continues to provide a plush and cozy setting where diners are serenaded with violins and cellos— and served food worth remembering.

THE OLD LOG THEATER

The Old Log Theater is America's oldest continuously running stock theater and the oldest theater of any kind in the Upper Midwest. For almost a half-century—since May 31, 1940—it has been entertaining the people of the Twin Cities with an ever-changing variety of stage plays. Since it moved to its present location on 10 scenic acres in Excelsior, not far from historic Lake Minnetonka, the Old Log has been open and active, packing them in 52 weeks per year.

The play is not the only thing at the Old Log. In addition to the 655-seat theater, a 400-seat restaurant serves dinner before the show. Summertimes, guests may find "chuck-wagon" dinners set up outside on the beautifully wooded grounds. An Industrial Show Division produces convention shows worldwide and numbers among its clients almost every major corporation in the Twin Cities.

The Old Log takes its name from the original log stable in which it spent its first 20 years. (The original building, which stands at the edge of the parking lot, is still used as a storage area.) During that era it produced a new play every week through the summer months, from the beginning of June through mid-September.

When it moved to its present

Nestled amid 10 acres of scenic woodland adjacent to Lake Minnetonka, The Old Log Theater entertains Twin Cities theater-lovers 52 weeks per year.

setting in 1960, it became a year-round operation and began to evolve toward its concentration on Broadway and English comedy. Its series of holiday Children's Shows are an annual Christmas tradition, as are the off-night series of Lenten productions each year.

A year after its founding a young actor/director who came to the Twin Cities by way of Kansas, Oklahoma, and the drama school at Northwestern University made his first appearance. Don Stolz stayed; in 1946 he became the theater's owner. Today he is the guiding hand behind both the theater and Don Stolz Productions, the industrial show side of the business. In 1986 he was named Small Business Person of the Year by the Greater Minneapolis Chamber of Commerce.

Stolz is not only the Old Log's owner. He is also its producer/director in residence (with more than 600 productions to his credit), occasionally a member of the cast, and often the host in the restaurant. His trademark "curtain speech," in which he welcomes his guests between acts and provides a sprightly perspective on the production in progress, is a Twin Cities tradition. The family business has come to include Joan Stolz, Don's wife, and their five grown sons.

The sense of family extends to the larger stage family. Its actors are members of Actors' Equity Association, the only union for professional actors in legitimate theater. The late Ken Senn was the first actor in the history of American theater to be associated with the same theater for 25 years. Others have gone on to make a name for themselves beyond the Twin Cities theater scene. Among the Old Log's better-known alumni are actor Nick Nolte, who did some 25 roles at the theater in the 1970s, and actress Loni Anderson.

In 1989 the Old Log embarked on its 50th season, a record unequalled by any other continuously running theater in the country. It takes special pride in the fact that the theater is entirely self-supporting. It has never asked for or accepted a single penny from grants or foundations, or resorted to pledge drives or membership campaigns. All revenue comes by way of the theater's box office—evidence that the Old Log Theater has been providing enjoyable entertainment to the people of Minneapolis, St. Paul, and the entire Upper Midwest.

In 1976 The Old Log Theater presented Relatively Speaking, *a comedy by Alan Ayckbourn. The theater concentrates on Broadway and English comedy.*

219

LEEF BROS., INC.

In the simple, comfortable lobby of a small but thriving company in north Minneapolis, a sign on the wall offers a brief explanation of the way the business is run. "Service," it says, "is an investment, not a cost." It's also the reason that the business started by Harry Leef in 1908 has grown over the years to become the largest independent industrial laundry and rental supplier in Minnesota.

A network of route representatives who average more than 20 years of service with the firm keep Leef Bros. responsive to customers' ever-changing needs. Their personalized service is enhanced by the latest advances in cleaning technology, a laundry facility rated among the best in the industry, and efficient, accurate, computerized support systems.

When it began, Harry Leef delivered overalls to local businesses, primarily railroad yards, by horse-drawn wagon. Today a fleet of 60 trucks with Leef's distinctive green leaf and red, orange, and gold stripes serves 8,000 businesses of all sizes and descriptions throughout the state plus western Wisconsin and North Dakota. There are distribution depots in St. Cloud

President Stephen D. Leef poses with a truck from the company's fleet of 60. In the Twin Cities and beyond, businesses are familiar with the trucks' distinctive design and with the high-quality service they bring.

and Waseca, and a branch plant in Fargo, North Dakota.

The firm is headquartered on James Avenue North, in the same near-northside Harrison neighborhood where Harry Leef grew up. He was 13 when he went to work pushing a handcart to make deliveries for a local linen supply company. At 20, based on his firsthand knowledge of the needs of local businesses, he started Minneapolis Overall Laundry (the building he rented cost eight dollars per month, plus another two dollars for the stall for his delivery horse). Later he added St. Paul Overall Laundry. In 1976 the two identities were combined into Leef Bros., Inc.

Harry Leef's knack for inventing and improving commercial laundry equipment helped the business grow: Many of the machines he developed were subsequently adopted by companies throughout the industry. That tradition continues to this day through a Leef Bros. subsidiary, Production

Design Products, that develops new equipment that initially will be used within the company but often is marketed to other firms, not only in the United States and Canada, but as far away as Belgium, the Scandinavian countries, and the United Kingdom. One such product development effort produced the High Roller® mat rolling machine now used by the mat rental industry nationwide.

Within the industry, Leef Bros. has augmented its penchant for good service with a zest for innovation. It was the first in the region to introduce rental coveralls, as well as dust-control products for modern businesses whose working environments—and the high-tech equipment in them—are much more sensitive to airborne debris.

Over the years there have been several sets of Leef brothers involved in Leef Bros., Inc. Harry's brother George worked with him in the 1920s. His sons, Stephen and Gilbert, assumed management of the company at his death in 1959. A third generation of Leefs have followed them into the business, as have second and third generations of many other employees.

OMNI NORTHSTAR HOTEL

The Omni Northstar is a 226-room business-class hotel uniquely located in a 17-story tower in the heart of downtown Minneapolis. It's the home of the renowned, four-star Rosewood Room Restaurant. It's centrally located on the Minneapolis skyway system. And it's at the forefront of an industry trend that finds discriminating travelers deciding that bigger isn't better—*better* is better.

Bigger has never been part of the Omni Northstar's outlook; better has. From its creation in 1963 as the downtown's first hotel oriented to the business traveler, through the complete and painstaking renovation that has prepared it for its second 25 years of operation, the Omni Northstar has focused the attention of its staff and physical resources on the traveler who welcomes more personal attention and a more manageable scale of operations.

Each of its guest rooms is tastefully appointed with custom-made furniture and draperies. Amenities such as in-room refrigerators, coffee makers, and complimentary cable television are standard throughout. A well-trained staff is on duty to provide support services with a personal touch at all hours of the day and night.

From the hotel's convenient, skyway-linked location at South Seventh Street and Second Avenue South, guests at the Omni Northstar are close to downtown business, commercial, and recreation destinations. But because the hotel's lobby is located not at ground level but on the seventh floor of the Omni Northstar tower, visitors can literally get above the hustle and bustle of the city, escaping to a secluded serenity rare in any downtown area anywhere in the country.

That escape includes access to the hotel's eighth-floor Skygarden, a 10,000-foot, open-air rooftop garden and retreat with a magnificent view of downtown Minneapo-

For downtown visitors and workers alike, the Omni Northstar's premier accommodations and attentive service provide a welcome respite from the pace of business.

The Omni Northstar and Rosewood Room greet visitors in the heart of downtown Minneapolis—but with a lobby seven stories above the street.

lis. For more conventional business and social needs, the Omni Northstar's three ballrooms plus a boardroom and five additional meeting rooms can accommodate groups from several to several hundred.

The Rosewood Room is a Minneapolis landmark in its own right. Its reputation as the ultimate experience in four-star dining has been earned and upheld over the years through an uncompromising adherence to standards of excellence in cuisine, atmosphere, and service. Over the years the Rosewood Room has won accolades from near and far, including

19 consecutive *Travel/Holiday* awards and four *Corporate Report* Silver Spoon Awards.

Rosewood Room guests are served on Royal Doulton china. Tables are covered in rose-patterned damask. Natural light and greenery combine with marble and, of course, rosewood to provide a relaxed, contemporary setting.

The Rosewood Room menu is constantly changing to reflect culinary trends, both nationally and abroad. Traditional continental cuisine and nouvelle American specialties are featured, complemented by the adjacent Rosewood Bar and Hors d'Oeuvre, a favorite gathering place for downtown business people and hotel guests alike.

The Omni name, with its attention to high standards and personal service, now unites approximately 30 fine hotels, primarily in the East, Midwest, and South. The company took on the management of the Omni Northstar in 1982, and has since invested some $2.5 million in refurbishing guest rooms and common areas to give the hotel a contemporary elegance in keeping with its reputation in the city.

As it celebrates its 25th anniversary in 1989, the Omni Northstar continues to provide a warm, friendly, personal form of hospitality to business travelers visiting Minneapolis.

NATIONAL CAR RENTAL

A global network one phone call away.

Dedication to classic, quality service.

Superior technology that sets new industry standards and attitudes, again and again and again.

These are the traditions—and the ongoing commitments—of National Car Rental. An enterprising, innovative transportation leader, its roots reach back to Joe Saunders, the man attributed with starting the industry itself in 1916. Today National and its international partners comprise the world's largest car rental network, spanning 129 countries and territories with more than 4,000 locations and 270,000 vehicles.

Minneapolis is home to National's worldwide headquarters and to some 1,100 of its 8,000 U.S. employees. More than 10 million calls and 7 million bookings are handled there each year through

National's 1,100 Minneapolis employees and their 7,000 co-workers nationwide participate in National's Quality Improvement Process, pledging to "Do It Right the First Time."

National features General Motors vehicles such as this 1989 Cadillac Sedan DeVille.

the Reservations Center, which was both the first computerized and first centralized system in the industry. National was also the first to offer a toll-free number, (800) CAR-RENT, and for the hearing impaired it provides a special reservations number, (800) 328-6323, answered by specially trained service specialists.

This highly advanced reservation system is only the beginning of National's leading-edge technology designed to benefit customers. National's Expressway Computer System maintains centralized profiles of National customers, including such information as the renter's personal data, company information, billing preferences, optional coverages, and frequent flyer numbers. One quick swipe of a customer's Privilege, Privilege Preferred, or Emerald Club card accesses their profile, providing all of the important details needed to complete the rental transactions and put customers on the road in a matter of seconds.

National calls its industry-leading car rental capabilities the Electronic Advantage, a complete menu of services based upon customers' car rental needs and fre-

quency of renting. The revolutionary Paper-Less Express, first introduced in October 1987, is the foundation of the Electronic Advantage. The industry's shortest, easiest-to-read rental agreement, it gives travelers a tailored, no-nonsense receipt in less than 20 seconds.

But the ultimate in car rental speed and ease is reserved for National's Emerald Club, the first frequent car renter program of its kind. In addition to upgrades and points for valuable awards, including free trips and car rentals, members can enjoy the exclusive Emerald Aisle. Unveiled in March 1988, National's Emerald Aisle involves no paper and no counter transactions. The fastest way from the runway to the freeway, Emerald Club members can bypass the rental counter, go straight to the Emerald Aisle for their cars, and be on their way in 23 seconds or less. The Emerald Club is National's way of providing a valuable array of benefits, in addition to superior service, to its most loyal customers.

ABOVE: The Paper-Less Express exemplifies National Car Rental's superior technology. With this short, easy-to-read rental agreement, National continues to set the pace in the car rental industry.

BELOW: National features fun and exciting General Motors classics such as this 1951 Oldsmobile 98 as part of its California Classics and Florida Funwheels programs for members of The Emerald Club.

As the global marketplace expands, so does National Car Rental. In addition to the firm's 1,000 U.S. locations, its international licensees can be found in Latin America, Central America, Australia, and Asia. In 1954 National formed a partnership with Tilden Rent-A-Car, Canada's largest Canadian-owned car rental company. In 1974 National joined forces with the largest car rental organization outside of the United States—Europcar—which serves Europe, the Middle East, and Africa. In 1988 National reaffirmed these partnerships by signing a 10-year pact with Europcar and a 25-year agreement with Tilden, renewing and strengthening their vital affiliations. The year 1988

also marked the completion of National's global network in the Pacific region when it signed a partnership agreement with Nippon, Japan's premier car rental company.

National has also built strong partnership arrangements with airlines and hotels, including Northwest Airlines and Radisson Hotels. National's travel partners also include resorts and amusement parks, and National is proud to be the official car rental company of Disneyland and Walt Disney World.

National also takes an active role in making the highways safe for its customers. That's why it supported the efforts of Mothers Against Drunk Driving (MADD) to make people of all ages aware of the dangers of drinking and driving. In fact, National was the first in its field to support an anti-drunk-driving campaign.

National realizes, however, that the vehicle itself is still the main object of the customer's attention. Accordingly, National offers a sparkling, well-maintained U.S. fleet of nearly 125,000 vehicles, featuring fine General Motors cars, some of them true classics. National's California Classics and Florida Funwheels offer Emerald Club members vintage convertibles from the 1950s and 1960s,

including Belairs, Corvettes, and Cadillacs. For families on vacation to Disneyland or Disney World, National offers minivans with bright Disney decals. Four-wheel-drives and ski packages are also available at popular ski locations.

Cleanliness and painstaking maintenance are high priorities for National. And to keep National's fleet current and customer-pleasing, its average car is kept in service for less than eight months. Because the company's reputation is on the line every time a customer gets behind the wheel, each vehicle in the fleet is selected, maintained, and serviced under the standards of National's Quality Process. National also offers the industry's first Buy-Back Guarantee in its retail car sales program.

Likewise, National's 8,000 U.S. employees are well-trained people whose commitment to quality is more than a slogan taped to a wall. Each year National employees receive training and development to make sure the skills they have and the technology they employ continue to result in satisfied customers. Just as important, National's Quality Improvement Process provides employees with awareness, training, and an avenue for correcting nonconformances. National employees are proud to be a part of a system-wide commitment. From top management throughout the organization, each National employee pledges to provide defect-free products and services to customers and each other, to fully understand the requirements of his or her job and the systems that support the company, and to fulfill these requirements on time, every time.

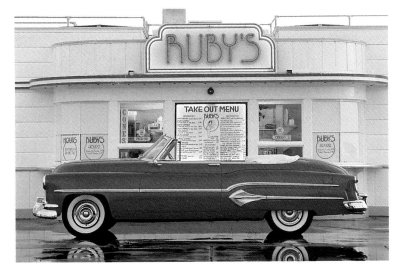

MARSDEN BUILDING MAINTENANCE COMPANY

When Adrian "Skip" Marsden decided to start a business that would specialize in cleaning offices and plant areas in the Twin Cities, the idea was just beginning to take hold on the East and West coasts. Up until then cleaning services were people that were called to wash windows occasionally. The concept of a business that served other businesses by cleaning up their premises in the off-hours on a contract basis took as much explaining as selling.

Marsden, then 23 years old, had been a hotel bellhop and a custodian at a Catholic church and school. He had learned about service in hotels, and he knew about cleaning and maintenance from looking after things at the parish. With a family to support and no formal education—he left his home in western Minnesota while still a teenager to enlist in the Merchant Marine during World War II—he figured his chances for success would have to come from recognizing opportunities and acting on his own initiative. In 1952, with a borrowed bankroll of $125, he quit his job and started knocking on business doors.

Today Marsden Building Maintenance Company is the largest locally owned commercial cleaning and maintenance organization in the region—and one of the largest

What was once Skip Marsden's second account is now the firm's corporate headquarters, located at 1717 University Avenue in St. Paul.

Adrian "Skip" Marsden, president and owner of Marsden Building Maintenance Company.

independent firms in the entire industry—with more than 2,500 employees and subsidiaries providing building security, armored car, and limousine services to businesses throughout the Minneapolis-St. Paul metro area. There is also a Marsden Building Maintenance Company in Omaha, Nebraska.

Marsden's first worker was himself. His wife, Jerri, handled the bookkeeping and accounting duties, and their home served as headquarters. His first account was the International Harvester parts depot on Eustis Street in St. Paul. The second was the nearby office building on University Avenue in the Midway District then owned and occupied by Skelly Oil Company. In 1986 Marsden bought the latter structure, some 65,000 square feet in size, and trans-

formed it into his firm's corporate home, renovating and remodeling it.

The business grew for one simple reason: Once a company became a Marsden client, it seldom left. Each new account meant real growth, not a replacement client for one lost to a competitor. Through the 1950s, even after the staff began to grow and the business to prosper, Marsden himself continued to log 18-hour days, seven days per week, much of it spent pushing a mop or running a floor-buffing machine or cleaning restrooms. That firsthand experience paid off both in quality control and Marsden's ability to make a convincing sales presentation.

In 1968, with growth straining the company's internal systems, Marsden turned to a consulting firm for help in computerizing. The consultant was a young man named Richard Lubbers, and the impression he made was so favorable that Marsden called the consulting company to warn it that he planned to steal their man; he did. Today Lubbers is executive vice-president and the guiding force in the administrative side of the business.

A 24-hour communications and dispatch center is staffed seven days per week. Integral to each customer's satisfaction is the assurance that Marsden is ready when they are.

The Marsden Building Maintenance name has become familiar throughout the metropolitan area. In Minneapolis, the firm developed its expertise in maintaining high-rise buildings. The first multi-story structure the company handled was the Lutheran Brotherhood Building (now home of Minnegasco), the first significant new building to be located in downtown Minneapolis, back in the 1950s. The firm still maintains the building for its new owners, while also servicing the striking new Lutheran Brotherhood headquarters built a few blocks away in 1981.

Building maintenance combines detail-oriented personal attention with sophisticated monitoring and management systems. Interior and exterior maintenance, while managed on a day-to-day basis, is carefully planned over a long-term cycle. A sophisticated database developed over the years by careful time management studies allows Marsden Building Maintenance to take the guesswork out of all types of cleaning and maintenance. A 24-hour communications and dispatch center is staffed seven days per week so building owners can be assured that Marsden is ready to respond to their needs, including emergencies and special situations, any time of the day or night.

The company's steady growth has led to the creation of a Special Services Division designed to meet the needs of larger clients and those with specialized needs. Services range from high-rise window cleaning to cleaning up construction sites, from application of special floor and surface sealants to cleaning carpets, drapes, and furniture upholstery. The division also handles out-of-the-ordinary situations, including cleaning up after floods, storms, fires, vandalism, and other disruptive incidents.

Marsden Building Maintenance has found new opportunities as well. The firm entered the building security business based on the understanding gained from the maintenance side, subsequently acquiring American Security Corporation to augment and extend its own building security accounts. With 700 employees and its own account base, American Security now operates as a separate, though wholly owned, affiliate business. It has branched its own service tree to include armored car, money-counting, and overnight vault services, and acquired Twin Cities Limousine to handle the needs of corporate clients.

Although building cleaning and maintenance does not require a college degree, one key to Marsden Building Maintenance's success is the degree of employee development effort invested in its

The backbone of every service organization is its people. In this classroom environment Marsden employees are being kept up to date on recent developments in equipment maintenance and repair.

people. A substantial portion of the company's headquarters complex is dedicated to training courses that provide both hands-on experience as well as classroom presentations involving the latest in instructor-led, videotape-based learning units. Workers learn the most efficient and effective techniques, stay up to date on new equipment and techniques, and must master the proper ways to maintain the various types of materials and surfaces used in the buildings—new and old—that the firm services.

Marsden himself has made contributions to the industry as well as to the community. His business was a charter member of the National Association of Building Services Contractors—now Building Services Contractors International—when the organization was founded in 1960, and Marsden has served in a number of officer positions, including president, as well as being a member of the board of directors.

Despite its modest beginnings, the business Skip Marsden built from scratch has long since achieved the important goal of supporting his family. Today Marsden's four children have followed in their father's footsteps and are active in the business.

225

SUPERAMERICA

"From the customer's point of view, if they can see it, walk on it, hold it, hear it, step in it, smell it, carry it, step over it, touch it, use it, even taste it, if they can feel it or sense it, it's customer service."

That's how SuperAmerica defines customer service in the training it provides to its employees. It's a fitting description when you stop to recall that what is now the pacesetting gas-and-goods retailer throughout the Midwest and beyond was originally a corner gas station—as they once were called—in the Twin Cities.

Today, from headquarters in Bloomington, SuperAmerica is a growing network of more than 500 locations in 18 states. With the exception of about two dozen Florida locations, most of those stores are spread across the northern tier of states from Washington and Montana through the Upper Midwest to Pennsylvania and West Virginia. Each year 30 to 50 new stores are added to the growing SuperAmerica family.

Now a subsidiary of Kentucky-based Ashland Oil, the nation's largest independent oil refiner and one of the largest industrial corporations in America, SuperAmerica is widely acknowledged as a leader in the evolving convenience retailing field—a modern hybrid that can offer more variety and selection than a convenience store, and faster than a supermarket. According to one convenience store trade magazine, the typical SuperAmerica sells three times more gasoline and about 30 percent more merchandise than the industry norm.

It all started in 1960 at the corner of East Seventh and Sibley in downtown St. Paul. For years the Erickson family's Northwestern Refinery had sold gasoline and other light oil products to independent distributors and gas stations. The new retail venture allowed it to sell direct from the refinery. But from the very beginning SuperAmerica was intended to be more

than another chain of corner gas stations.

The initial question was what to sell *inside* the store to augment the gas pumps *outside*. Fishing and outdoor gear was tried. So was an inventory of sporting goods, small appliances, even lawn mowers and bicycles. A few food and nonfood household items were stocked. Then SuperAmerica decided to watch what its customers were buying and act accordingly.

Before long the sporting goods were replaced by a growing selection of convenience foods and groceries. More gas islands were added (24 to 48 pumps per store is the standard) to make sure customers could count on fast access with little or no waiting. People-pleasing touches such as canopies over the gas pumps (to protect customers from the elements) and microphones on the canopy pillars (so customers could talk to and get help from someone inside the store) were added, too.

Pumping gas isn't the most pleasant of activities, SuperAmerica reasons, but it doesn't have to be unpleasant. Consequently, each store's staff makes a concerted ef-

SuperAmerica convenience stores feature a wide range of consumer goods and groceries, including sandwiches, salads, and baked goods from SuperMom's Kitchen in St. Paul Park.

fort to keep the gas islands moving, the pump hoses clean, and the stores bright and cheery. Customers are greeted personally—and personably. As formulas for success go, it's nothing out of the ordinary. But the way it is fulfilled by SuperAmerica's people has led to nearly 30 years of extraordinary results.

By the time Ashland Oil acquired Northwestern Refinery in 1970, SuperAmerica had more than 100 locations and a growing reputation as an innovator and service leader.

The typical SuperAmerica store combines fresh food, packaged food, and a wide variety of non-food items—from automotive parts and film to household goods, magazines, and greeting cards—in a bright, accessible format that is always staffed by at least two clerks for fast service no matter when a customer stops in. Since customers like to stop in at their convenience, most SuperAmericas are open 24 hours per day.

At the same time SuperAmerica continues to be far more than a conventional corner convenience store. The company constantly experiments with new ideas, new formats, and new offerings. If customers like what they see, they're likely to see more of it. That's how SuperMom's Bakery got its start back in 1981. Today Twin Cities customers can call in a bakery order to the central SuperMom's commissary and pick it up the following day at a nearby SuperAmerica store.

There really is a SuperMom's Kitchen—in St. Paul Park. It supplies SuperAmerica stores in the Twin Cities and surrounding areas with a wide selection of baked goods: 10 varieties of bread, 4 kinds of rolls, 30 different kinds of donuts and pastries, 14 varieties of cookies, and nearly two dozen other cake and refrigerated dessert items. For the deli section of the store, SuperMom's also fixes 15 varieties of sandwiches and several different types of salads. And SuperAmerica has a growing line of homemade, store-branded products, from SuperSoda to SuperCare Diapers.

Similarly, SuperAmerica constantly looks for new services to add to its product mix. It was the first to install automated teller machines in some of its locations. When customers indicated they liked the service, it was expanded. Nearly one-half of all SuperAmerica stores—including more than three-quarters of those in the Twin Cities—now have ATMs. In a continued effort to explore new ways to enhance services to its customers, SuperAmerica has introduced video rentals to almost all locations, and even has a few stores with full pharmacies. SuperAmerica employees are told their "first and foremost responsibility" consists of making sure that every customer they serve will want to return to their store again. More than any other duty on their to-do list, bringing customers back is their job.

To see how well that customer-focused philosophy has paid off, all one has to do is note the more than 80 busy SuperAmerica stores found throughout the Twin Cities metropolitan area. More than 500,000 times per day, a customer, somewhere in 18 states the company serves, experiences service the SuperAmerica way.

LEFT: SuperAmerica brings new meaning to the word "convenience." Most stores are open 24 hours per day and many feature ATMs.

BELOW: Constantly expanding the services available to its customers, SuperAmerica has added such innovations as video stores and pharmacies to some of its locations.

DAYTON HUDSON CORPORATION

In the early days of the new century, an outstate banker spent some time standing on street corners in downtown Minneapolis, comparing traffic patterns and trying to decide where to locate a new retail business for maximum visibility. Although "downtown" in those days was mostly clustered along the west bank of the Mississippi River, George Draper Dayton figured on the city's growth turning the corner of Seventh Street and Nicollet Avenue into a prime business location.

Dayton's educated guess ranks among the most perceptive—and profitable—in Minneapolis history. The original dry-goods store he established on that promising street corner is now the cornerstone of a national retailing corporation with $12 billion in annual revenues and more than 600 locations in 38 states: Dayton Hudson Corporation. Today the Dayton Hudson retail family of companies includes Target, a national upscale discount company with 349 stores in 27 states; Mervyn's, a promotional department store company with 219 stores in 14 states; Dayton Hudson Department Store Company,

Lechmere is a hardlines retailer that sells brand-name merchandise in four specialty categories: home electronics, home appliances, housewares, and leisure/sporting goods.

with 37 stores in seven states; and Lechmere, a hardlines retail company with 27 stores in nine states. The corporation employs more than 135,000 people on a full- and part-time basis, approximately 20,000 of them in the Twin Cities area.

The Dayton Hudson name has come to be associated with a continuing record for innovation in quality retailing. The basic Dayton Hudson strategy is to provide value through multiple retail formats, each of which has five critical traits in common: dominant assortments, so that customers can count on finding what they want most; quality merchandise that provides safe, durable, satisfying use backed by capable, consistent, and personal service; fashion that stays close to customers' changing desires and responds quickly to their changing needs; convenience in location, organization, and easy-to-shop environment; and finally, competitive pricing that assures the "value equation" will build long-term loyalty based on years of personal satisfaction.

Dayton Hudson Department Store Company emphasizes fashion leadership, innovative merchandising, and an exciting store environment, as well as offering its patrons the ultimate in customer service.

With sales of $1.7 billion annually, the more than three dozen stores of the Dayton Hudson Department Store Company throughout the Upper Midwest continue to play a leading role as the nation's largest department store family. The division and company names reflect the 1969 merger of Dayton Corporation of Minneapolis and J.L. Hudson Company of Detroit.

When the 1960s opened up a market for quality-oriented discount retailing, Dayton Hudson launched Target as an upscale discount concept offering low prices on a broad assortment of high-quality fashion and basic hardlines and softgoods in easy-to-shop, self-service stores. The original store in suburban Roseville, and almost 400 others in 27 states nationwide, make Target the country's premier upscale discounter. Combining modern retailing technology and offering nationally known brand-name products at low prices, Target's self-service format now rings up annual sales well in excess of $6 billion.

Mervyn's, based in the San Francisco Bay Area, became part of the Dayton Hudson family in 1978. A well-established favorite for its mixture of brand-name and private-label apparel, accessories, and household goods, Mervyn's stores in 14 states post annual sales in excess of $3 billion. From its strong West Coast roots, this value-oriented department store organization has now moved into

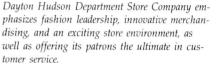

Popular for its mixture of brand-name and private-label apparel, accessories, and household goods, Mervyn's joined the Dayton-Hudson family in 1978.

the Southwest, Midwest, and the South.

Lechmere operates primarily in New England and the southern Atlantic Seaboard states. It concentrates on consumer electronics, major appliances, housewares and hardware, and sports and leisure equipment.

Minneapolis has been the site of a number of important business milestones for the company. It was there that Dayton Hudson forever changed the style of shopping in America by developing the nation's first indoor mall. Southdale opened in 1956 in what had been a peaceful cornfield well out on the fringes of the city. Six years later Rosedale provided the first market test of Target.

Over the past three decades, while many cities nationwide watched helplessly as their downtowns declined, Minneapolis not only made a success of the nation's pioneer indoor suburban shopping mall and its premier upscale discounter, it also experienced true renewal in its central core. Dayton's provided a retail anchor for the development of the Nicollet Mall; as a result, Seventh and Nicollet has remained an exceptionally busy and attractive corner.

Today skyways link the original department store—still the corporation's flagship location—to offices and retail operations throughout the downtown. Hundreds of thousands of Twin Citians still come back to that pivotal corner in downtown Minneapolis for such special events as the an-

nual Christmas display (which attracts a quarter-million people annually) and the Spring Flower Show.

Not only has the original store been totally refurbished in recent years, but similar attention will result in new facilities for Dayton's department stores in Southdale and Rosedale by the early 1990s. The new stores, built adjacent to the existing ones, will allow those regional centers to grow in turn by expanding into the previous Dayton's space to provide more stores and services for their customers.

Dayton Hudson has developed a philosophy of service based on the value that strong and healthy communities add to the long-term success of the corporation—that businesses flourish in prospering environments, a belief that traces all the way back to George Draper Dayton himself and is actively shared by Kenneth A. Macke, the architect of Target's success and chairman and chief executive officer of the parent corporation since 1983.

That quality of life concern shows up in everything from the company's long tradition of em-

ployee volunteerism to financial contributions through which Dayton Hudson invests back in the communities that have made it successful. Innovative programs such as the Department Store Company's JobPlus—which helps teenage mothers and other young women at risk of long-term dependency to upgrade their skills and become successful in the regular economy—are further evidence of the firm's tradition of matching business needs to the needs of its community. The community gains through people who are more productive and self-supporting, less likely to need public assistance; the company gains by learning how to train and work with employees from nontraditional backgrounds in a time of severe and worsening shortages of entry-level workers. These are also potential customers and employees of Dayton Hudson.

Since 1946 Dayton Hudson Corporation has contributed an amount equal to 5 percent of its federally taxable income to social action and arts programs in communities where it does business. Through its operating companies, that commitment now exceeds $20 million.

Target is a national chain of upscale discount stores offering a broad range of quality-oriented general merchandise at low prices.

NASH FINCH COMPANY

Nash Finch distributes food, taking it from the grower and the processor, the baker, and the others who produce foods and moving it to the grocer quickly and efficiently. The heart of its business is distributing wholesale and retail lines of food and related products, plus a broad selection of general merchandise.

As part of its role as "Supplier to Successful Food Stores," Nash Finch provides operational expertise and support to 6,000 grocers, discount stores, and convenience stores in more than 24 states. From the Upper Midwest down the Mississippi Valley, east as far as the Carolinas and west as far as Colorado, Nash Finch has been helping food businesses succeed for more than 100 years.

In recent years the scale of that success has been growing steadily: Through the 1980s Nash Finch doubled its annual sales to more than $2 billion. Yet the firm itself remains relatively unknown outside its industry. For years Minneapolis has been the home base of a publicly held but still family-oriented enterprise that started as a confectionary store in Devils Lake, North Dakota, way back in 1885.

The three Nash brothers, who left their native Vermont for the Upper Midwest in the 1880s, had learned retailing in their father's general store back east. Fred, Edgar, and Willis Nash lived in the back of the store in the early years, often fixing their meals from the food in stock. By 1889 the business had grown enough for them to hire their first nonfamily employee, a 14-year-old boy named Harry Finch.

The business officially became Nash Finch in 1921. Fred Nash

was the organization's first president, succeeded in 1926 by Harry Finch. Today Harold B. Finch, Jr., is chairman of the board and chief executive officer, and Robert Nash is the company's vice-president and treasurer, but the Nash Finch family has grown to include more than 9,000 employees, including 250 in the company's Minneapolis headquarters.

The rare combination of management continuity and managed growth is an important element in Nash Finch's continuing success. For more than a century the firm has concentrated on doing the things it does very well instead of dissipating its strength in activities outside its areas of expertise.

In the trendy management books, that is called "sticking to the knitting," a tactic Nash Finch mastered early and has never forgotten. Year after year it has systematically reinvested its earnings in the core business, improving the services it provides to its customers, preserving its financial soundness by limiting its dependence on borrowed capital, yet paying a dividend every year since 1926.

The backbone of the modern Nash Finch is a network of 17 distribution centers. Each is strategically located to supply the complete food and non-food needs of the various customer businesses it serves. That can range from a

The Nash Brothers Grand Forks store, circa 1889, in the company's oldest photo. This address was home to the brothers as well as their first wholesale fruit building.

carefully managed selection of items for small, all-night gas-and-goods stores to the broad array of products offered by massive warehouse-style grocery operations.

Each distribution center operates relatively autonomously, focusing its activities and developing its growth by satisfying the specific needs of the unique mix of customer stores in its region. To keep the distribution network close to its customers and customize crucial delivery schedules to the varying needs of different sizes and types of stores, Nash Finch maintains its own truck fleet. To provide high-quality, low-price alternatives for its retailers, Nash Finch offers its own extensive line of private-label products under the Our Family and Golden Valley names.

In the Nash Finch system, zone managers also function as retail counselors. With their experience, depth of knowledge, and access to the company's total resources, they are valued advisers who can respond as needed to questions and requests from customers. They also serve as an information source for independent operators competing in a fast-changing industry, providing up-to-the-minute knowledge and assistance on emerging consumer trends and business developments.

Firsthand experience is as important today as it was when the business began a century ago. Nash Finch operates a selection of approximately 100 stores throughout its service region—everything from combination food and general merchandise stores to warehouse stores, conventional supermarkets to "super stores" with almost twice as much area under their roofs as the grocery store of years past. The company-owned stores serve as field laboratories where Nash Finch can test and fine tune new systems and ser-

vices for its affiliated and independent customers.

Nash DeCamp, a wholly owned subsidiary based in Visalia, California, owns and operates packing, shipping, and cold-storage facilities for the distribution of fresh fruits and vegetables throughout the United States, Canada, and many overseas markets.

Other products are produced under contract by farmers who receive in return the same kind of operational support—advice on growing practices and harvesting, financial support, market analysis—that Nash Finch provides to food stores. The more than a dozen independent, California-based shipping organizations that pack their own fruit while taking advantage of Nash DeCamp's extensive sales and marketing expertise assure Nash Finch customers a year-round supply of fruits and vegetables.

Nash Finch also provides support services that include financial management systems, merchandising programs, marketing and advertising campaigns, complete data-processing services, human resource support—from training of frontline workers to the development of supervisory and management skills—and store development planning.

Econofoods is Nash Finch's super warehouse grocery operation, with stores throughout the Midwest. This new Bismarck, North Dakota, store is typical of the format, which offers shoppers traditional grocery inventory as well as a scratch bakery; full-service deli; a fresh and live seafood department; sausage kitchen; floral department; juice bar; a large, diverse produce department; and a store-within-a-store video department.

The Minneapolis-based Retail Support Center is an additional service and is known informally within Nash Finch as the Help Desk. With one toll-free telephone call, a Nash Finch customer can get technical and service support to keep its electronic scanning systems up and running smoothly. Help Desk personnel are specially trained as trouble shooters and problem solvers. If they can not solve a problem, they serve as a liaison between the store owner and the equipment vendor to make sure field service is provided quickly and accurately.

Operations large and small turn to Nash Finch for both the systems and the expertise that can help them more effectively monitor merchandise, increase sales, improve profitability, solve personnel problems, and plan for the future growth and expansion of their businesses.

ALBRECHTS

When the Nicollet Mall began to take shape in downtown Minneapolis in the early 1960s, it represented a rebirth for retailing in the heart of the city. Albrechts quickly established itself along the city's new prestige address as a family-run furrier and women's clothier; its roots in the Twin Cities already stretched back more than a century.

Today Albrechts on Nicollet Mall is both a local landmark and a vigorous, growing business—the nation's oldest and largest full-service furrier. Its collection of more than 2,000 distinctive furs is matched by a reputation for integrity and craftsmanship that is known coast to coast. Two satellite stores—one in Edina, the other in St. Paul—make Albrechts the name to be reckoned with in local fashion circles.

The name of the branch of the founding family that continues to dedicate its efforts to maintaining and extending the business' century-plus reputation is Jerrard. Five generations of Albrechts and Jerrards have nurtured and managed the business over the years.

The full-service furrier label is a mark of increasing rarity. Albrechts serves its customers by continuing to sell, manufacture, store, and repair fine furs—one of only a handful of such businesses remaining in America. At all three stores—Nicollet Mall, Edina, and in the Highland district of St. Paul—the retail floors are augmented by workrooms and storerooms as well as dressing rooms and private showrooms. That full-service touch is valued by residents of the Twin Cities and customers who come from outstate Minnesota, Wisconsin, Iowa, the Dakotas, Nebraska, Montana, and even from abroad.

Computers sit on wooden desks dating back to the turn of the century. Sensitive temperature and humidity controls regulate the storage vaults, while people still cut and sew furs by hand or on spe-

cialized machines, many of which have not been made for decades. Up-to-date marketing and business practices are filed away electronically next to wooden and iron cabinets that contain records dating back to the city's infancy.

The informal family of Albrechts employees has grown to more than 125, including almost 30 with training and expertise in the care and repair of fine furs. These experienced craftsmen are joined by knowledgeable salespeople to carry on the family business in the traditional way.

It is a "no-games" approach to fine furs. Almost one-third of the fur garments Albrechts sells are custom made to the customer's order; all are custom fit. Any alterations on the furs are done by Albrechts' own people, as are repairs should anything unfortunate befall the fur. Only top-quality American furs from labels such as Black Diamond are used in the manufacture of custom garments.

Salespeople are prepared to explain and counsel as well as fit and sell, and quick to point out that in fine furs, as in fine woods, it is the natural texture and quality and not the added veneer of dyes that truly determine quality.

And "service" is the key word.

Albrechts, on the corner of Nicollet Mall and Ninth Street, is America's most established and successful furrier.

With the change of seasons each year, Albrechts' temperature-controlled vaults open and close, accepting thousands of furs for cleaning and storage through the summer, then returning them to their owners when the region's notoriously cold winters once again approach. Pickup and delivery in the Twin Cities are free, a long-standing courtesy to customers whose loyalty often spans several generations.

Albrechts' roots in the Twin Cities stretch back to 1855, when Ernst Albrecht brought his family's fur business (originally founded in Germany by Johann Christoph Albrecht in 1723) to downtown St. Paul. By the late 1880s the family had opened a store in downtown Minneapolis. In its early years Albrechts numbered such local luminaries as James J. Hill and Theo. Hamm among its customers—and one Jesse James, whose gang once paid a visit and stole a fur coat at gunpoint, was an early visitor who liked what he saw, even if he did not see fit to pay for it.

It was John Jerrard, a fourth-generation descendant of the Albrechts, who set up shop in the Medical Arts Building on the Nicollet Mall in 1962. Previously its location on Nicollet was in the Harold Building (between Eighth and Ninth on the west side of Nicollet from 1938 to 1962—now the site of The Conservatory), across from the current location on the east side of Nicollet near Ninth. At the same time he also expanded the business into women's apparel (sportswear and ready-to-wear) and accessories. That was four years after he became president of the company at the death of his father in 1959. In 1988 Albrechts' downtown store expanded to the corner of Ninth, providing the opportunity to further enlarge its fur salon and extend the variety of women's fashions offered.

In recent years sons Steve and Paul have joined John in the business—Steve working out of the downtown Minneapolis headquarters as vice-president and advertising manager, Paul as vice-president and manager of the Albrechts on West 50th Street, in the prestigious 50th and France district of Edina, that his father opened in 1974. Both learned as

their father did—from the ground up, starting as janitors and working in every part of the business.

Inspired by the elegant styles displayed by characters in popular television series, furs have enjoyed a rebirth of popularity in the 1980s. In actuality, however, they have never gone out of style. The quality and usefulness of a high-quality fur, not its price or perceived elegance, continue to be the true measure of its value. A well-made fur cuts the harsh winter wind and chill like no cloth coat ever made, regardless of the high-technology synthetics that might be involved. Well cared for, a good fur will stand the test of time far better than cloth and synthetic fabrics.

Albrechts continues to accumu-

More than 1,000 furs and an impressive selection of women's apparel await shoppers at Albrechts.

late old coats for its refurbishment efforts: matching fur pieces of similar age and texture to repair older garments that have been damaged but still have years of useful life in them. In recent years, in fact, its fur experts have taken in a growing number of coats for "remodeling"—garments in an older style inherited by younger women that, with some well-crafted attention, can be remade into a new coat reflecting more contemporary styling.

For five generations—and with no end in sight—Albrechts has been a family name valued for far more than its business acumen.

RADISSON HOTELS INTERNATIONAL

As the world shrinks and Minnesota expands far beyond its borders, the Minneapolis Radisson Plaza Hotel is an ever more dramatic symbol. It occupies the vital Seventh Street location between Hennepin Avenue and Nicollet Mall that was the original home of the first Radisson Hotel, built in 1909. At the same time it is the flagship of a global fleet directed by Radisson Hotels International, which is emerging to be one of the dominant corporations in an increasingly important industry.

In 1909 the newly opened Radisson Hotel, built at a cost of $1.5 million, was considered the finest, most luxurious establishment to be found between Chicago and the West Coast. It boasted 425 rooms, two restaurants, a close relationship with Dayton's Department Store next door, and a deep artesian well providing fresh, cool water from 975 feet below the ground.

Since the new Radisson Plaza opened on the same spot in 1987, the same reputation as a hospitality landmark has held true. The plaza offers 357 rooms, two restaurants, an even closer link with the Dayton's store (via the Skyway-connected Plaza VII Shops retail arcade), and the same artesian well water. It is a powerful, popular emblem of a corporation dedicated to excellence on both an international scale and in its own home community.

The Minneapolis Radisson Plaza is the outgrowth of a far-reaching business decision. In 1960

Close to home or across the globe, the Radisson name sets the standard for quality. At left is the Radisson Plaza Hotel, Carlson Hospitality Group's flagship property in downtown Minneapolis; at top left is the Park Lane Radisson Plaza on Causeway Bay in Hong Kong.

BELOW: Juergen Bartels, president of Carlson Hospitality Group.

Curtis L. Carlson decided to diversify his sales promotion business, founded largely on Gold Bond trading stamps, by joining nine other investors in purchasing a 5-percent interest in the original Radisson. Within two years he was the hotel's sole owner. And he was hooked on hospitality. By the early 1970s there were more than two dozen Radisson hotels, inns, and resorts in the United States.

Today Radisson Hotels International is one of the key operations within the Carlson Hospitality Group, one of the three corporate wings of Carlson Companies, Inc. With more than 200 hotels spread among 17 countries, the Radisson name is visible in Beijing, Lausanne, Stockholm, Mexico City, Budapest, Hong Kong, Istanbul, and near Australia's Great Barrier Reef, among many other locations.

Under the leadership of German-born Juergen "J.B." Bartels, who assumed the presidency of the division in 1983, the corporation has taken the hospitality industry by storm. It is widely considered the fastest-growing upscale hotel company in the nation, and is increasingly recognized as an innovator and leader.

In recent years Radisson has led an industry-wide process of segmentation that has redefined the word "hotel." Radisson guests now rest in any of six categories of lodgings. Five are variations on the traditional hotel theme. Plaza Hotels are premier, upscale properties, usually in a city center or prestigious suburban location. Suite Hotels feature guest rooms with both a sitting room and a bedroom, designed especially for commercial and weekend travelers. In the Radisson definition, hotels are business-oriented properties with spacious, well-equipped meeting and convention facilities, while inns are smaller properties, often in second-tier cities, emphasizing upscale executive services. And resorts provide luxurious recreational facilities in a setting designed for both work and play.

The sixth—and newest segment of the family has been christened Pierre Radisson Inns. The industry's newest wrinkle, this category is designed for the discriminating individual traveler who does not need large meeting and conference space but has high expectations for lodging quality and personal amenities.

All are served by one of the hospitality industry's most sophisticated computer reservations systems and a management philosophy embodied by three short, customer-focused words: "Yes I Can."

Radisson also offers an industry-leading frequent-guest program, award-winning restaurant, and meeting and catering services tailored to the individual or corporate client.

Attention to detail, outstanding service, and sensitivity to rapidly changing trends earned Radisson Hotels International the prestigious five-medallion rating from the American Association of Travel Editors three years in a row (1986, 1987, and 1987-1988).

Yet if the new Radisson Plaza Hotel can be said to represent a combination of global vision and corporate history, it also deserves to be seen in its own light—as a premier hotel and office complex. A Japanese business travel magazine saw fit to put the hotel's executive boardroom meeting facilities on its cover as a new standard of quality. Its sleek profile blends into the modern skyline, but its impact on Minneapolis as a growing center of business and commerce is measured in far more than guest

Since the days of the original downtown Radisson Hotel, fine dining has been a hallmark of Carlson Hospitality. Today that tradition lives on in the Festival Restaurant in the Radisson Plaza Hotel.

rooms and corporate offices. The Minneapolis Radisson Plaza Hotel is not so much the tip of an iceberg as it is one bright light in an ocean-spanning strand.

And the end is nowhere in sight. For the past few years, new hotels have been added (by acquisition, franchise, or construction) at the rate of one every 10 days. Plans call for the Radisson collection to number 350 by the end of 1992. The properties will share a common commitment to high standards and guest-focused services, a theme appropriate to an organization that describes its operations as "worldwide and world class."

Patrons

The following individuals, companies, and organizations have made a valuable commitment to the quality of this publication. Windsor Publications and the Greater Minneapolis Chamber of Commerce gratefully acknowledge their participation in *Minneapolis: City of Enterprise, Center of Excellence.*

Aeration Industries International, Inc.
Albrechts
Ambassador Sausage Corporation
Arthur Andersen & Co.
AT&T
BCE Development Properties Inc.
E.W. Blanch Co.
Carlson Companies, Inc.
Dayton Hudson Corporation
Doherty, Rumble & Butler, Professional Association
The Dolphin Corporations
Eberhardt Company
Ernst & Whinney
First Bank System
Hammel Green and Abrahamson, Inc.
Jostens
Juno Enterprises
The Kerr Organization
KMSP-TV
Leef Bros., Inc.
LifeSpan, Inc.
Lutheran Brotherhood

Marquette Bank Minneapolis
Marsden Building Maintenance Company
Merchant & Gould
Metropolitan-Mount Sinai Medical Center
Miller, Johnson & Kuehn, Incorporated
Minneapolis Heart Institute
Murray's
Nash Finch Company
National Car Rental
Norwest Corporation
The Old Log Theater
Omni NorthStar Hotel
Opus Corporation
Piper, Jaffray & Hopwood Incorporated
Popham, Haik, Schnobrich & Kaufman, Ltd.
Precision Associates, Inc.
Radisson Hotels International
Sandoz Nutrition
Star Tribune
SuperAmerica
Thermo King Corporation
The Toro Company
U S WEST, Inc.
Whitney Mill Quarter by CitySide Development

Participants in Part Two of *Minneapolis: City of Enterprise, Center of Excellence.* The stories of these companies and organizations appear in Chapters 6 through 11, beginning on page 140.

Bibliography

Abercrombie, Thomas J. "Tale of Twin Cities." *National Geographic,* November 1980.

Abler, Ronald, et al. *The Twin Cities of St. Paul and Minneapolis.* Cambridge, Massachusetts: Ballinger Publishing Company, 1976.

Baerwald, Thomas J. "The Twin Cities: A Metropolis of Multiple Identities." *Focus,* Spring 1986.

Blegen, Theodore C. *Minnesota: A History of the State* (revised edition). Minneapolis: University of Minnesota Press, 1975.

Breckenfeld, Gurney. "How Minneapolis Fends off the Urban Crisis." *Fortune,* January 1976.

City of Minneapolis. *State of the City 1986.* Minneapolis: 1987.

Deziel, Francine K., ed. *Corporate Report Fact Book,* 1987 edition. Minneapolis: MCP, Inc., 1986.

Ervin, Jean. *The Twin Cities Explored.* Minneapolis: Adams Press, 1972.

——————. *The Twin Cities Perceived.* Minneapolis: University of Minnesota Press, 1976.

Finley, Michael. "As Minneapolis Experiences Another Growth Spurt, It Once Again Looks to the River." *Corporate Report Minnesota,* July 1987.

Flanagan, Barbara. *Minneapolis.* New York: St. Martin's Press, 1973.

Gebhard, David, and Tom Martinson. *A Guide to the Architecture of Minnesota.* Minneapolis: University of Minnesota Press, 1977.

Godward, A.C. "Minneapolis, 1979." *Minneapolis Journal,* September 15, 1929.

Greater Minneapolis Area Board of Realtors. Centennial brochure. Minneapolis: 1986.

Greater Minneapolis Chamber of Commerce. *Economic Profile.* Minneapolis: 1987.

Kane, Lucile M. *The Waterfall that Built a City: The Falls of St. Anthony in Minneapolis.* St. Paul: Minnesota Historical Society, 1966.

Lanegran, David A. and Ernest R. Sandeen. *The Lake District of Minneapolis: A History of the Calhoun-Isles Community.* St. Paul: Living Historical Museum, 1979.

Larson, Don W. *Land of the Giants: A History of Minnesota Business.* Minneapolis: Dorn Books, 1979.

Lass, William E. *Minnesota: A History.* New York: W.W. Norton & Company, 1977.

Morrison, Don. *The Face of Minneapolis.* Minneapolis: Dillon Press, Inc., 1966.

Pine, Carol, and Susan Mundale. *Self-Made: The Stories of 12 Minnesota Entrepreneurs.* Minneapolis: Dorn Books, 1982.

Rottenberg, Dan. "Marvelous Minneapolis: It's Anything but Wobegon." *Town & Country,* December 1987.

Salisbury, Harrison E. *Travels Around America.* New York: Walker and Company, 1976.

Stavig, Vicki, ed. *Twin Cities Guide.* Minneapolis: Dorn Books, 1983.

Stelling, Lucille Johnsen. *Frommer's Guide to Minneapolis St. Paul.* New York: Prentice Hall Press, 1988.

Stipanovich, Joseph. *City of Lakes: An Illustrated History of Minneapolis.* Woodland Hills, California: Windsor Publications, Inc., 1982.

Svendsen, Gustav Rolf. *Hennepin County History: An Illustrated Essay.* Minneapolis: Hennepin County Bicentennial Commission, 1976.

Tice, D.J. "The Ties that Bind." *Twin Cities,* October 1967.

Worthy, Ford S. "The Could-do City Could Do It Again." *Fortune,* January 19, 1987.

NEWSPAPERS AND PERIODICALS
City Business
Corporate Report Minnesota
The Star Tribune
Minnesota Monthly
Mpls. St. Paul
Twin Cities

Index